Making Plays

Interviews with Contemporary British Dramatists and their Directors

Introduced, Interviewed and Edited by

Duncan Wu
University Lecturer in Romantic Studies
St Catherine's College
Oxford

First published 2000 by
MACMILLAN PRESS LTD
Houndmills, Basingstoke, Hampshire RG21 6XS
and London
Companies and representatives
throughout the world

ISBN 0–333–74001–7 hardcover
ISBN 0–333–91561–5 paperback

A catalogue record for this book is available
from the British Library.

This book is printed on paper suitable for recycling and
made from fully managed and sustained forest sources.

10	9	8	7	6	5	4	3	2	1
09	08	07	06	05	04	03	02	01	00

Printed and bound in Great Britain by
Antony Rowe Ltd, Chippenham, Wiltshire

Making Plays

Contents

List of Illustrations

A photograph of each writer and director is printed at the beginning of the interview. Photographer credits: Donald Cooper (photographs of David Hare and Nicholas Hytner); John Haynes (Richard Eyre and Max Stafford-Clark); Conrad Blakemore (Michael Blakemore); Chris Davies (David Edgar); Duncan Wu (Michael Frayn, Howard Brenton, Alan Bennett).

Plates

1. Sian Thomas as Mary Shelley in Max Stafford-Clark's 1988 revival of Howard Brenton's *Bloody Poetry*. Photo: Sarah Ainslie.

2. 'The Coronation Anthem finally reaches its climax ... as the King struggles, howling, in the chair': Nigel Hawthorne in the restraining chair in Alan Bennett's *The Madness of George III*. Photo: Donald Cooper, Photostage.

3. Jan Ravens as Gabriella Pecs and Charles Kay as Oliver Davenport in Michael Attenborough's production of David Edgar's *Pentecost*. Photo: Shakespeare Centre Library.

4. Judi Dench and Samantha Bond in David Hare's *Amy's View*. Photo: John Haynes.

5. From left to right: Matthew Marsh (Heisenberg), Sara Kestelman (Margrethe) and David Burke (Bohr) in the Royal National Theatre production of Michael Frayn's *Copenhagen*. Photo: Conrad Blakemore.

Acknowledgements

Only some weeks after it was suggested to me did I recall that the title of this book was used by Richard Nelson and David Jones for their recorded conversations, also concerned with the writer–director relationship, published by Faber in 1995. I hope they will forgive me for recycling it, and that they might regard the present volume as an extension of their valuable labours.

In fact, it was not my original intention to produce a book about theatrical collaboration at all. When I visited David Edgar at his home on 9 July 1997 I knew that I wanted to conduct a series of interviews with contemporary dramatists, and that Edgar's *Pentecost* would be the subject of the first I was to record, but was unclear as to my approach. Over lunch prior to the interview, Edgar suggested that I talk to both dramatists *and* directors about their working methods, helpfully establishing the device of the present volume, even going so far as to suggest some of its subjects. In retrospect, I realise how fortunate I was in having chosen to visit Edgar first. As one of the foremost teachers in the craft of playwriting, he was ideally placed to offer this advice, and his suggestions have proved sound and wise. I owe him a great debt, which it is a pleasure to acknowledge here.

This book is a record of research undertaken in the field, guided by my experience of particular stage productions. It will be evident from what follows how much I owe my interlocutors, who have given freely of their time and energies (in alphabetical order): Michael Attenborough, Alan Bennett, Michael Blakemore, Howard Brenton, David Edgar, Richard Eyre, Michael Frayn, David Hare, Nicholas Hytner, and Max Stafford-Clark. For valuable assistance in making contact with these subjects, and arranging interviews, often in the midst of hectic production schedules, I thank Jane Tassell of the RSC, Suzannah Bedford of Out of Joint, Drew Barr (assistant to Nicholas Hytner), Stuart Burge, and George Fenton.

Work on this volume has extended over the course of some three years. It was begun during joint tenure of a research grant from the British Academy that exonerated me from teaching duties during the academic year 1997–98, and a Visiting Fellowship at St Catherine's College, Oxford, for which I am indebted to the Master and Fellows. I am grateful to my colleagues at the Department of English Literature at the University of Glasgow for taking care of my tutorial responsibilities during that time, and to my head of department, Richard Cronin, for permitting the necessary research leave. Charmian Hearne, my editor at Macmillan, has supported this volume from the outset, and it has been a pleasure to work with her again. As my editor at the *TLS*, Lindsay Duguid sent me to Howard Brenton's 3 Plays for Utopia at the Royal Court in 1988, a formative experience for which I remain grateful. Pat Devlin has proved a rapid and accurate transcriber of many hours of tapes. My wife Caroline has encouraged me in this work from the outset, and has proved the most perceptive of my critics.

Glasgow, June 1999

Introduction

> The sublimity of Mrs Siddons's acting is such, that the first impulse which it gives to the mind can never wear out ... The impression is stamped there for ever, and any after-experiments or critical enquiries only serve to fritter away and tamper with the sacredness of the early recollection.
>
> Hazlitt, 'Mrs Siddons's Lady Macbeth'[1]

What is it that distinguishes theatre from any other art form? No doubt it has much to do with what Richard Eyre calls its 'human' scale.[2] Film enlarges and distorts everything it touches; the medium is inherently larger-than-life, and inherently alien from the viewer. Its characters pass through the consciousness of the audience in disembodied form. But theatre is more direct: its audience is engaged with the lives of other human beings in the same time and place. And it is that immediacy that makes the theatre more intense, more compelling, than any other medium. It is what makes it a more potent vehicle of what Hazlitt calls the 'sublime' than any other.

The most widely held theory about the origin of theatre is that it evolved from rituals created symbolically to act out natural events, thereby bringing them down to human scale and making the unknown more easily accessible. The aspiration to realise the sublime is thus embedded in the origins of the tradition; that is its hallmark. Which is not to claim that all theatre comprises great literature: much eighteenth- and nineteenth-century British drama is buried beneath the rubble of critical neglect, and deservedly so. And no doubt the children of the twenty-first century will remember only a small fraction of post-war theatre writing of the present century. But then, the dramatic sublime is not to be found in the printed text. In that sense, it differs from other literary genres. Poems and novels depend for their existence on the coincidence of ink and paper; they don't need a performer to mediate them. It is, of course, possible to 'act out' a dramatic work within the theatre of the imagination (the only arena for which Shelley and Byron wrote), but in the case of most plays that would be to miss the point. Words matter in drama, but comprise only a small part of a much larger and more fragile phenomenon.

This book sets out to trace the relationship between the dramatic text and the nonrational hinterland that lies behind it. By 'nonrational' I refer to those elements in a dramatic production that transcend the spoken word. They

---

[1] From *The Selected Writings of William Hazlitt* ed. Duncan Wu (9 vols, London: Pickering and Chatto, 1998), iii. 207.
[2] Both Eyre and David Hare discuss this; see pp. 180–1, 205–7, below.

often comprise mythic elements within the narrative, such as parent–child relationships – stories such as the Oedipus legend, or that of Phaedra and Hippolytus – or certain religious rites and rituals in secular form. It has been said that myth provides the libretto for ritual. One of the most important such motifs is the enactment of the cycle of the seasons, dramatised by a battle in which winter gives way to spring, in the course of which a year-king figure was ritually killed and supplanted by a new one. At first this was probably a human sacrifice of propitiation; later the killing was mimed. In a further development, the two kings were reduced to a single figure who underwent a process of repeated death and resurrection. The oldest ritual in the world tells the oldest story: that of the death and revival of a single figure. It is a story that continues to compel and fascinate audiences in its various manifestations, from the death and resurrection of Christ to all its variants: in Shakespeare, the apparent 'revival' of Cordelia and Desdemona *post mortem*; in modern drama, Isobel's final reappearance in Howard Davies' production of David Hare's *The Secret Rapture*. Edgar's *Pentecost* invokes the Christian story in order to discuss the life of works of art, and the very function of storytelling within society. In each case, the theatrical experience could be claimed as one in which the observer is reconnected to the roots of drama itself – the enactment of processes that are felt to be essential to the continued health of society.

Behind these ancient narrative patterns lies a vast reservoir of emotional power; that's why good storytellers return incessantly to them. Even very stylised theatre depends for its impact on its fidelity to those primeval forms. The theatre, Hare has written, 'is a place where the playwright's ultimate sincerity and good faith is going to be tested and judged in a way that no other medium demands'.[3] This is partly because theatre, while clearly not being the same as 'life', is life-like. It is enacted before us by real people in real time – and our reactions to it are correspondingly more immediate than, for instance, those to a story told by the silent voice of the novelist, or those to an image mediated through poetry. Of all literary forms, it is only in theatre that dramatic action and the nonrational are so intimately intertwined, to such intense and inescapable effect. The obvious comparison is with a charismatic religious experience – indeed, the best theatre offers something similar to that – in which the individual and the mass are brought together, however briefly. Any child who has left a pantomime in tears because of his or her engagement with stage characters knows what it is. Such experiences are easily forgotten. They slip through the fingers as soon as they are rationalised, because theatre is not the product of analysis. Indeed, the nonrational in contemporary drama is no more susceptible to discussion than it is in any

---

[3] 'The Play is in the Air: On Political Theatre', *Writing Left-Handed*, pp. 25–6.

other sphere of human activity. To that extent, a degree of futility is built into the process of verbalising one's responses to it.

The nonrational may be ineffable; it is also the product of a thousand practical judgements as to how it can be invoked. How was it that Richard Eyre created the final moments of *Amy's View*? How did Michael Attenborough and David Edgar create the stage magic of the storytelling scene in *Pentecost*? What is the appeal of such works as *The Madness of George III* or *Copenhagen*? Why was the Plato's Cave scene in *Bloody Poetry* so haunting? My aim has been to enquire into the generation of dramatic intensity, to trace the passage made by the text as it is translated from script to stage. The conscious decisions made by directors, actors and actresses, in collaboration with the writer, as they make the journey from text to performance, can be shadowed, even reconstructed, in retrospect. Theatre is written in the wind, but its effects can endure long after it is witnessed, and may continue to work its magic on the receptive mind.

I was first made fully aware of the power of the nonrational in contemporary drama when I saw Howard Davies' production of *The Secret Rapture* at the National Theatre in London in 1987. Having read the play in advance, I thought I knew what to expect. In fact, there were many elements in the production beyond the imagination of even the most dedicated student. This was most evident in the final scene. With the female protagonist (Isobel)[4] dead, her sister Marion[5] stood in the garden of Isobel's country house, and spoke the final line of the play: 'Isobel, where are you? Isobel, why don't you come home?' The published text ended there. But Davies had an audacious touch up his sleeve. At that moment, the actress who had played Isobel appeared at the back of the stage, very dimly seen, behind layer upon layer of stage gauze.[6] The 'ghost' was barely present, barely perceptible, and, almost before it had registered on the mind's eye, the curtain descended. The image resonates whenever I recall that production. It taught me that there is an unquenchable appetite within the theatregoer for more than pure entertainment; the theatre is the empire of the sublime – of the immaterial, the transcendent, and the ephemeral.

It may no longer be possible to say of drama, as Durkheim says of ritual, that its referent is the belief system of a society.[7] In spite of the statistical evidence, which suggests that large numbers of people regard themselves as 'religious', late twentieth-century society is characterised more by scepticism

---

[4] Played by Jill Baker.
[5] Played by Penelope Wilton.
[6] This is discussed by Hare, p. 183, below.
[7] Durkheim (1858–1917) discussed religion in his book, *The Elementary Forms of the Religious Life* (1915).

than by conviction.[8] Institutionalised religion may have broken down, but the capacity and need to believe remains undiminished; it is a constant in the human psyche. At the same time, literary studies has become less like biblical exegesis, on which it was once based, and more like a subdivision of philosophy. This is due partly to a fear of the powerful forces represented by religion, and partly to the increasing politicisation of literary studies. Whatever the cause, it is an abdication of responsibility. The elimination of faith from most peoples' lives has left a vacuum, and instead of attempting to fill it, literary critics have made their discipline more abstract, more inaccessible, and more redundant.

At a time when society as a whole is alienated from a common belief system, there is more need than at any other for the critic to recognise that great drama, like any literary form, is symbolic of social, psychological, or numinous realities. And if drama cannot refer to a shared religion in the present, it can nonetheless invoke shared understandings from the past. Drama may resemble ritual in the same way that it resembles reality. But those resemblances are the least of it. What is most important about great dramatic moments is not what we recognise, but what appears strange. There is a tendency within the human mind to ground what it perceives, however alien, within what is known. The tension between the rational and the nonrational pervades English Literature. This is most obvious during the Romantic period when, against the transcendentalism of Wordsworth and Coleridge, Byron purported to describe the natural world (including humanity) as essentially material. Despite the difficulty of envisaging the insubstantial in a profoundly positivistic world, contemporary dramatists have not lost sight of symbolic elements. Among the plays covered here, they include the storytelling scene in *Pentecost* (which functions both as ritual and invocation); the father–son relationship in *Copenhagen*; the purification rite at the end of *Amy's View*; the reading of *King Lear* in *The Madness of George III*; and the ritualised burning and rebirth of Shelley at the end of *Bloody Poetry*. Not that there is anything like a 'school' or 'movement' among those writers covered by this book. Admittedly, Hare, Edgar and Brenton were associated at the outset of their careers, but they are very different three decades on. They are of a later generation than Michael Frayn and Alan Bennett, both of whom were at Cambridge shortly after the war. Both are underrated, because they are assumed to be 'comic' writers, and therefore to have little to say. Analysis of the mythic elements of their work reveals them to be every bit as ambitious and 'serious' as the other writers interviewed here.

---

[8] In his lecture, 'When Shall We Live?', David Hare notes that while researching *Racing Demon* he was told by a number of inner-city vicars that we are living in 'what they were happy to call a post-Christian era' (*Via Dolorosa and When Shall We Live?* (London: Faber and Faber, 1998), p. 50).

There seems to be a point in the literary work at which the reader, or audience, is admitted to a realm beyond that discovered by exclusively naturalist narrative. There may be an overt attempt to invoke it, as in the culminating image of Richard Eyre's production of *Amy's View*[9] – which might be described as transcendental – or it may be embedded within the structure of the narrative, as in the case of *The Madness of George III*. Nonetheless, whether by design or not, that elemental function of the dramatic process, which prefers the nonrational to the rational, the symbolic to the real, the sacred to the profane, the deific to the humanistic, and tradition over experiment, is the subject of this book.

Questions of justice, of what constitutes a fair society, permeate the culture, and will always form the bedrock of intellectual discourse. Romanticism may be characterised by a prevailing optimism towards those questions. The period 1798–1832 was one of several in history when the aspiration to universal betterment predominated over conservatism. A comparable moment might be the 1960s, when, partly as a result of aspirations first expressed by the Romantics, British society began to declassify itself. To the extent that the writers surveyed here are political, they are inheritors of an age in which such ambitions were legitimised.

It would be odd not to invoke that shared tradition, given the way in which, during the last twenty years, history has repeated itself. Romantic writers knew that they were living through a peculiarly repressive period in English political and social history. From 1793 to 1815 England was inter-mittently at war with France (and much of Europe), the consequence of which was widespread social deprivation and suffering. The government of the time was largely intolerant of dissent, and sought to stifle it for fear that it would mutate into Revolution, as it had in France (an anxiety that would last well into the twentieth century). Britain during the 1980s was not at war with Europe (or at least, not openly), but under Mrs Thatcher it studiously defended its rights against what were regarded as the encroachments of the European Community (portrayed by the popular press as the 'enemy'). Events at home make parallels with the Romantic period rather more striking. After several decades during which the existence of a welfare state had been taken for granted, the Thatcher government embarked on the ambitious project of dismantling it. At the same time, the power of trades unions was drastically curtailed. The consequences of this were revealed most obviously in the running battles that occurred on a daily basis during the miners' strike in the mid-1980s. They mirrored the mass meetings and protests that had occurred from the 1790s through to the 1810s, when working people campaigned, and died, for their rights. If Britain in the 1980s was not at war with Europe, it

---

[9] See p. 203, below.

can at least be argued to have been at war with itself. That conflict manifested itself in various ways. Most insidiously, the government exerted pressure to compel the BBC, the state-funded broadcaster, to toe the party line. Tory placemen were given top jobs. Funds were threatened. Editorial impartiality could no longer be taken for granted. In the arts world, where funding was constantly under threat, a bunker mentality prevailed. Political bias or indecency was used as an argument for curtailing subsidies to the theatre (and, for that matter, to schools), the most obvious example being the row generated by Brenton's *The Romans in Britain*. Indirect though it was, the state exerted a degree of influence over cultural life in the 1980s that found its response in such works as *Bloody Poetry*, as its author observed in the programme note to the 1988 revival at the Royal Court: 'Byron, Shelley, Mary and Claire are moderns. They belong to us. They suffered exile from a reactionary, mean England, of which ours in the 1980s is an echo.'[10]

As the 1980s recede in the memory, one detects an increasing desire among those affected by it – understandably, no doubt – to put it behind them. To those who feel they lost out, it is a nightmare from which one has to awaken. Among those interviewed here, Max Stafford-Clark and David Edgar are inclined to accept many of the changes introduced by Thatcherism. David Hare has written, 'It is clear we need to move on.'[11] The period under which they lived brought irrevocable changes to the way in which Romantic writers saw the world. Shelley could not have composed *The Mask of Anarchy* or even his *Ode to the West Wind* had it not been for the Peterloo Massacre. Similarly, such plays as *Pravda*, *Greenland*, *Serious Money*, and *Racing Demon* are the result of prolonged meditation on the state of the nation. They reflect life in Britain during the 1980s, and comment upon it. For left-leaning writers of the time, that decade can only have been traumatic. The great project of the 1960s, with which they had been brought up, was a socialist one. It had been stalled by the multiple incompetences of the Labour government of 1974–79, but the more optimistic among them must have believed that the Thatcher government of 1979 was a blip. It wasn't. It marked the end of the experiment begun by the Labour government of 1945. That generated crisis in the arts generally, and, more importantly, in the vision of some of the writers profiled here.

Those who had taken a particular set of circumstances for granted in the 1960s and '70s were compelled to accept that they were now invalid. In 1981, as Max Stafford-Clark recalls, he and his colleagues at the Royal Court had planned to turn the theatre into a co-operative; no one would conceive of such a thing today. No one writes plays any longer about latter-day Marxist

---

[10] Brenton's programme note is reproduced in Appendix I, pp. 251–2, below.
[11] *Asking Around: Background to the David Hare Trilogy*, p. 8.

revolutionaries, and anyone who did would be thought out of touch. The events of the Eighties made idealism unfashionable. The result is nowhere clearer than in the work of the latest generation of playwrights. Take the late Sarah Kane, who was pre-eminently a writer of the 1990s. 'Fuck God. Fuck the monarchy', Hippolytus says to the Priest in *Phaedra's Love*.[12] Spiritual absolutes have no place in her world; dramatic action is rooted in the realm of the material. *Phaedra's Love* is close in mood and form to the Jacobean tragedies, and its cathartic conclusion licensed by the spirits of Webster and Tourneur. That said, it would be rash to view Kane's work in purely literary terms. Extreme it may be, but it is nonetheless exquisitely reactive to the world in which it is wrought, and offers the logical response to a world in which idealism has been systematically voided of significance.[13] It is the utterance of a sensibility profoundly aware of the state of the nation at the millennium. Or, for a similar kind of writing, take *Shopping and Fucking*, by Mark Ravenhill:

> It's summer. I'm in a supermarket. It's hot and I'm sweaty. Damp. And I'm watching this couple shopping. I'm watching you. And you're both smiling. You see me and you know sort of straight away that I'm going to have you. You know you don't have a choice. No control.
> Now this guy comes up to me. He's a fat man. Fat and hair and lycra and he says:
> See the pair by the yoghurt?
> Well, says fat guy, they're both mine. I own them. I own them but I don't want them – because you know something? – they're trash. Trash and I hate them. Wanna buy them?[14]

This artful speech establishes the play's central theme with remarkable economy. It's about the peculiar powerlessness of being owned by someone else – a phenomenon only too familiar to most young people of the 1990s. The play is set in a world in which love is displaced by mammon, in which people are objects to be sold from one owner to the next. Once again, it is a world rooted in materiality. Kane and Ravenhill are distinct from their elders in that their work reflects a universe stripped of soul, and it is difficult to resist the observation that theirs is a vision shaped and nurtured by Thatcherism. Conversely, the writers profiled here have comprehended the world through the aspirations that resulted from the war. Their work, not surprisingly, has

---

[12] Sarah Kane, *Blasted and Phaedra's Love* (London: Methuen Drama, 1996) p. 90.
[13] I take issue with Peter Ansorge's recent contention that Sarah Kane and her contemporaries have 'almost nothing to say' (see Peter Ansorge, *From Liverpool to Los Angeles* (London: Faber and Faber, 1997) p. 119).
[14] Mark Ravenhill, *Shopping and Fucking* (London: Methuen Drama, 1996) p. 3.

often returned to it: *Heading Home*, *Plenty*, *The Churchill Play*, *Destiny* and *Copenhagen* spring to mind as obvious examples. David Hare has written:

> The most important fact of my life happened before I was born. In the Second World War millions of people died in defence of a belief, and the sense of squalor and disappointment of the post-war period seems to me inexorably to have stemmed from the feeling that the sacrifice they made has somehow been squandered.[15]

Hare's language is revealing – 'belief', 'sacrifice': terms that imply the existence of something beyond the purely material. It is a perspective utterly distinct from that of *Shopping and Fucking*, and is shared by the other writers in this volume. The challenge that has characterised their recent work is that of resisting the lure of a perspective in which human existence is seen to function primarily, or even largely, on the level of the material. Primo Levi once observed that 'it's a good thing, a moral thing, to behave as though there's still hope'. That statement is as resigned as it sounds, and within a year of having made it, Levi was dead by his own hand. Nonetheless, it accounts to some degree for the position adopted by the writers in this volume. Their claims are curtailed – more so than in the 1970s. But by reflecting the world in which they live, and commenting upon it, they are engaging in an act of faith with their audience. That act is inseparable from a perspective geared to accommodate nonrational elements. Of all the plays examined in this volume, *Copenhagen* may seem the least congenial to these ideas. After all, it features three characters who discuss the scientific developments that led to the invention of the atom bomb. What could that have to do with the nonrational? In fact, the play is underpinned by the relationships between the characters; Niels Bohr remembers his first encounter with Werner Heisenberg as a 'spot of time':

> Beautiful summer's day. The scent of roses drifting in from the gardens. Rows of eminent physicists and mathematicians, all nodding approval of my benevolence and wisdom. Suddenly, up jumps a cheeky young pup and tells me that my mathematics are wrong.[16]

The darker aspects of the play are given depth by such moments, which set the speculations and histories of the characters within an emotional context. And that, perhaps, is the essence of the nonrational. 'Poetry is passion', wrote Wordsworth, 'It is the history or science of feeling.' What all of the plays

---

[15] David Hare, *Via Dolorosa and When Shall We Live?* (p. 72).
[16] *Copenhagen*, p. 22.

1: Sian Thomas as Mary Shelley in Max Stafford-Clark's 1988 revival of Howard Brenton's *Bloody Poetry*. Photo: Sarah Ainslie.

2: 'The Coronation Anthem finally reaches its climax
... as the King struggles, howling, in the chair': Nigel
Hawthorne in the restraining chair in Alan Bennett's
The Madness of George III.
Photo: Donald Cooper, Photostage.

3: Jan Ravens as Gabriella Pecs and Charles Kay as Oliver Davenport in
Michael Attenborough's production of David Edgar's *Pentecost*.
Photo: Shakespeare Centre Library.

4: Judi Dench and Samantha Bond in David Hare's *Amy's View*.
Photo: John Haynes.

5: From left to right: Matthew Marsh (Heisenberg), Sara
Kestelman (Margrethe), and David Burke (Bohr) in the Royal
National Theatre production of Michael Frayn's *Copenhagen*.
Photo: Conrad Blakemore.

analysed here have in common is that they are Romantic in that supreme sense: they document a history of the emotions.[17] The pay-off may be geopolitical, as in *Pentecost*, or philosophical, as with *Copenhagen*, but the pulse by which the play registers is its truth to the emotions. No one element can be abstracted from the equation, but if that component is absent, it is hard to see how dramatic action can partake of the 'poetry' of which practitioners such as Richard Eyre speak.[18]

My central preoccupation is with how abstract concepts are transformed into stage action, and from the outset it seemed most useful to talk to the writer and director: the writer because he has the task of formulating the ideas behind the work; the director because he is in charge of its staging. Of course, I could have spoken to others involved in the business of production – designers, lighting designers, sound technicians, and so on. But that would have been a less focussed kind of investigation. The director is the architect of each production, and I wanted to understand how different practitioners went about their job. As my investigations have continued, this has emerged as the dominant subject of the volume. Romanticism, myth, the nonrational, and the Thatcher decade all remain elemental to my approach, but at the conclusion it is clear to me that the book has taken on a shape I could never have anticipated. Although my preoccupations have often determined the questions I have asked, and the assumptions I have brought to each encounter, the answers I have been given (which I could never have predicted) add up to something more revealing, and more important: a unique insight into the business of *making plays*.

In the first place, it is a highly intellectual affair. All the works analysed in this volume are the work of people who have first thought long and deeply – and who, in most cases, have engaged in extensive background research. In the second, it is eminently practical. In several cases examined here, the director is the editor of the text, helping to bring it to completion, as he takes practical control of it, mediating it to those involved in its production. It may be that all literary processes are collaborative, but theatre is more so than any other. As the text is translated into stage action it may acquire qualities entirely dependent on the collision of talents, the precise nature of which remains incalculable. To take just one example, Alan Bennett says that he was delighted by Robin Bailey's reading of Thurlow in the first read-through of *The Madness of George III*.[19] This was not anticipated, and the nature of dramatic collaboration dictates that it could not have been. Stage alchemy is

---

[17] Hare writes of being 'unafraid of being passionate' as a writer; 'Looking Foolish: On Taking Risks', *Writing Left-Handed*, p. 50.
[18] See p. 203.
[19] See p. 86, below.

by nature unpredictable, and permits the receptive audience access, without warning, to those realms I refer to as the nonrational, the sublime, and the transcendental. The primary task of this book is to retrace the route taken by some of those responsible for such happy accidents.

Much has been written and said about the writer–director relationship in recent years.[20] The only way of approaching the subject with any rigour is through specifics. In each case, my strategy was to take a single play as the focus of each interview; within it, I chose a scene, or moment, at which a crisis of some kind had been reached. Having established that frame of reference, I asked my interviewees to address themselves to it. In the case of *Amy's View*, the obvious moment is the final scene in which Esme and Toby prepare to go on stage; in *Pentecost*, the storytelling scene; in *George III*, the climax of Part I, when the King is put in the restraining chair, and the 'Lear' scene in Part II, when he is returned to sanity; in *Bloody Poetry*, the 'Plato's Cave' scene and the final scene, in which Shelley is cremated on the beach; and in *Copenhagen*, the third and final re-enactment of the meeting between Bohr and Heisenberg.

To those inclined to note the absence here of the numerous female practitioners in British theatre, I would respond that it was always my intention to include some but, for reasons beyond my control, they have eluded me. It is no criticism of their talents that I have failed to represent them here, and I hope that, although none of my interviewees is able to offer a distinctively female perspective, readers will nonetheless acknowledge the heterogeneity of technical and intellectual approaches dealt with in this study.[21]

Methodology

Interviews are transcribed from tape and presented much as they happened, prefaced by brief introductory commentaries on the works and productions concerned. Interviewees were given a free hand to edit transcriptions prior to publication. By and large, they have restricted themselves to minor adjustments to iron out the kind of solecisms – syntactical errors and the like – which everyone makes in conversation. On occasion, interviewees have substantially revised or rewritten their remarks, but the result has invariably been to make their written words even clearer, more detailed, and more accurate, than their spoken utterances.

---

[20] See, for instance, Richard Nelson and David Jones, *Making Plays: The Writer–Director Relationship in the Theatre Today* (London: Faber and Faber, 1995); Maria Delgado and Paul Heritage, *In Contact with the Gods? Directors Talk Theatre* (Manchester: Manchester University Press, 1996), and Arthur Bartow, *The Director's Voice: Twenty-One Interviews* (New York: Theater Communications Group, 1988).
[21] For some helpful interviews with modern female playwrights in Britain see Heidi Stephenson and Natasha Langridge, *Rage and Reason: Women Playwrights on Playwriting* (London: Routledge, 1997).

Introductions have been provided to each interview with the aim of establishing, for the benefit of the reader, my interpretation of the dramatic work I wanted to discuss. This includes aspects of each production and points of information related to it. I hope that these materials are sufficient to enable most readers to enjoy the interviews, but those with a serious interest in these works will wish to consult published texts of the plays under discussion, all of which are in print at the time of writing. Suggestions for further reading can be found at the end of each essay and in the bibliography.

It is my hope that this book will reveal to the reader in what ways drama is distinct from other literary forms, and something of what is entailed in the creation of great theatre.

Howard Brenton

Howard Brenton, *Bloody Poetry* (1984–88)

Bloody Poetry was commissioned by Foco Novo Theatre Company and presented at the Haymarket Theatre, Leicester, 1 October 1984, in a production directed by Roland Rees.[1] It was revived as one of Brenton's 3 Plays for Utopia at the Royal Court Theatre, directed by Max Stafford-Clark, 7 April 1988.

> BYRON: Y'bloody hypocrite! Where is your legal wife? In England! The two women you are with, Mary y'call your wife, Claire y'friend – concubines, sir! Y'mistresses, sir! All your idealism, revolution in society, revolution in the personal life, all trumpery! The practice of it, sir, the practice doth make us dirty, doth make all naked and bleeding and real![2]

Byron's speech in Act Two spells out the central conflict of *Bloody Poetry*, between Shelley's aspirations and the wreckage of his personal life. In the face of Romantic aspiration, the play presents a portrait of lives that were, in every sense, 'naked and bleeding and real'. That tension amounts to a trenchant critique of the characters and the impulses which they represent; as Byron remarks of Wordsworth: 'Romanticism rears its ugly, look-both-ways, have-it-both-ways head! Though something be nonsense, feel the feeling.'[3] It is an observation typical of Brenton's Byron, whose response to Shelleyan (and Wordsworthian) optimism is to deflate it. A little later in Act One, Polidori puts it slightly differently: 'Shelley has tuberculosis, Byron has syphilis, and these are the men whom the intelligent among us worship as angels of freedom.'[4] That sardonic commentary

---

[1] Roland Rees was the founder and guiding spirit of Foco Novo, and his first production of *Bloody Poetry* remains highly regarded. Unfortunately I did not see it, and first encountered the play in the Royal Court revival of 1988. I therefore chose to interview Max Stafford-Clark rather than Rees. Readers interested in Brenton's working partnership with Rees should turn to the interview in Rees' useful volume *Fringe First*, pp. 201–21.

[2] *Brenton Plays: Two*, p. 273.

[3] *Brenton Plays: Two*, p. 258.

[4] *Brenton Plays: Two*, p. 262.

can't be said to summarise Brenton's position, but it does encapsulate the argument of the play as a whole. It could be expanded to apply to almost all revolutionaries; Brenton is concerned with whether moral inconsistency, even failure, invalidates the larger political project. An answer, insofar as there is one, is provided by Claire Clairmont:

> All of us, we will become magnificent. The men and the women of the future will thank us. We are their great experiment. We will find out how to live and love, without fear.[5]

It is a painfully ironic speech within the context of the play. By its conclusion, the characters have experienced both the highs of their first encounter at Geneva in 1816, and the lows of suicidal despair. And yet, though deeply flawed, Brenton asks us to value them for their attachment to ideals which were impossible to reconcile with the reality of their lives. They were adventurers, and their example is a promise of new realms to be discovered.

That promise informs much of Brenton's work: it is, for instance, the intensity of sensation that compels Christie, the serial killer, in *Christie in Love*,[6] as early as 1969: 'I don't remember what happened', he says, 'But I must have gone haywire.'[7] Despite his appalling crimes, Christie experiences a sublimity that gives his life a meaning lacking in others'. For the constable who apprehends him, love is a series of cheap clichés: 'Love's the bleeding moon. And bleeding doves cooing. And bleeding Frank Sinatra crooning.'[8] There is no intensity in his life; his feelings are deadened. Like the characters of *Bloody Poetry*, the squatters in *Magnificence* (1973)[9] are aware that their ideals are compromised by reality: '"Mobilize the people?" We can't mobilize a tin opener.'[10] The culmination of their zealotry is when Jed blows up himself and Alice, the Paymaster-General. That explosion is cast by Brenton as an image of waste; it is also one of sublime aspiration, and is echoed in subsequent works. Christie and Jed are characters about whom Brenton is deeply ambiguous. They are on the one hand extreme visionaries, and, on the other, responsible for acts which neither he nor his audience could endorse. In the first of the Plays for Utopia, *Sore Throats*,[11] Judy nurses a similar dream:

---

[5] *Brenton Plays: Two*, p. 242.
[6] First performed by Portable Theatre, Oval House, 23 November 1969, directed by David Hare.
[7] *Brenton Plays: One*, p. 27.
[8] *Brenton Plays: One*, p. 28.
[9] First performed at the Royal Court Theatre, 28 June 1973, directed by Max Stafford-Clark.
[10] *Brenton Plays: One*, p. 66.
[11] First performed by the Royal Shakespeare Company, 8 August 1979, directed by Barry Kyle, and revived as the first of Brenton's Plays for Utopia, Royal Court Theatre, 15 April 1988, directed by Nancy Diuguid.

Burn what's left of the money, and steal if we have to. Nail the door up if we have to. Block the windows with bricks. Move. Sleep in the open. Sell ourselves. Get guns. Kill, if we have to.
I'll not go back in that front room.[12]

The desire for liberation is as intense in Judy as in Jed, but far less damaging. Money and sex are seen to have confined her and her violent ex-husband Jack to the fallen world, and her rejection of them is what leads to this escapade. The destruction of her remaining cash is seen as a final attempt to open the door to Utopia; as she sets light to the banknotes, her concluding speech is a kind of manifesto: 'I am going to be fucked, happy, and free.'[13] (In a pre-AIDS world, sexual permissiveness was seen as a kind of Utopia.)

All Brenton's revolutionaries are in some way failures. They know that another, better world is somehow attainable, but can't find it. The strategy chosen by Jed and Christie is too extreme; that taken by Judy isn't, apparently, quite extreme enough. Like Judy, Claire Clairmont believes 'I am going to be loved, happy and free',[14] but that expectation turns out to be horribly thwarted, when Byron abandons her and takes away their child, Allegra. Shelley's first wife commits suicide; discord enters the Shelleys' marriage, and Percy is finally drowned in a storm. But were they really failures? The answer to that can be found in Brenton's images of ambition, originating with the explosion at the end of *Magnificence*, and continuing with the lighting of the banknotes at the end of *Sore Throats*. It is repeated at the end of *Bloody Poetry* with Byron's funeral oration, delivered over Shelley's decomposed body:

Burn him! Burn him! Burn him!
Burn us all! A great big, bloody, beautiful fire![15]

Hellish and consuming on the one hand, the flames are symbolic also of an ultimate victory: that of the work, the poetry, which extended its influence into an unknown future. The flames of future revolution would sweep the world during the succeeding 150 years, partly thanks to the inspirational force of Shelley's verse. On a spiritual level, those flames describe something else: release from the physical realm in which Shelley's visionary hopes are grounded. It is as if death, the final barrier to the realisation of his Utopian dreams, has finally been conquered. Through the burning of the pyre, Shelley is translated out of earth into air. And perhaps there is an echo of the Monster at the end of Mary Shelley's *Frankenstein*, who envisages his destruction in similar terms:

---

[12] *Brenton Plays: One*, p. 376.
[13] *Brenton Plays: One*, p. 390.
[14] *Brenton Plays: Two*, p. 244.
[15] *Brenton Plays: Two*, p. 310.

I shall ascend my funeral pile triumphantly, and exult in the agony of the torturing flames. The light of that conflagration will fade away; my ashes will be swept into the sea by the winds. My spirit will sleep in peace; or if it thinks, it will not surely think thus. Farewell.[16]

Brenton transfers the Monster's note of triumphant resignation directly into *Bloody Poetry*. But unlike the Monster, Shelley will not be forgotten; as Claire remarked, he was part of a 'great experiment'. The conclusion to this argument is presented in *Greenland*, the third of Brenton's Plays for Utopia.[17] Claire had envisaged people who had discovered how to 'live and love, without fear'; they are the Greenlanders, 700 years hence, who have shed the concept of property, and forgotten the meaning of pain and misery.

Despite its setting, *Bloody Poetry* is a play of its time, as Brenton recalled in a recent interview on BBC Radio:

> It was the early 1980s, and Thatcher's government had taken hold because of the Falklands war. The country was awash with sudden jingoism, and all the things that a number of us had believed in – that we were socialists, or Labour Party-ists, or quasi-Marxists – all writing theatre in the 1970s, we seemed to be really washed up on the beach and in a state of internal exile. Indeed, we were beginning to be called 'loonies'. And this reminded me of the attitude towards Byron and Shelley ... And I thought, 'There's an empathy here between my generation and theirs.' So I looked on it as a play about the exile of idealists.[18]

It may be historical, but *Bloody Poetry* is intimately rooted in the time and place of its writing – more so, perhaps, than any of the works examined here. It is about spiritual dispossession, alienation from one's homeland. That's why it is so important to Brenton that the characters, for all their shortcomings, are redeemed by their attempt to live and love without fear: for *Bloody Poetry* is also a rallying cry to radical spirits of the 1980s. This is more transparent still in the case of *Greenland*, set on election night 1987, when the Labour Party suffered crushing defeat. The second and third of the Utopian plays are, emphatically, about surviving in the face of hostile opposition.[19]

As Brenton remarks below,[20] the 1980s was a productive decade for him; he wrote many plays, some inspired directly by current affairs. By comparison, the

---

[16] Mary Shelley, *Frankenstein* ed. M. K. Joseph (Oxford: Oxford University Press, 1969, p. 223).
[17] It was first presented at the Royal Court Theatre, 26 May 1988, in a production directed by Simon Curtis.
[18] *Adventures in Poetry: Shelley, Ode to the West Wind*, BBC Radio 4, transmitted 11 April 1999. Produced by Sara Davies.
[19] Brenton describes all too vividly the uneasiness of radical life in Thatcherland in one of the best novels of that bleak era, *Diving for Pearls* (London: Nick Hern Books, 1989). See also my review of it, 'Out of the gutter', *New Statesman and Society*, 16 June 1989, p. 37.
[20] See p. 48.

1990s has been quieter. His most important work of the ten years is *Berlin Bertie*.[21] It would suggest that, like David Edgar, he has renewed himself as a writer by turning his attention towards Europe. Into this haunting tale of betrayal and deceit, he has incorporated another Greenlander, Joanne, who nurtures a vision of how men and women may live and love without fear:

Turn a strange corner
                    arch your back
And SLIP in through

Open a door in the air
                    free
Human flight

It's in us
                    I know
It's a KNACK

All you've got to do
                    is just
Slip through[22]

Fear grounds the hopes of the Greenlander in the palpable; fear is the enemy of idealism. The tension between the two has provided Brenton with his subject-matter for the last three decades. It is what makes those occasional moments, when visionaries like Joanne see beyond the post-lapsarian universe into a redemptive future, so vitally important. Another such moment occurs in *Bloody Poetry* when the characters dramatise Plato's Cave:

> The fire in the cave is the past, by which we see now. The sun on the hillside, is the future of mankind. It is our future that is the absolute good! Plato himself was a prisoner, religion a flicker in the cave! The mind of man, that is the true sun! We are the instruments of that future light![23]

On one hand, the play is designed to show how painfully acute was the failure of the second-generation Romantics to realise the ideals they held most dear (indeed, that was the aspect of the work that caused disquiet among such Shelleyans as Paul Foot); at the same time, Brenton sets out to value their achievement for what it was. In the Plato's cave episode, he succeeds both in illustrating a complex piece of philosophy, and in explicating the Utopian hopes of his characters.

Brenton seems to me a remarkable writer. He is a propagandist, a provocateur, and one of the few dramatists of our time who might credibly be described as

---

[21] First performed at the Royal Court Theatre, 9 April 1992, directed by Danny Boyle.
[22] *Berlin Bertie*, p. 54.
[23] *Brenton Plays: Two*, p. 267.

the inheritor of the Brechtian tradition. It is a point worth making, because at the time of writing he is also one of the most underrated of those profiled here. This is partly because he remains at odds with the spirit of the age, a point underlined by the criticism that greeted his recent critique of Blairite double-dealing, *Ugly Rumours* (co-written with Tariq Ali). The complacency of 1990s Britain requires Brenton's adversarial vision no less than the more despotic reign of Mrs Thatcher. Since recording my interview with Brenton, he has written a debate about the war in Kosova, *Collateral Damage*, with Tariq Ali and Andy de la Tour.[24]

I visited him at his home in Camberwell, south London, 24 March 1999. Brenton is a generous interviewee: besides taking a retrospective view of his career, from *Christie in Love* to the present, we covered a number of general issues, including situationism, Thatcherism, Brecht and Ibsen, queer theory and much else. In fact, this interview confirms the impression one gets from his work – that, intellectually, he is an adventurous writer, unafraid of risk. Besides *Bloody Poetry*, Brenton discussed his partnership with Max Stafford-Clark, which dates back to 1972 when *Hitler Dances* was first produced at the Traverse Theatre, Edinburgh, and which embraces *Epsom Downs* (1977), which evolved out of a workshop with Joint Stock, as well as the revival of *Bloody Poetry* at the Royal Court in 1988.

Interview

Duncan Wu: *Do you regard the theatre as an instrument of change?*

Howard Brenton: I would think any artist has to, given what they're doing.

What kind of change?

Well, it's very grand and naïve. To make a better world.

Better in what way?

Well, I'm a socialist, so I'd like to see a more communitarian world, and the ravages of greed and exploitation diminished. You write hopefully for that to happen. But it depends how you see the world. You have no choice but to see the world in the way you do, you're caught in the solipsism of this, so when you're asked, 'Are you a political writer? Do you want to change the world?', you reply, 'Yes' and 'Yes' – but that doesn't seem an extraordinary thing. The questions then are, 'Well, how does this play work like that? How

---

[24] It was performed 19–30 May 1999 at the Tricycle Theatre, Kilburn, London.

does that play work like that?' Like with any other writer, like a writer who wants to retain *status quo*. Someone who says, 'I want purely to entertain' will be a *status quo* artist. And they can achieve things by accident which actually do change the world.

One has a kind of Lutherian pomposity about this – 'Here I stand, I can do no other!' But no; I do dream about people rushing out of the theatre saying, 'The very molecules of the air have been rearranged by this piece of work! We're breathing in different ways.' Of course it doesn't happen ...

Doesn't it?

Very rarely, but that's what you aim for. I think you have to claim higher naïveté as a writer, no one else will.

Your 3 Plays for Utopia, and many of your other works, have addressed concerns that are very important to me as a Romanticist. The Romantics believed that it was possible to reclaim Paradise. Do you have a concept of Paradise behind your work?

I was very cross when a children's sci-fi film thought of the title *Back to the Future*: that was a brilliant title, and you do have the sense of how things could be do inform the things you do now. In other words, your tradition is future possibilities. It's the other way round from a conservative point of view where you construct a style of life like classicism. We construct a view of what it was like in Greece and want to get back to it – which I know the Romantics did in some ways; Goethe got heavily involved in that. I did a version of *Faust*, we did Part II,[1] and I thought, 'This is the life I want, this is how I want things to live, this is the way I think things could be lived.' There was a Utopian feel in that, it was extraordinary.

Tell me more about that. There's a section in Faust *where they go to Greece?*

Yes, in Part II. They're looking for a classical ideal. Mephistopheles is deeply put out because he doesn't exist in that time era, his powers don't work because it's a pagan world. Mephistopheles, as an agent for the Devil, can only work after Christ is born. So Goethe in some extraordinary way is by-passing the whole of the neo-platonic difficulty concerning mind and body; it's one of the great, deeply-crazed pieces of writing, and utterly unstageable!

---

[1] Brenton's translation of *Faust* was produced by the Royal Shakespeare Company at the Swan Theatre, Stratford, 2 September 1995, and is published by Nick Hern Books.

I'm interested in Christie in Love.[2] *Is Christie, as he appears in your play, a sort of proto-Utopian?*

Well I won't know, because that was an instinctive piece of writing. I was young, and when you start writing you're just so pleased you can do it, you don't really ask what you're doing. The craft overwhelms you, the fact that you can get through an hour. I was so pleased I could tell jokes in some short earlier plays I wrote before *Christie*. And then the idea of how you do a serious play? – well, you kill off the jokes. So *Christie* is built on a system of incredible bad timing, and all the jokes must never be laughed at. The limericks should be done in such a way that no one could *possibly* laugh at them. You don't really know what your themes are. It's when you get a bit older, when you start to write two-Act, full-length plays, that you have to be able to answer the question of what you actually are about. 'Jokes about what?' you have to ask – that process takes over. So I couldn't honestly say, 'Oh yes guv, of course I set out to write this whole span of work on Utopian themes, even when I was twenty-five!'

Fair enough. What drew you to Christie?

It was a series of accidents. One was that Portable Theatre, run by David Hare and Tony Bicât, had a grand scheme of making a number of shows called *The History of Evil* – which seemed a really silly idea! None of the plays got written, but *Christie* was meant to be one. They said to me, 'Would you write *The History of Evil?*' and I said, 'I don't know what that means, really.' But I suddenly realised that at that time my wife and I were living, in straitened circumstances in a basement, just round the corner from where Christie had lived. I realised that this was a whole area of interest, so I began to think about Christie. The theme was sort of self-generating.

The play was against easy thinking. A number of the books that I read said that he was a displaced person, a Yorkshireman with emotional difficulties; he came down to London and didn't know anyone. He became a Special Constable to project himself more, so people would notice him. I thought, there are hundreds of thousands of displaced Yorkshiremen who have uneasy relationships with their mothers, and they did not all kill six people and bury them under the floorboards. I could not find an explanation for it, and so I suppose that was the definition of evil, that it has no explanation. I was fumbling after something like that. Which is why the coppers, the police, cannot make sense of the man's sexuality.

---

[2] *Christie in Love* was first produced by Portable Theatre at the Oval House, London, 23 November 1969. It was directed by David Hare.

He says, 'I must have gone haywire.'[3]

Yes.

Which is no explanation at all.

No explanation at all. It's just an observation. I remember thinking a lot about that. I wanted to make it a piece which was deliberately end-stopped. In other words, it deliberately had no message – at all, so you were face to face with what it was about.

So what you were looking at was just an evil being.

That's it, that's it. And the question it begs is, what does this mean to us? I think that's what was disturbing about it. It's so easy to moralise in the theatre. Most TV dramas are full of moralising. The reason is you can write it very quickly. *Neighbours*, the TV soap, is full of moralising statements, because they have to write each episode in half an hour!

With Christie, *you're standing back from all that. In a way you're reacting against it.*

Yes, that's it. I do remember that's what I was trying to do.

Magnificence *was produced at the Royal Court, 1973.*[4]

It took me a long time to write.

I wonder whether you'd agree with me that characters such as Jed in Magnificence *are not so far from those in* Bloody Poetry. *They have aspirations which are thwarted. Like the characters in* Bloody Poetry *they're dealing with the sordid realities of living and trying to realise some kind of aspiration.*

I was very disturbed in the early Seventies because I knew of people like that. I didn't know them personally, though I met someone who taught them. They were a group called the Angry Brigade, in England, who copied the Baader-Meinhof[5] in the early 1970s. They set off a bomb on a window-ledge in the Ministry of Defence. I say bomb, but it was more or less a big firework.

---

[3] *Christie in Love*, Scene 10; see *Brenton Plays: One*, p. 27.
[4] 28 June 1973, to be precise; directed by Max Stafford-Clark.
[5] Also known as the Red Army Faction; West German leftist terrorist group formed in 1968 and popularly named after two of its early leaders, Andreas Baader (1943–77) and

And there were a couple of other attempts. They were quickly arrested and went down for a long time. These were kids from Essex University, and I think a London college too. They had bought the Baader-Meinhof revolutionary line, and it seemed to me that the Sixties had decayed in its thinking. But I was very disturbed, I couldn't work it out, and I wrote the play to work it out, saying, 'Should we be on their side or not?' And I came to the conclusion not. There was a book which I'm reading again, it's still in print, called *The Society of the Spectacle* by Guy Debord. He was a Belgian philosopher. He wrote a book which began the situationist movement, and it's one of the key texts of that movement – which was anarchic, no movement at all.[6] It's a brilliant analysis. It popped up again in punk, oddly; those punks weren't totally ignorant! It certainly influenced me. And the speech about disrupting the spectacle is out of Guy Debord.[7] 'You will not destruct it. What you will destruct is yourself', that's what my argument was. There's a good pamphlet by Lenin entitled, *Left-Wing Communism: An Infantile Disorder*. That's the conclusion I came to, and I wrote the play to try and say, 'Don't do this.'

Did you find yourself attracted to situationism?

Enormously, because I believe their analysis is probably right.

Could you summarise it?

It's become *very* strong in the last couple of years. It's that the state runs a spectacle, which is like a printed circuit board – that is, the way you speak, the way debates are conducted, the way news is put out, the way you can think something and cannot think something, the span of time you have to say something, the length of lessons, the syllabus in schools. All of it is like a printed circuit board, so that things will run in an orderly way. The state puts up a show, a spectacle, in which you say, 'I am a ...; I am a ...' But in actual fact, no one lives in the spectacle. It's like a giant projection which dictates the way which, if you're going to be understood or make your way in the world, you've got to follow.

It's like a politician who stands up and says, 'We all grieve today at the news from Uganda.'[8] And then goes into his office and says, 'Fuck those

Ulrike Meinhof (1934–76). From its early years, the members supported themselves by robberies of banks and other businesses and engaged in terrorist bombings and arson, especially of West German corporations and businesses and of West German and US military installations in West Germany. They also engaged in kidnappings and assassinations of prominent political and business figures.

[6] Brenton comments further on situationism in his essay, 'The Spaceman Amongst the Tower Blocks', *Hot Irons*, pp. 38–43.

[7] Brenton refers to Jed's speech in Scene 7; *Brenton Plays: One*, pp. 95–6.

[8] Eight tourists captured by rebel Rwandan soldiers were hacked and clubbed to death while on safari in Uganda; the news was reported on 3 March 1999.

fucking tourists.' The spectacle is the statement that we grieve today for the death of the tourists, but no one is actually living in it; what they're living in is, 'Fuck the tour company, I'm going to screw them!'

The spectacle is there to control us.

That's it. But even more, it's so we know what to live by. It's because we live in huge, crowded, urban populations. Fantasies have to be orchestrated, so you have to have a Madonna, you have to have certain values, and they have to be increasingly worldwide – so that everyone can think together and more or less do things together, and accept their place in the world, or else you're going to have chaos.

The situationists would want to undermine that.

They say it's an oppression. They say it's replacing the work of the ruling class. A mechanism is replacing the work of the ruling class. That's a very brilliant analysis, and it has a certain truth, particularly in the spin-doctored world of this tiny island. The spin-doctors are managing the spectacle very consciously these days, saying 'There are certain cultural things you can think, and certain things you can't.'

It's very strong in the theatre at the moment – you can't have messages, you can't have political speeches out of characters' mouths. That's really out of fashion. It's been put out of fashion because there's a general consensus. There's a reason why, commercially, you really don't want that kind of work in the theatre any more. To be petty about it.

That at least is what I take to be the situationist argument. It's written in the most impenetrable French – you know, that French academic style where you think, 'Wittgenstein is like the *Sun* compared to some of this stuff!' It is very beautiful though, Guy Debord's book. A new translation came out not long ago.[9]

Were you conscious at the time that you were addressing an audience that was as conversant as you were with those intellectual notions?

No. I thought people *wouldn't* know about it, particularly in England. And I thought they wouldn't care: that's a good reason for dramatising it. I've often thought that. The theatre can do that. I thought that people wouldn't care about nuclear physics, particularly, so in *The Genius*[10] I thought, 'I will actually try and dramatise this.'

---

[9] Guy Debord, *The Society of the Spectacle* tr. David Nicholson-Smith (New York: Zone Books, 1995).
[10] *The Genius* was first performed at the Royal Court Theatre, 8 September 1983.

Do you have a strong feeling about who you're talking to?

I prefer it to be strangers, that's why I liked it when I had plays on at the National Theatre.[11] It was full of people who wouldn't like your plays normally, and maybe you could get it to them. Or perhaps they wouldn't be interested in what you were interested in. It's a matter of addressing strangers. You feel you're speaking for someone, but you don't necessarily know to whom you're speaking, I think that's the position that writers are in. I worry that the theatre's very difficult for that. I think it's easier to have heretical books that make their way than it is to have heretical plays.

Why?

A heretical book can be read in secret, and can get hammered by reviewers, and yet still recover and persist. Take *American Psycho*,[12] which is beginning to look like one of the most terrific American novels written since the war – and yet when it came out it was looked on as an absolutely disgraceful piece of work. A play needs a kind of instant consensus. If 90 per cent of people don't agree with you, you're not going to have a hit: it's getting very strong, the demand for consensus.

The Romans in Britain, I suppose, was a heretical play.[13]

That's right. It recovered, interestingly. It was said to be heretical, had terrible reviews on the whole, but actually was middle in the running order at the National Theatre.[14] Peter Hall put it on for another season because it passed the box-office test! It wasn't sold out, they kept on saying it was sold out.

People are reluctant to go out to the theatre if they think, 'This is going to frighten me.' Drama's not a frightening genre. It's easier in the cinema, really. People say, 'Let's go and see that horrendous film', but they don't say that about plays so easily.

David Edgar tells me that in the early Seventies he was very aware that he was addressing a group of people much like himself.[15] But you didn't have that particular feeling?

---

[11] Namely, *Weapons of Happiness* (1976), *The Life of Galileo* (1980), *The Romans in Britain* (1980), *Danton's Death* (1982), and *Pravda* (1985).

[12] Novel by Bret Easton Ellis, 1991.

[13] For further comment on this, see Brenton's 'Writing in Thatcherland: Five of My Plays', *Hot Irons*, pp. 28–31.

[14] It was first performed on 16 October 1980 at the National Theatre in a production directed by Michael Bogdanov.

[15] See p. 122.

Not particularly. But certainly, the theatre audience was always middle class. In London, they came out of bedsit-land, which was very strong in the Seventies – from which, indeed, the bombers would come after they'd stopped being students (as in *Magnificence*). So the notion of people in a squat, or near a squat, meant that the play had a whole subgroup that it could address; there was a social reality within the general middle-class span of the theatre audience. Indeed, it was possible that there would be an audience for a certain kind of play but not for others. People who went to the Royal Court would not, at that time, readily go to the National Theatre. The National was associated with Olivier and camp style, whereas the Court was carrying, however briefly, a more youthful, out-of-the-bedsit, rock and roll public. Denim.

Denim?

When he went to see a play of mine at the National, Tom Stoppard said to me, 'You've got a lot of denim in tonight.'

Magnificence *ends with this incredible explosion and blackout. There's something very deliberate about that, and I'm wondering whether that's an image you had in your head from the start.*

I had an endless debate with myself, and indeed with the theatre, about whether the bomb goes off or not. The theatre got very nervous about it, and Oscar Lewenstein, who was a dear soul and is no longer with us, was incredibly nervous (he was the artistic director). He thought it would be controversial, and people would ask, 'Why have you put this anarchist play on?' He couldn't understand the politics of it because he was an old Communist Party member. He said, 'What is all this pissing about, what is all this soulbaring?' And I said, 'People have to be responsible for their actions.' He replied, 'Yes, you join the party or you don't, you see?' That would be Oscar's clear-cut answer. This was a millionaire out of the East End of London talking! A millionaire ex-communist!

It's a theatrical set-piece, isn't it? Everything blows up.

I came to the conclusion that *Magnificence* was, in a rather grand phrase, a tragedy of waste. I thought, when they die, how many people were wiped out?

Bombs *were* going off. I met members of the Baader-Meinhof gang a few years afterwards. It was very, very creepy. I was at a Human Rights conference – writers go to these things, there are fewer of them now. You would be rounded up to go to a Human Rights conference and be completely out of your depth. This was in Germany, and I was with Trevor Griffiths, and one night he said, 'There's some people who want to come up and see you in your room and have a discussion', so I said fine. And we went up and these three young women walk in, and they're the women of the Baader-Meinhof men who are in jail. They wanted us to make a human rights statement for their men, and one of them – her name was Rosie – took out a knife and put it on the floor. It was as if the discussion in some way concerned this object.

That is creepy.

That is very creepy. But what was creepy about the discussion was that they had gone over a certain edge – and I wish I'd understood this when I wrote the play. If you say, 'I'm prepared to kill for this', you go over a line. You are out of the discourse. The Germans are particularly critical on this point. If you tell them that violence puts you beyond the discourse, they'll reply, 'You only use words, you will not use actions!' Writers are very susceptible to that. When you say that to writers, their eyes sort of crumple. They worked on guilt. That's what they were doing, and you suddenly realised that there was only one thing they wanted, which was for us to make a statement about the men in jail, about their conditions in a place called Stanheim. They would do anything for that, it didn't matter. They would agree to anything, they would say anything. There was no discourse about it, no argument along the lines of 'Are the conditions bad? Are they rightfully in jail?' This idea that you can cross a certain line and take yourself out of the loop of political argument, I should have realised that that was what would happen with Jed.

So you very definitely don't come down on the side of crossing that line, there's no doubt about that.

Well, look what happened to the Baader-Meinhof Gang! Many of them died: some killed themselves in jail, some may have been bumped off in jail, several have recanted and become very wise people.

There's a sump under Romanticism, isn't there?

A sump? What do you mean?

Certain things fall out of Romanticism, like the bad oil, the tar. One of them is terrorism. Sometimes you feel Shelley is near it. 'Let's shoot someone', that was Byron's feeling – 'I have to go and shoot someone': that was a personal quest. That's why he ended up in Greece, in a way. 'I have to fight for it!' That can lead you to thinking about terrorism. Then there's the Wagner stuff about what's underneath Romanticism. I've been reading a book about that; I've begun to think about that quite a lot.

Would you agree that Byron and some of the other characters in Bloody Poetry *have a good deal in common with the characters in* Magnificence*? There is that idealistic element, the aspiration towards a better life. There's a line that the people cross in* Magnificence *that they don't cross in* Bloody Poetry.

At the time I had a strong sense of internal exile which a lot of writers felt. Thatcher had come to power. What we'd been trying to develop in the Sixties and Seventies had failed or receded. The tide had gone out, and you were more and more called a 'loony'. I remember talking to Caryl Churchill about that, saying, 'Why do they think we're completely mad? What has happened? We're totally reasonable people, Caryl.' You suddenly open the paper and finding something saying you're insane and unrealistic! I think that there was a strong feeling of that, and that's why my mind turned to what are now seen as apostles of English heritage. Now of course, thanks to Richard Holmes' biography, *Shelley: The Pursuit* (1974), and the academic work that has followed, Shelley's no longer regarded as a cottage-industry lyricist.

For me, one of the most memorable scenes in the play was when the characters act out the parable of Plato's Cave. It seemed an incredibly ambitious thing to do, to take a philosophical discourse like Plato's Cave and dramatise it. How did you arrive at that?

It was all predicated on the Brechtian principle that you should respect the audience's intelligence but assume they're ignorant; assume they're bright but don't know about what you're talking about. If you start at zero you can win, you can get something across. I knew that the Shelleys and Byron were reading the *Symposium* in the Villa Diodati, and I thought, I'll have to say what the Plato ideas are, so I'll stage Plato's Cave and explain it. In the end you can deliver this idea about a demon love, and it doesn't come out of nowhere. Then I worked out that you could probably do it with lamps. They were playing games. I don't think I read anywhere that they did stage the cave, but you could imagine them doing that. Shelley was very playful.

Do you see Bloody Poetry *as quite a realistic play?*

I wanted it to be quite accurate about them. Realistic in that sense. It's slightly like when you recall a period of your life when you were very busy, and you see it in some heroic terms, and you don't remember having baths, or going to the loo, or eating, or bad days, or much small talk; it has a slight feel of that. I wanted the sense that they were myth-making – that was strong amongst them. They were diarists. You read Mary Shelley's notes. There's this drive to live this construct, and make it honest, so everything was shown. I think that does make the play rather unrealistic in many ways.

If you're working on the Plato's Cave scene with actors and a director, is it part of your job to give your colleagues a kind of tutorial in the intellectual background to the piece?

Oh yes, they'll ask you. It's quite simple really, Plato's Cave as presented there.

The one thing I was always terrified of was that the lamps wouldn't be strong enough, so the shadows wouldn't be strong enough. It's difficult to achieve that on the stage because light spills all over the place. And to be able to light the actors, so you can see the actors *and* see the image – it's actually a swine to pull off because the stage is awash with photons. It always looks brown for some reason. It's one of the worst things about the stage. You get this yellowy light if you're not careful. It's technically very difficult.

It's a multifaceted scene that brings many elements of the play together. How much of that would you explain to the actors?

You'd explain Plato's Cave but the actors would discover for themselves how it fits into the play thematically. They would see for themselves how the play moves from the rationalism of Plato's Cave. Then there's Byron's intervention. He reads it crudely, and slips in the dark side of Romanticism, Coleridge's *Christabel*, and that freaks Shelley out.[16] But you tend to leave the second part of that to actors, who have to find it convincing that they can freak out, that the events have a kind of emotional logic. You restrict yourself to technical things. It takes some time to learn when you're a playwright that, in rehearsals, you're there to guard the text and explain it when necessary, if you can (though sometimes you can't!). Your task is to protect the text, and judge, if they're really having difficulty, whether it's their fault or yours. If it's yours then you should rewrite. You start with a very narrow view – just look after the text. By the end of successful rehearsals you'll be talking about everything: costume, acting – they'll ask you about it. But you must start by making it a very technical matter. That way you'll get, in this godfather-like way, respect.

If, when you're inexperienced, you go in and you want to philosophise and get excited by the actors, they won't like that, because they're athletes really, they're not intellectuals. Some actors are bright, some aren't – but basically it is an athletic gift that they have.

How did you find the characters of Shelley and Byron? How did you discover them?

They seemed to me to be like that. I got a lot out of Byron's letters. Just the way they're written with all those dashes, and the way they suddenly stop –

---

[16] See *Brenton Plays: Two*, pp. 268–9.

he gets bored so he stops. The way that he *tries* to be ungenerous but he finds it difficult. He can be malicious. I thought he was a precursor to Oscar Wilde, and what happened to him was oddly very like what happened to Wilde about sixty years later. He thought he had the establishment on the run, but he didn't. They turned round and did him.

His cruelty to Claire Clairmont about the child was incredible.[17] Absolutely terrifying. I thought, this mustn't destroy the character in the audience's mind. It's got to be in, but you mustn't destroy it. The rush to easy moral judgement is a danger in the play. I think some people have difficulty with the play asking are they good or bad?[18]

That's not a stupid question though is it? I mean I can understand people saying that. Is there an answer?

No, there isn't an answer, because people in action is what matters. And they did have successes, amongst them the bloody poetry. Mary, who suffered a great deal at Shelley's hands in many ways, because of the madness of the escapades and the travelling, nevertheless knew that they had done something worthwhile and spent the rest of her life preserving it, editing it, and getting the editions out. She makes Shelley sound older and wiser than I think he was. I sometimes wonder whether he would have talked a lot and driven you mad; I imagine a kind of Julie Burchill rant would have been coming out of him all the time. He fizzed, didn't he?

You just said, 'people in action is what matters'. Can you tell me what I should understand by that?

There are two views of human nature that have dominated drama throughout this century. One is Freudian, as represented by Ibsen. It's a belief that we are repressed, and that repression can be removed to reveal a real self in some way. It produces a kind of onion drama, if you like, of which Ibsen is the great example – indeed the inventor. According to this notion, a character is stripped down, layer by layer, until you reach some central truth, like, for instance, the revelation that his father had syphilis. End of play. It's usually set in small rooms with small characters who talk about the past a lot: theatre of revelation.

The opposite of that, if you don't believe that personality is fixed and that what you must express is your true nature (an idea on which American civil-isation is founded – 'be true to yourself', as if 'yourself' is something set), is

---

[17] Dramatised in Act Two, Scene 7; *Brenton Plays: Two*, pp. 294–5.
[18] Brenton refers to Paul Foot's comments; see *Fringe First*, p. 217.

the existentialist, or Brechtian, notion that our behaviour makes us what we are, that the way we interact with the world makes our character, and that we're born and make ourselves and do well or perish *in action*. That's a Sartrean view: existence before essence.

What do you mean by saying that it's a Sartrean view?

Well, you wake up in the morning and for a split second you don't know who you are, and then you remember who you have invented by the life you've led: that you are Duncan Wu, you are an academic, you are involved in certain things which are defining the way you're talking and thinking and being. And that view (which has an almost mystical feeling at the centre of it, although it's atheistical, really), that we burn a very bright flame which you can't really know, is Sartrean. It says that the *cogito* is false, because as soon as you think 'I think therefore I am', you are looking at what you thought, but what is looking at it? You can never get to that prime *cogito* because you burn a bright flame and you enter the world, and you make yourself – by actions.

If you believe that, you'll invent a completely different drama, because you'll show people in action, and what you'll end up with is an epic theatre which is Brechtian, which shows, scene by scene, people in crisis, doing something about a crisis, making themselves by their deeds. Christ said, 'By their deeds you will know them', and that's what Brecht believes. In other words, we can change, we are malleable; and he tried to show this. *Mann ist Mann*[19] is a comedy about a gentle, retiring, shy, cowardly figure, who's transformed into an efficient SS-type killer by the society he's in, and by his own choices. That's what I meant by studying character in action, and by the principle that action makes the character. It may be a crackpot view but it's something I have pieced together over the years!

The latter view, as you've described it, is totally opposed to the Ibsenesque, onion-skin view. The onion-skin view seems to me to lead to a drama of moments, as it were ...

A drama of revelation. Indeed the thriller is based on it, and most TV drama, and most drama in the theatre. It's still the dominant theory about our psychological make-up. It came out of Freud and it's individualistic. It's also rather fatalistic – 'he's a bastard' (full stop), 'that's the truth about that guy', you hear characters talk like that.

---

[19] Translated as *Man equals Man* by Gerhard Nellhaus, edited by John Willett and Ralph Mannheim (London: Methuen, 1979).

Whereas the Sartrean / Brechtian theory would say?

Whereas we would say, 'he's a bastard, and then he was capable of doing a saintly thing – so is he a saint or a bastard?' Well, he was a bastard when he did this, and a saint when he did that. And if you say that's morally ambiguous, I'd reply that it isn't, it all depends on what day you met him – which is a completely different view, and it's one that hasn't held out in the culture.

Interestingly, it's what Goethe believed, and was regarded at the time as a kind of heresy. The church was always criticising him for it; it's called anti-nomianism. It means being against universal moral laws because you can't apply them to what people do. An interesting view. It's lain there since the enlightenment, but it's not won out, and that explains why people can't understand Brecht. People say, 'Is Galileo a good or a bad man?'[20] The dramatist must, in his last scene, surely show what his final view, the final truth about Galileo is.' He doesn't. In fact his last scene doesn't have Galileo in it at all; it has a book Galileo wrote crossing the stage, as if that's what the three and a half hours you've been in the theatre watching this man, is all about. And the best judgement about him is that that book went to Protestant northern Europe and started modern physics, modern mechanics. It's morally difficult from the revelatory onion-view.

I think these two views have been fighting it out, and modernism is basically on the side of the unknown flame, the character in action. I don't know which side postmodernism is on. There is a feeling in this last decade of people giving up these debates, unresolved and exhausted.

There's something very nihilistic about postmodernism. If you're a good postmodernist you wouldn't go to the theatre at all, you'd just watch cable TV.

The theatre has become deeply unfashionable in some sections because of that. It's that wonderful phrase, 'breakfast in the ruins', isn't it, postmodernism?

Was there a point at which you became aware that with Bloody Poetry *you were writing a play that was extending an argument you had begun with* Sore Throats?

I think I thought that *after* writing *Bloody Poetry*. The real conscious decision was to move on to *Greenland*. To begin *Greenland* was to say, 'This *is* a trilogy,

---

[20] Brenton translated Brecht's *The Life of Galileo* for a production in the Olivier Theatre, National Theatre, 13 August 1980, directed by John Dexter. Dexter's production notes may be found in his fascinating collection of notes and journals, *The Honourable Beast*, pp. 228–39.

this is a three-arch play.' The other two were, in a way, about defeat, so I felt I should go on, because people came up to me and said, 'Why don't you write about what you believe in?' I'd reply, 'No, no, what about dialectical drama?' But they weren't convinced by this, and *Greenland* was a comic attempt to have a crack at that, at a real Utopia – at least in its long second Act.

   Bloody Poetry was written very quickly; there were emendations later. I changed a bit for Max Stafford-Clark's 1988 revival. In the first version, which Foco Novo produced, the scene with the madman is somewhat mystical, and Max being Max wanted this sorted out. 'What is being said?' he wanted to know. And I clarified it – I think to the better.

The endings of some of these plays are similar. There's the explosion at the end of Magnificence; *the equally spectacular end to* Sore Throats *– 'I am going to be fucked, happy and free';*[21] *the 'great big, bloody, beautiful fire' at the end of* Bloody Poetry.[22] *Do you think those resemblances are important?*

I suppose they are similar. At the end of *Sore Throats*, I wanted to say, 'What would they do without money?' There was a very good American production of it, and the women in it had this long talk about, how would Judy survive now, what would she do? And would I write a sequel? Being Americans they wanted it resolved. The play asks, how can she be 'fucked, happy and free'? So it's more of an open-ended one, perhaps. It has a comic structure, whereas I suppose *Magnificence* has a tragic ending: they die, the project goes to waste, lives are lost.

And Bloody Poetry?

And *Bloody Poetry* looks like a tragedy, but then they became Byron and Shelley after they were both dead.

So it's a bit of both. It's bloody because it's a bloody failure.

Yes, and it's cost them.

I think of the end of Sore Throats *as revolutionary; you're setting fire to banknotes. It's a subversive thing to do.*

Yes, that's right. She's going to go off and do something else, yes.

---

[21] *Brenton Plays: One*, p. 390.
[22] *Brenton Plays: Two*, p. 310.

It's a new society, a new world.

The end of *Bloody Poetry* is a tragic ending.

I wrote a play last year called *In Extremis*, which was about Abelard and Eloise, and I may have done a similar thing there, because at the end of the play she goes to see Bernard of Clairvaux[23] who in their time wiped the slate with them. He had Abelard destroyed, many of his books were banned. Bernard ruled the roost in the Catholic world; he made the new pope, he was totally in control. And at the last second in the play the elderly Eloise tells him, 'We wrote letters.' He says 'Letters?' She says, 'Yes. In the next 700 years they're going to be published all over the world; look, I have a copy here!' She holds up a Penguin paperback: blackout. Bernard is now unread, except by the really devout. That was, I suppose, a similar ending to *Bloody Poetry*.

Literary longevity is the consolation.

Yes, they survive. They do what they wanted to do. They achieved what they wanted to achieve.

Could it be argued that many of these characters are doomed? The Romantics of Bloody Poetry *(bar Mary Shelley) seem to be doomed; Christie's doomed.*

There was a lot of talk when we started writing about whether it was possible to write a new tragedy, a modern tragedy. I think I've asked that question a lot in the plays I've written, about what a modern tragic sense is. Sometimes it's waste, sometimes it's being out of step with your time (which is certainly true of *Bloody Poetry*; it's certainly true of all the people at the beginning of *Greenland*, who go into the dream in the second Act).

It was asked first by George Steiner, who when I was a student began teaching with enormous controversy. He took me and my friends to dinner several times; we'd go round and talk to him, even though we weren't in his college.[24] He was a fantastic teacher. I don't know how sound he was academically; he was hated by other dons at the university, but he made you read books and think things. He told us that it was impossible to have a modern tragedy because of the holocaust. That tragedy makes no sense before that. These were devastating ideas at the time (this was in the early Sixties). The question is, can you have a modern tragic sense? Well, of course you can. People lose their lives, people are ruined who should not be. Tragic anguish is there in everyday life. I've thought about that again and again.

---

[23] 1090–1153; one of the most influential churchmen of the day.
[24] Brenton read English Literature at St Catharine's College, Cambridge, 1962–65.

Is tragedy partly a structural thing, or would you place the emphasis wholly on content?

It's about content, yes; it's a matter of destruction, of self-destruction, or of being destroyed by something when you shouldn't be destroyed. It's a matter of anguish really. There's an existentialist view about tragedy which I'd embrace.

What is it?

It's that you can't live with the predicament that you put yourself into. Not a bad faith in the Sartrean sense. I mean, you've defined yourself as a poet, you can do no other. *A la* Luther: you're in Italy. You are in a sense doomed. You put yourself into that predicament and it's tragic that you have. You can't live with it really.

I only ask about structure because I'm thinking about the end of Magnificence *again.*

Traditionally at the end of tragedy people die, of course. But I remember going to this literary seminar when I was a student at Cambridge – a swine of a seminar! 'What is tragedy?' the speaker asked. So we all said, 'Everyone dies at the end.' He said, 'These are tragedies in which people do not die at the end', and he named many famous tragedies in which people do not die at the end, so that definition didn't work! At the end of the seminar he came to the conclusion, he said that, 'As a philosopher I have to tell you (it may be of interest to you as literary people or not) that there is no definition of tragedy.'

We all tore our hair out because he was so much cleverer than we were! And at the time we didn't realise who this bugger had been taught by. His name was Bamber, and he was this very bright student of Wittgenstein's, who had died not long before.[25] Without knowing it, I was getting the full Wittgenstein treatment – which was typical, absolutely typical! You are in a solipsism, there is no definition within a solipsism. You are using a word which has no definition, so you can only say a tragedy is a tragedy because it's tragic. That is the Wittgensteinian line!

You don't agree with that do you?

No, I don't. Because writers are interested in experience and action. It's about action. But then you go away and say, 'No, you have nothing to say about

---

[25] Ludwig Wittgenstein died in Cambridge, 29 April 1951.

literary process, Mr Bamber.' You can't say it at the time but ten years later you suddenly can.

So would you want to offer your own definition of tragedy? Or is it something you'd say is shifting?

I'd say there was a tragic sense, and it entails being caught in a predicament that you can't live with. You can apply it to Lear, he *makes* his predicament and he can't live with it. The consequences of it destroy him. And you can see that happening with exiles like Shelley and Byron.

I can see it happening to the characters in Sore Throats.

At the end of it Judy wants to make a predicament. Or she could say, 'Let's suck this one and see.' There's a strong suck-it-and-see attitude in *Sore Throats* that she has – which is breaking out of her predicament. She's in a predicament with her marriage, then she goes into this pre-AIDS festival of fucking everything in sight, which is inexplicable to audiences now! She was a good character, Judy, wasn't she? She was an invention. I don't doubt whether there are many Medeas around, or many Judys. I'm not comparing her to Medea but I was trying to make her really special. I hope there are people like this alive.

I keep coming back to the sublime in your work. It's there in such episodes as the Plato's Cave episode in Bloody Poetry. *Firstly, do you think I'm projecting that? Secondly, is it a component in the way you think as a writer? And thirdly, is it anything at all to do with what we've been saying about tragedy? Three questions!*

I think it's a way out. In *Sore Throats* they dream of a hole in the wall and on the other side is Greenland, and in moments of ecstasy people glimpse it.[26] The idea that you can glimpse a better way of living is essential in this kind of writing. It's often ecstatic, so, no, I don't think you're projecting it.

I always feel you've got to really earn it on the stage, and it can't be there for long, because you're not really describing something that you personally know will work. You've got to be absolutely certain, be convinced, that there *can* be a better way of living, or that the ecstatic view of a more reasonable, or beautiful, future is won at some level – usually instinctively, or emotionally, or just in the storytelling. Otherwise you could become very

---

[26] 'See a country, the other side of the wall. Sweet fields, rivers, forests. All you have to do is knock a few bricks out, wriggle through a hole onto the grass'; *Brenton Plays: One*, p. 378.

sentimental, couldn't you? You could disappear, like the worst Romantic painters, under endless heavens.

That must have been one of the difficulties with Greenland,[27] *in fact.*

Yes, that's why I tried to make it a Romantic comedy, a magic wood comedy. I wrote a first version which was set 700 years from now, and it was just incomprehensible! They were conducting games, they were kite-flying, but the only piece of drama was the figure who had a mental illness – a mental illness of paradise, which is that you empathise so much that you disappear into other people. That's the only mental disease, and that character's in the finished version of the play. But it was incomprehensible, and it also seemed horrible.

I thought the magic wood way was the way to do it. That's why I chose six characters, and by a quaint device they all fall into the Thames at the same moment, and they blip somehow. They wormhole or something, by device of science fiction, into the second Act. Then you have the comedy of people who achieve what you want to achieve, but you hate it. You ask, 'Where is your nearest committee?' And they say they don't have any. You say, 'But you're living in some kind of socialist Utopia, where's the agenda?' But there is no agenda. You can make that work as comedy. There's the religious person who can't get the congregation to be afraid of guilt, so she can't preach because they don't get the point! And they try hard, because the Greenlanders are interested. 'This could be really interesting', they say. So that's how I tried to do it. It's written in a series of routines. It's a difficult play.

Because it's written as a series of routines?

Yes. In a way the first Act would be great on a proscenium arch stage, because it's like the satires we were writing in the 1980s. But the second act needs to be in the round in a different theatre. It has to be *so* radical, and it's very difficult to achieve that. The production looked rather pretty when it was done. Yes, it was difficult. There's also something very difficult in that people do want to know the history of what's happened, and I do tell them, but only very near the end of the Act.[28] I couldn't bring myself to do that earlier because it seemed boring. I wanted the actual thing to be staged. I don't know if I made a structural mistake there or not. Shaw's fine in *Back to Methuselah* because they're constantly talking about past history. It's written in those terms, their speeches: 'In the first hundred years of the post-disaster era ...' Off

---

[27] The third of Brenton's Plays for Utopia was first produced at the Royal Court theatre, 26 May 1988.
[28] In Act Two, Scene 13; *Brenton Plays: Two*, pp. 392–4.

he goes, nine hours! But I wasn't trying to do that, I wanted the routines of the comic meetings to be very realistic. Anyway, we had a lot of fun with it.

Has it been variously produced around the world?

No, not much; I think there were some German productions, although I never saw them. There were a handful. It was a nasty time to put a socialist Utopian play on – it was 1987 for Christ's sake! The Thatcher apogee!

I remember it well.

It was just pre-crash as well.[29]

That was a horrible time in human history.

It was extraordinary, wasn't it? *Serious Money* got hold of it so well, didn't it?[30] And they went to see it! That was what was so extraordinary, it was full of traders and brokers. The champagne bottles were rolling around in the bar!

They probably didn't understand it, did they?

I thought they understood it all too well. They understood that it was a critique. And the sight of them being shits – I think they loved it, loved it!

Don't you find that rather depressing? Wouldn't you prefer it if those people had come out of the theatre feeling ashamed of themselves?

I don't think that you've got a chance in hell of that! If you want to understand that phenomenon in the Eighties then *Serious Money* is the play to look up – as much as any essay, I'd have thought. If you read Milton Friedman's description of why Hong Kong is Utopia, you think, this man is insane, why didn't they realise it? Now Hong Kong's going down the tubes. He argued that Hong Kong is the way we should run the British state – the world! It's a role-model. And the early Thatcher government took this on board. They had him round to dinner!

---

[29] The London Stock market crashed in October 1987.

[30] Caryl Churchill's play evolved from a workshop by the English Stage Company and was first performed at the Royal Court on 21 March 1987, directed by Max Stafford-Clark. Its success, helped by its popularity among those who worked in the city of London, led to a run in the West End.

I'm interested in Berlin Bertie[31] *with what Joanne calls turning a strange corner, the opening of a door in the air.*[32]

Joanne was like the witches in *Thirteenth Night.*[33]

How would you describe that kind of character?

She's a Greenlander, she's involved in Greenland activities. All this hopeless artwork she's doing! So she can't have any character at all, it's very odd. It's the nearest I've come to putting a mythic figure on the stage. No one knows what the witches are on about in *Thirteenth Night* because they're destructive, but they seem to be some kind of party, they've arrived, they trigger the nightmare, and then they mop it up at the end.

They're the weird sisters aren't they?

Yes, they are.

And you just called Joanne a mythic figure.

Yes, like an angel or a time-traveller. If a time-traveller arrived you'd think they were an angel, or you wouldn't understand what they were talking about. It would be so difficult.

They're mythic in the sense that they're larger than mere humans?

Yes, they're mythic in that you cannot characterise them. You can say, well she's a Goth. But that's from the outside.

I've often thought there is Greenland activity, and the reasons why people go hang-gliding (for instance) are not wholly selfish. It's not about making money. Of course, it can be all of those things, but the actual thing of doing it, this idea of something done for an effortless purity of intent – it's a wonderful thing to do, full stop – is terrific.

Is there a religious element to this?

No, I don't think so. I suppose I do have a belief (and this may be ex-hippie stuff) that if you and your body can be at ease, unthreatened, you could

---

[31] First performed at the Royal Court theatre, 9 April 1992, directed by Danny Boyle. Brenton has published his rehearsal diary of that production in *Hot Irons*, pp. 229–70.
[32] See introduction to this interview, p. 17.
[33] Brenton's 'dream play' in nineteen scenes was first performed by the Royal Shakespeare Company at the Warehouse, London, 2 July 1981.

suddenly develop the most extraordinary ideas. If a balance with nature is possible, then you must try and find that way of living. I don't live like that, I'm not preaching! It's just this idea that for a moment you can fly because you're in balance. Which is what hang-gliding probably is about, that's why people love doing it. They say, 'That flight went like a dream.' You could imagine somebody saying that – like a dream, perfection.

Equilibrium with nature.

Yes, that's it. Balance, wholeness.

Is that a mystic thing or is it a physical thing?

No, I think it's a humanist aim, it's a humanist notion.

That word, 'humanist': is there a particular meaning that you would attach to it?

I do believe that it is possible to say, 'I can understand human nature. In the end we can understand human nature, and understand the nature of your predicament.' That's the Sartrean thing. He wrote a great little essay, *Existentialism and Humanism*,[34] in which the argument is: understand your predicament, and you'll become truly human. The project is to become truly human, and that phrase, 'truly human', assumes that there is a right way of thinking and living, and I think that's what I'm talking about.

The modernists believe it. I feel like an unreconstructed modernist. I do believe progress is possible, that you can change human nature, or find out its true nature and live by it. Postmodernists don't. Queer theory in California says the body is a construct – the *body* is a construct! You can change it, you can make it into anything, there is no reason why it should be any particular way – let's invent a way for our body to be, let's go into surgery. Literally! Let's go into surgery! Why not implant a foetus in your stomach wall? We're near to the technology, do it! Make yourself a new body. That's a postmodernist view. Whereas I'd say, there's something human that you gravitate towards, and it's with the grain of nature. Put babies into the stomach walls of men and you will screw up!

Modernism flourishes when there are areas of crisis. The great Picasso paintings were painted during World War I, during the Spanish civil war, at the beginning of the Second World War – fantastic stuff in the Forties! He was responding in the way that anyone who believes in progress will be outraged at crisis. In the way that anyone like that would react, saying, 'We need a new

---

[34] Sartre's *Existentialisme est un humanisme* was first published in 1946 in Paris, and 1948 in Britain.

art for this new time, or a new art for this dangerous new time' – which Brecht thought. There's a lovely book by Fredric Jameson just out, called *Brecht and Method*.[35] His argument is that Brecht was a modernist, that he has all the shapes of modernism, all the techniques – except that he's not a reactionary like Joyce or Eliot. And actually they're in the same camp, and were doing the same things; it's just that they're from different political divides.

Brecht has been quite influential in your work, hasn't he?

He believes in people in action, that human nature is very difficult to find out. He doesn't have the Ibsen-like view – that the human soul is an onion which you can peel; he thinks that in some ways we have to make our own lives, so he's a storyteller. Anyone on the left would agree with that, so you naturally tend to write epic stories, epic plays – many scenes, with crucial moments, crucial events. Although it's all domestic in setting, *Bloody Poetry* follows the same pattern, and the scenes can be self-contained, and also, as in *Magnificence*, can be in any style. You're just getting over the content of the scene, so if you use pantomine in one and realism in the next, it doesn't matter. The audience will be fine about it, critics will get upset perhaps, but actually they'll receive the reality of the scene. Whether it's done with cardboard in one, puppets in another, and then full-blown David Storey realism in the next!

Your work with Max Stafford-Clark, who directed Bloody Poetry *for its revival at the Royal Court in 1988, extends to a Joint Stock classic:* Epsom Downs.[36] *How did that come about?*

I wrote a chaotic first draft, and then we began to workshop on it, and go to the races, meet the trainers, jockeys, punters, sports journalists. I had material that I took to them, and knocked it around in the workshop.

They were going through a Maoist period, and interviewed me for the job. 'Which project, which writers shall we hire?', said the actors. Then you had to go into a room, and say, 'I want to do this, this and this, and I've got this material'. It was a bit like going to an audition.

You mean they were asking several writers in?

They were, yes. Because of the success of *Fanshen* they decided to be a Maoist collective – manipulated, one suspects, by a two-man Politburo of Max

---

[35] Published in Britain by Verso, 1998.
[36] Two-act play, written in collaboration with Joint Stock. It was first performed at the Roundhouse, London, 8 August 1977, directed by Max Stafford-Clark. See *The Joint Stock Book*, pp. 130–7.

Stafford-Clark and Bill Gaskill. It was made clear that I had to make sure, because it *was* a collective, that all the actors got equal parts. There were eight actors, so I gave them six parts each, making forty-eight parts in all. Mad doubling!

How different was your original draft from what you actually wound up with? Was it totally different?

Oh, it was chaotic. I didn't really know enough about racing, which is why it was a good workshop project. I'd had the idea that it had to be set on the day of an actual Derby, and I was inventing one, I didn't know what the outcome of the race would be. I knew 1977 would be a good year for it because it was the Queen's Silver Jubilee year, and there would be a lot of bunting and British flummery around, and that would make it interesting.

As we came to know more and more, I realised you could nominate six main characters, and it would be interesting to follow them.

Were you and the actors and the director all there at Epsom?

Yes, everyone fanned out and took notes. We went to see trainers. I was given a tip which an eminent trainer assured me was going to win the race, and the thing came last! It was the only bet I made. I think he saw me coming, and thought, 'I'll teach this arty-farter to write about horseracing, give him the worst tip in the world!' It was a horse called Million Dollar Man. We were lucky because it was a classic Derby, and I thought, whatever happens, whether Piggott wins it or not, we'll record that Derby. It was perfect because Piggott was riding Minstrel – one of the most famous horses, it was a small horse for a Derby winner, incredibly strong.

Was horseracing something you'd been interested in before?

No, I had the idea just sitting watching a play the year before at the National, thinking, what could I follow this up with? I suddenly had the idea of writing a state of the nation play. It seemed to me that you could look at the state of the nation just by writing the stories and keeping close to it. It would be like a national cake; you would cut through it and see all the layers.

I loved Epsom. I first had the idea when we went up there with our kids who were small then, like Sharon's kid in a buggy, trying to wheel a buggy over the grass. There wasn't a race on, but they were training horses over on some gallops, you could see them, a magnificent sight, and it was a wonderful summer day and a kite was flying, and I thought, this is magic, I should really try and do this.

As far as I remember, the process – the memory is faulty of course – is that after we'd done the workshopping and been to the races, there were betting breaks. Actors went off to lay bets. And we had people come in. Lord Wigg talked to us. He was Wilson's hatchet man, but he'd started betting shops. He'd got that legislation through, and he had this weird social vision of the betting shop as a sort of community centre, where there'd be a little coffee shop at the back, and a little crèche for the kids, and that all went straight in the play. It looks bananas in the play, but this is what he believed in![37] Poor old sod. He'd just been done for kerb crawling[38] and he burst into tears in the rehearsal room – that was *really* weird. Then we spoke to other people like gamblers anonymous. And then we went to interview trainers, at Upton Newmarket.

And then the company did improvisations based on that material?

Yes, that's right – 'I saw this at the races, can you do it?' It was what's now regarded as conventional workshopping. 'Can you fit that into a scene?' Then that night or the next morning you try to draft a scene using some of the things that have come up during the day. It's hard work for a writer, because you're working both in and out of hours. Then they all buggered off for a holiday for a fortnight while I was expected to sit down and write the final draft – which I did. There was some rewriting; we rehearsed it convention- ally. It was a great undertaking really.

What was so wonderful was the reality of the world you were dealing with. You could craft it because you had all this material which was coming at you straight off racecourses. I'd have thought about a quarter of all the lines in the play were heard on racecourses in 1977. When a Bunny Girl says, 'Don't give me a hard time',[39] that was her: a Bunny Girl was heard to say that to someone.

I was wondering about the acid spurting out of the batteries, is that real?[40]

Yes, that was one of the problems at Epsom. We talked to people in the Romany council, and then went down to talk to the gipsies as best you could, but they were very guarded.

What are your feelings about the Evangelists in the play? There's a great exchange at one point:

> MRS MOTROM: They could have builded a New Jerusalem here.
> MR TILLOTSON: Yeah. 'Stead they built a race track.[41]

That's a sort of index of what's going on, isn't it?

---

[37] See, in particular, Act Two; *Brenton Plays: One*, pp. 313–14.
[38] Lord Wigg was prosecuted for kerb-crawling in 1976.
[39] In Act One; *Brenton Plays: One*, p. 290.
[40] In Act One; *Brenton Plays: One*, p. 272.
[41] In Act One; *Brenton Plays: One*, p. 276.

Yes, it's a feeling that the country is shabby in the mid-Seventies, and the play reflects that. There's a dream of peace and democracy, but it's shabby and declines as the play goes on. And that seemed to be the temperature that the play is taking.

Epsom Downs is roughly contemporaneous with Light Shining in Buckinghamshire, which also expresses a somewhat jaded view of the Labour government of the time.[42]

Yes, it had been a terrible decade in many ways. The whole Left experiment in France had petered out. Amsterdam, which had been an enlightened city in the Sixties, had become a heroin hell. The oil crisis had wrecked social policies. There were terrible problems with the pound which had been the result of the oil crisis. There was a great crisis in 1976. Inexplicably as it seemed at the time, Wilson gave up and left office.[43] He now seems like one of the most extreme socialists in Labour Party history compared with what we've got now! We were all cursing him at the time. There was certainly a feeling of shabbiness creeping over everything. That said, it's a Jonsonian comedy ...

It's Bartholomew Fair, *isn't it?*

I suppose so. I don't know *Bartholomew Fair* well, but that was the idea, yes. It's interesting how, in the theatre, you can stage a Derby of forty horses and half a million people with eight actors – and people believe it. You can do it, it's *very* interesting – unfilmable, of course. The cost of filming it would be beyond reason, and you couldn't use the invention. The invention that comes out of the theatre, when you're under pressure! You think, 'God, there's only eight of us, how are we going to do this?' So you say, 'Well, you'll have to have a speech about the race and a speech about the course, that's how it will start.' And you do it and it works! And most of the people in the theatre will be on the course. About 10 per cent won't be.

I've got a theory that there's a kind of colour blindness, imagination colour blindness. About 10 per cent of every audience don't get it, and those people usually don't go to the theatre again because they only see something shabby going on in the middle distance. Angela Carter was one of them. She said, 'I hate the theatre, these people in the middle distance wearing stuff on their faces and you can't hear them.' The thing was it was like being colour blind, it didn't work for her brain. She was not transported.[44]

---

[42] *Epsom Downs* was first performed 8 August 1977; *Light Shining in Buckinghamshire* on 7 September 1976.

[43] Wilson announced his resignation as Prime Minister on 16 March 1976.

[44] Carter's harshest remarks on British theatre are made in her essay about television drama, 'Acting it Up on the Small Screen', *Nothing Sacred: Selected Writings* (2nd edn, London: Virago, 1992), pp. 145–7.

What would you say are the disadvantages of the Joint Stock method?

A workshop show tends to have certain characteristics: short scenes, lots of material. It gets cartoon-like very easily, it's usually manipulating clichés about peoples' types – it encourages a theatre of types. If you're doing something like *Epsom Downs* that's great, because it *is* a theatre of types. You aren't trying to manipulate it, but that's the nature of it: 'Enter the Lord, the drunk, the religious nutter, and so on.'

Epsom Downs was perfectly with the grain; if you're trying to workshop something else, it's very difficult. Actors in workshops like things to be logical, they don't make leaps, and it's difficult to get the leaps that other kinds of writing need. You suddenly just go from A to K, and you don't know why you have. You could never workshop a Pinter play because he goes from A to K all the time. It would just collapse, you couldn't do it.

Workshops naturally tend to produce a certain type of drama. You can always tell with a workshop show when it's not really working because they'll have taken, say, a more domestic thing, or they'll have tried to run one big complex character. The problem with that is that they can't make him or her complex enough because they can't sense mystery. It's hard in a workshop show to stage something which is mysterious, because everyone will talk him out.

Is there a sense in which the workshop method is Brechtian?

Brecht used to write with a big long table, and often in the rehearsal room. There'd be new stuff on the table in the morning. Indeed anyone who had a bright idea would find their bright idea in the text before they knew it. There was a hoovering sort of method about the way Brecht thought, and he always wanted it to be collective – though of course he always dominated it. There was a Stalinist paradox about his collective work! Epic plays lend themselves to rewriting and second thoughts in a way that an Ibsen or a Pinter play doesn't. Pinter's one of the main inheritors of Ibsen; the subtext is mysterious, but the ache to reveal something is palpable. 'I had your Nelly away in your taxi in 1945', do you remember that line?

The Homecoming, *isn't it?*

It's almost a parody of an Ibsen line – revelation. The character falls backwards and dies!

It's not all that revelatory either, when you boil it down to the bare essentials!

I know; God knows what games he's playing! You couldn't do that for a workshopped play. There were dramas of the Sixties that David Storey wrote, he would write them in three to five days, and never change anything.[45] There's a logic to that, in that (in the case of *The Contractor*)[46] they put the tent up that day this way, and I can go through the day and have them put the tent up and take the tent down. If you start fiddling around and saying, 'Wouldn't it have been better if they'd had an argument about the pegs?', then the whole house of cards could collapse. So there's a logic to that kind of play.

What would you say were the advantages of workshopping?

Richness – maximalist rather than minimalist drama. The ability to go very quickly through a hell of a lot of stuff, a lot of routines; also to change the temperature a lot, some stories more serious than others. And *Epsom Downs* had a social feel to it. Speed and richness really.

It must be helpful working with a cast before you've actually written the play.

It's not so easy writing directly for actors because you tend to play towards what you think are their strengths, but actually those are the things they do easily. And that's often bad. Good casting is often against the grain of what they usually do. For half his career Michael Gambon was looked on as a light West End actor. It was only John Dexter who said, 'You should play the heavy classical roles', and persuaded him to.

And was Galileo one of the first he did?[47]

Yes, it was, and he went on to do many more, Lear included. He's still a great comic actor, but that was against him. If you'd sat down in the late Seventies and found Michael in the cast, you'd have written a light part for him, because he's so great at that. Whereas you actually should have written a totally unfunny heavyweight part for him to see what he could do. But you wouldn't have thought of that. That's the problem with writing for actors: you write often for their worst traits.

---

[45] Writing of *The Contractor*, *In Celebration*, and *Home*, Storey has observed that 'none of the plays took me more than five days to write and, once written, none required more than nominal correction' (*David Storey Plays: One*, pp. x–xi).

[46] *The Contractor* was first performed at the Royal Court, 20 October 1969, directed by Lindsay Anderson.

[47] Gambon played Galileo in Brenton's translation of Brecht's play, produced 13 August 1980.

Is it helpful working with the director before you write the play?

Max is a very good but reluctant play-doctor. He's become more reluctant. His instinct in setting up Joint Stock was almost as an *auteur*. It's very un-English: he wants to see certain shows about certain things, so he finds writers and actors to do them. If he can't find a writer, he'll improvise the thing. His show about the Falklands war,[48] I don't think it had a writer. It was Max saying, 'Let's just make the show that no bloody writers have got off his or her bottom to write!' It's an *auteur*'s instinct, it's quite continental really.

I think he's unrecognised as a great director. The temperature is often quite low in his work, he doesn't like rhetoric much. But the innovation was incredible with Joint Stock, the sense of reality that he was able to bring into the theatre was very strong. *Fanshen* was a great piece of directing – I know it was co-directed,[49] but to present middle-class actors with middle-class accents on a stage, and convince you that this was a religion, this was actually how people thought in a village in China, took terrific drive, and was totally consistent. A lot of it came from Max and Bill, as I'm sure David would acknowledge. That's all out of fashion at the moment because he's looked on as too dour.

He ran a new playwriting policy to get young new women writing, new feminist writing onto the stage when he took over the Royal Court.[50] Now that's so common that people don't look on it as remarkable. He got some fantastic work out of Caryl Churchill that, if she'd gone to the National, I don't know whether she would have done. They were era-defining shows. Today people curse the political drama of the Royal Court of that era, but it was a great invention and when it worked it was enlightening.

Are you saying that, from the writer's point of view, you feel almost that you were serving the will of Max?

No, not really. *Epsom Downs* was my idea; I'd brought it in, I always felt it was my play, and I put in it whatever I wanted. He thought the beginning wouldn't work so we reworked that; he was happy with the end. It was mainly the first quarter of an hour that he had objections to, and I partially solved them. I saw what he meant: he thought it didn't begin quickly enough. I thought, you've got to have a slow beginning, but Max isn't a slow man. Slow moments in the theatre he has to be very secure about. He's usually quite quick.

---

[48] *Falkland Sound*, produced at the Royal Court, 1983.
[49] With Bill Gaskill.
[50] Max Stafford-Clark was Artistic Director of the English Stage Company at the Royal Court, 1979–93.

Do you like your directors to be editors?

No, but it's good if they point out something to do with one's craft – there's a repetition, or something's too slow, or the audience are not getting this. With a show which is not working, everyone knows what's wrong, and everyone knows what should be done to put it right, and usually only you (the writer) *can* put it right. A collective mind does take over on a good show, and most of the actors will know that the end of Act Two is a bummer and that something will have to be done, and how many previews do we have to have before this writer realises it?

Is somebody deputed to talk to you?

Max would, that's why he's such a good play-doctor. *Epsom Downs* was a play that I brought in, as I explained, in a very rough draft, and it was just wonderful writing it in the environment of the rehearsals.

How would you characterise the ideal relationship between the writer and director?

It's a hard lesson to learn as a writer, but you should not look on yourself as an *auteur*; that is, someone who knows everything about how your play should be done. The best way (and this was often true with my work with Max) is to go into the rehearsal and look after the text. Is that line working? If not, is it their fault or mine? And be able to make that judgement, and look after the text. If people begin to ask for cuts that are wrong, speak up for why they shouldn't be done, or if you think cuts should be made, get in there and convince them that they should. Sit in your corner with the text on your lap all the hours of the rehearsal and concentrate on it. In the end, if the show is working, actors will say, do you think I'm playing that right? Do you think that's right? The set designer will start asking your advice; the director will start saying, am I botching that scene or not? In the end that will happen. That's the ideal thing, to occupy the position of the craftsman. And Max is like that; he likes to be secure in craftsmanship.

He's an actions director. It's a theory of directing where you give each line in the play a transitive verb. You can say, 'cueing him', 'helping him', 'loving', 'stopping'. And you say the verb behind every line, and you write it in the text, so the whole text is a web of actions that characters do to each other with the lines.[51] The first days of rehearsal are mindbending because he goes through the text line by line with the actors, and they all have to write down these actions. He's a good games player, Max, he likes playing games, and

[51] Stafford-Clark's technique is explained and illustrated on pp. 65–7, below.

he'll say, 'Is that right? Marks out of ten.' 'Seven out of ten? Change it, let's give it eight out of ten.' It's like a game. Finally, after the first days of rehearsal, the whole text will be this palimpsest of action words. And it has an effect. The actors know what they're doing quite early on. They may not know *why* they're doing it, but they know what the lines are doing to each character. It's a good test with a play, because actors will turn to you and say, 'This line doesn't do anything to anyone!' It's interesting. It's a theory worked out at the Central School of Speech and Drama by Jan Kat.

It brings clarity to peoples' thinking. Later, when they forget what the actions are, they can go back and say, 'What was the action for that?' And Max will look it up, or the stage-manager will look it up.

Both David Hare and David Edgar pointed out to me that Thatcherism created a kind of crisis for playwrights insofar as everyone thought that society was going in one direction and exactly the opposite happened. David Hare said that he didn't find his way out of that until he sat down with you and wrote Pravda. *Is that a view of Thatcherism that you would endorse, in terms of how Thatcherism affected your vision?*

Well, you didn't expect yourself to be in early middle age in this situation. You didn't expect the triumph of capitalism in the country. On the other hand you knew exactly what to write, and they were productive years in the theatre, and produced a lot of very good plays.

You mean fighting against it?

Yes, fighting against it, satirising or showing personal disasters or strategies, or just knowing what this new beast was. I produced a lot of good writing. *Bloody Poetry* came out of a sense of exile in that period, then there were later, more political, attempts like *Pravda*. It was very productive. The theatre was up for its duty really, and had the audience for it because there was a massive disaffection going on throughout those times. The theatre picked up that audience, even in Peter Hall's National Theatre. Bravely, too, because Hall's job was on the line several times for putting our plays on and keeping us going. He was aware that the theatre should try and do this. The Nineties have been far more difficult.

How do you mean?

Because the battle between modernism and the conservatism of human nature has exhausted it. I have a feeling that the culture has got exhausted. The solution is to not worry about anything except your job and your pleasures. The arts has become a pleasure industry, and you've got a kind of market realism: who can sell the most pleasure has taken over in the arts – in TV, film and, I'm afraid, theatre too. The culture's got into a terrible problem because of this.

The blandness of the Blair government reflects it. When Oskar Lafontaine, the last socialist in Europe, fell,[52] *Allgemeine Zeitung*, the German newspaper, said, 'We all know what reality is. Reality is how things are, and Oskar Lafontaine did not know how things are. He still dreamt of socialism and equality and redistribution of wealth, and they are not how things are.' So settle for this vision of how things are, as if they are naturally this way, and you will be alright. And you can go and have your pleasure-art and your *GQ*, and in the postmodernist world you can look up women's skirts, or you can be a feminist. It doesn't matter any more. It doesn't matter. The culture is exhausted, fragmenting. I think that may have happened.

It's more difficult functioning in this atmosphere than in the 1980s. In a way the Thatcher project has half-succeeded and is now itself becoming grubby, and you begin to sense even at the last budget that they are going to backtrack from this, and that social engineering is going to be re-asserted, or else things are really going to go to pieces.

So what's the proper role for the artist in a society like that, a deeply deluded society?

Well you want to strike against the delusion but will you get an audience? If you set up the Anti-Delusion Theatre Company you're going to get three a night; if you set up the right delusions you'll probably get an Oscar!

So what do you do then?

I don't know, I think you have to peg away. I think you have to look for what opportunities there are. Artists are opportunistic. It's been the same since Euripides. He saw the opportunity in a state-run theatre to put on stuff which wasn't really pro-state. The young Shakespeare probably did, Christopher Marlowe certainly did. I don't really know what you do. All I can say is, you do the three projects I've got on my table upstairs. See whether any of them work!

That gives a context to Ugly Rumours, *which I see as belonging to that strand of your work that's satirical, and stems from the satirical plays you wrote during the 1980s. I guess it's very much against the temper of the times to be presenting a play like this.*

---

[52] Oskar Lafontaine, the German finance minister, resigned on 11 March 1999, following a turbulent five and a half months in which he caused dismay among bankers and fellow EU politicians with his tax-and-spend agenda.

It's been an interesting experience, *Ugly Rumours*. It's not a play, really; I don't think of it as a play. It's theatre journalism, theatre cartoonery, which isn't like *Bloody Poetry* or *In Extremis*. It's a completely different operation really.

It's like A Short Sharp Shock![53]

That's right. I did something with David Edgar that started it – which, embarrassingly, was called *A Fart for Europe*.[54] That started my interest in this kind of thing. I don't know whether I'm very good at it or not, because you've got to be really brutal with it, it's got to be really outrageous. Shows like that will always get terrible flak. All of them got terrible flak. I did one about the Rushdie affair with Tariq Ali: *Iranian Nights*.[55] And we went on to do *Moscow Gold*,[56] which combines living history and satire. And then *Ugly Rumours*. They're knockabout outrages; there's a savage theatre cartoonery about them.

Ugly Rumours was a classic theatrical disaster. We had ten previews which were sold out with the audience falling over itself with laughter; we took out forty minutes so it looked very lean to us by the very last preview. We had West End backers, we had the Comedy Theatre ready to move into, on the last preview the people who'd put the money up came and it was nigh champagne before it had opened. They were absolutely convinced they had a winner; they thought it was going to run for months. Tariq and I were going to rewrite it as it went along. There was a feeling in the air of celebration. We had the first night on the Monday, and there were two laughs in the whole evening. Seventy-five critics turned up in the little theatre, occupied nearly all the downstairs, and these actors came on with silly lines, silly voices and rather silly costumes, and went, 'la de dah de dah', to a silent house. It went on and on and on, and I thought, when is this going to stop? When is someone going to start giggling? We had rounds of applause on lines in the middle of scenes on the Saturday, and here we were at the opening, and it was a nightmare. We got slaughtered. Terrible reviews, except, I think, for *The Scotsman*. They said, 'We understand this in Scotland!'[57]

---

[53] Two-act play written with Tony Howard, first performed Theatre Royal, Stratford, East London, 21 June 1980, directed by Robert Walker. It transferred to the Royal Court, 16 July 1980.

[54] One-act show written with David Edgar, first performed at the Royal Court, 18 January 1973, directed by Chris Parr.

[55] First performed at the Royal Court, 19 April 1989, directed by Penny Cherns.

[56] First performed by the RSC at the Barbican Theatre, London, 20 September 1990, directed by Barry Kyle.

[57] In an informed review, Joyce McMillan described it as 'extroverted, cabaret-like, Brechtian, constantly challenging the audience to do something about the abuses they're laughing at or have the grace to shut up', adding that it 'is fundamentally more radical than any critique of Blairism I've seen in Scotland'; *The Scotsman*, 11 November 1998.

It's a play about two Scotsmen.

It never really recovered. We got some of the audience back and the houses really dipped and then began to build up again, and we began to have some good evenings. But the pre-lapsarian ten performances never really quite returned.

Do you think previews are untrustworthy?

I think previews are innocent, people don't know what they're seeing, and if they've gone it will be on pure word of mouth, so you get enthusiastic audiences and they get more and more enthusiastic. Once the imprimatur of 'this is good' or 'this is bad' is put on it, odd things happen. Even with a hit it's never quite the same, because people are carrying in their heads a single line from a critic, usually one critic, explaining why they've decided to go, or a single really bad line from a critic, which makes them think, 'I can't cancel for this because I paid for it by Visa card!' With an audience thinking that, it can be pretty grim, particularly if it's an attempt at a kind of silly seriousness!

The show was vulnerable in that you *had* to think it was funny or you were sunk. Most comedies can be taken as art: if you've got a house that doesn't laugh at a Chekhov you'll be alright, because it will look like a serious glum drama. The next night you may get a laughing house and it will look like it had that wonderful Chekhovian froth that you can develop, and you'd be alright. But with *Ugly Rumours*, if they didn't find it amusing then you were done for. Even friends who wanted to get the show working, and had seen it before, couldn't physically laugh. Someone described to me this rictus feeling, of not being able to get it out, because it was frozen in this dreadful atmosphere. Dreadful!

I don't know really what it taught us. Some people said the satire was too early, and that, unfortunately in the theatre these days, the shows that succeed 90 per cent of people agree with. It's a very cynical thing, but 90 per cent of people were not agreeing that the Blair government was a national disaster back in October 1998.

David Edgar thought that the possibility of staging a political show like that has gone, because it needs a larger attention span and more background knowledge than people actually have. We were trying to keep it very simple, but unless you have read one of these big articles about spin-doctoring it is all news to you. My friend Terry Jones said, quite interestingly, that that was the problem, that you were both teaching someone something about what's going on, and sending it up. Comedy usually works by taking something that everyone knows and sending it up. With this the audience may have felt there was stuff they didn't realise about how the cabinet office worked. It felt, more than I realised, like a teaching show and a piss-take at the same time. And that is a very difficult act to pull off.

People may have just thought Tariq and I were overweening bastards who deserved to be taken down a peg. I think there was a strong feeling of that, partly because we had done pre-emptive strikes in the press and given a heap of interviews trying to get your own good reviews in before they get at you. I don't know. My God, it nearly broke me, because I spent all the summer on it, earned no money out of it, and I suddenly thought, 'God, we haven't earned a penny!'

What are you working on at the moment?

I've just completed my play about Abelard and Eloise, *In Extremis*. And I've been working for a long time on a play which is called *One Once*. I began it six years ago, after *Berlin Bertie*. It was commissioned by the Deutsches Theater in Berlin and is based on a Calvino story called 'The Cloven Viscount', about a seventeenth-century prince who goes to war. He's a renaissance man, interested in how cannon work, and is warned on the battlefield not to look at them too closely. But he steps in front of one as it's fired and is cut in half. Half of him returns to his estates, but it's the bad half, and everyone suffers intolerably. Then the good half returns, and the bad half goes away, and people are really bored by the goodness – they'll have to go to church all the time! Then an English surgeon turns up in the area, and stitches the two of them together.

I was trying to adapt this, and work German reunification into it. I produced an enormous, incomprehensible version. It was full of jokes about Berlin, which they were rather offended about. It also had science-fiction elements. Anyway, it was a mess. But I've carried on with it, and at the moment I'm doing a series of workshops on it with some drama students. My hope is to complete a new version soon.

My adaptation begins with an unfortunate accident in 1989 at a Soviet research station for visiting pro-Gorbachev lefties somewhat like myself. I was over there during the Gorbachev era, thinking, this is it! Isn't it pathetic when you look back? This unfortunate accident with a Soviet-designed laser cuts the lefty in half, and one half goes incredibly authoritarian – Stalinist – and the other goes Taoist (that is to say, passive but cunning). And the two wander around Europe looked after by their sponsors and end up in the drains of Berlin for some reason, in those tunnels that run under the Deutsches Theater. Under the Max Reinhardt Platz, outside the Deutsches Theater, there's a tunnel, running from the air-raid shelter nearby. This tunnel goes straight to Hitler's bunker about 300 yards away! I thought, 'This is a gift!', so I set all these scenes underneath the theatre. I got a feeling they weren't too amused by it. I admit the play was a mess, but I haven't stopped working on it. I'm finding a way of redoing it completely, so I've got two new ones, and I'm ready to go!

Max Stafford-Clark

Max Stafford-Clark

Max Stafford-Clark joined the Traverse Theatre, Edinburgh, in 1966, where he was Artistic Director, 1968–70. As Director of the Traverse Workshop Company, 1970–74, he specialised in new plays. That provided a foundation for his work with Joint Stock Theatre Group, which he co-founded in 1974. Joint Stock developed the workshop approach by which writers collaborated with actors in researching the subject of their plays (explained below). This was the means by which some of the most important plays of the 1970s were produced, including David Hare's *Fanshen*, Brenton's *Epsom Downs*, and Caryl Churchill's *Cloud Nine*. Stafford-Clark continued his association with those writers during his period as Artistic Director of the Royal Court Theatre, 1979–93. Notable successes during that time included Churchill's *Serious Money* (1985), which also evolved out of a workshop, and Brenton's 3 Plays for Utopia, which featured the first production of *Greenland* (1988). In 1993 Stafford-Clark co-founded an independent company, Out of Joint, with Sonia Friedman. Since then he has been responsible for commissioning the writing and production of some of the most important new works of the 1990s, including Mark Ravenhill's *Shopping and Fucking* (1995) and Caryl Churchill's *Blue Kettle* (1997).

I visited Stafford-Clark on 11 February 1999 at the Out of Joint offices near Holloway Road, London. I began by asking him about the evolution of Joint Stock, and went on to ask about the revival of Brenton's *Bloody Poetry*, which he directed in 1988. I was particularly interested in the staging of such scenes as the Plato's Cave episode. Joint Stock remains one of the milestones in post-war British theatre; further information on its history and evolution may be found in *The Joint Stock Book* ed. Rob Ritchie (London: Methuen Theatrefile, 1987). And for anyone wanting to know more about Stafford-Clark's work as director, his diary of his 1988 production of Farquhar's *The Recruiting Officer*, *Letters to George* (London: Nick Hern Books, 1989), remains indispensable.

Interview

Duncan Wu: *You co-founded Joint Stock in 1975 with David Hare and David Aukin. I wonder whether you could tell me what it was, and what it set out to do?*

Max Stafford-Clark: I think, really, it defined itself as it went on. I don't think it had a declared agenda at the point when it started – it wasn't a company started in order to promote a particular political or aesthetic idea.

The first thing to say is that life as a freelance director rates along with sewage maintenance as one of the grimmer professions. As soon as you're a freelance director you want to change that situation. I'd been working at the Traverse Theatre in Edinburgh,[1] and had come down to London. What you get, as a freelance director, are the plays other people don't want to direct. So starting a company was not just a good idea but a prerequisite to sustain a career. In fact, although David Aukin and David Hare are, as you correctly say, nominally the people who supported this endeavour – because David Hare had finished with Portable Theatre[2] and David Aukin had been running the Freehold theatre company[3] with his wife Nancy Meckler, so they were at a loose end – the real partner was Bill Gaskill. Although history records that all three of us founded it, in fact *I* started it, and very soon after it had got going Bill Gaskill joined. The first play we did together was *The Speakers*, which was an adaptation of Heathcote Williams' book.[4] Although we asked Heathcote, in fact he didn't play very much part in the adaptation (though he came to see it and approved of it). It was a kind of cut-up job, and the characters he was writing about, the people who spoke at Hyde Park Corner, were largely still alive. There was a man with tattoos; Axel, a German refugee who spoke to a Marxist agenda; and McGuinness, an Irishman who was rather psychotic, who had died since the book had been written.

The first thing to emphasise is how stimulating it is for a director to work with another director, and how rarely that happens. I was thirty – I'd been at the Traverse, I wasn't just starting off – and Bill was forty-two. He had been running the Royal Court; he was the second director after George Devine. What he had to offer me was the kind of precision that came from working

---

[1] Stafford-Clark was artistic director of the Traverse from 1966 to 1970, directing new plays by a range of writers including Stanley Eveling and David Mowat.
[2] Hare wrote his first play for Portable Theatre, *Inside Out*, in 1968. He describes the conclusion of his association with Portable, and involvement with Joint Stock, in 'The Awkward Squad: About Joint Stock', *Writing Left-Handed*, pp. 64–72.
[3] The background to the Freehold, and the theatre culture in London at that time, is recalled by Aukin in conversation with Bernard Pomerance and Roland Rees in Rees' *Fringe First*, pp. 48–65. Like Portable Theatre, the Freehold ground to a halt in 1973. See also *The Joint Stock Book*, pp. 100–1.
[4] *The Speakers* was Heathcote Williams' first book, published 1964. The play was adapted by Bill Gaskill and Max Stafford-Clark, and first performed at the Birmingham Repertory Studio, 28 January 1974.

in a proscenium – and an astute political analysis that I certainly lacked. And what I had to offer him – which was a lot less clear to me at the time but which I now realise was equally important – was having come from working with a band, working on the fringe where what is now called site-specific or promenade performances (although we didn't use those words at the time) were part of that world. And I'd seen not just Grotowski[5] but another Polish company who performed all over dining tables; the audience sat at the tables, and the actors performed in and out of the plates and knives and forks.

Having got the script of *The Speakers* we set about producing it as a promenade production. There was a central tower which acted as a kind of refreshment counter, and the actress who ran it sold tea and coffee as well as playing a part in different scenes. And there were overlapping scenes of different people speaking that took place in different corners of the hall where we were performing. The audience had, to a certain extent, a free choice at certain moments as to which speaker they would listen to. At other moments there was only one thing going on, and they were more focussed and directed. It was terrific, it worked very well, apart from an attempt to do a late-night performance at the Abbey Theatre in the Dublin Festival, which ended in a drunken riot. It was an invitation to the audience to transcend the usual boundaries, without in any way involving their active participation. It didn't invite their participation, but it often happened, because the staging meant the ground rules had shifted.

We learnt a great deal during rehearsals for *The Speakers*. We did a workshop for four weeks, and then we had a prolonged rehearsal period for seven weeks – none of which was paid for, we were all working for free at that point. But you could learn skills, you could teach an actor to improvise extempore on paperweights, or traffic wardens, or the Albigensian heresy. Some of the actors became very skilful at nonsense talk. But one thing we didn't – and couldn't – rehearse was how to cope with heckling.[6] So we rehearsed how to cope with heckling by having some of us actually doing the heckling. Some of the actors playing speakers became *viciously* skilled in how to cope with hecklers, far more so than a real speaker, because they had really given it some thought. And when we came to the odd person heckling in the live audience, they were humiliated in the most vicious way and we had to learn to do that not quite so well. And we learned also that couples, a man and a woman together, would very rarely heckle or risk anything unusual. Girls together were quite

---

[5] Jerzy Grotowski, international leader of the experimental theatre who became famous in the 1960s as the director of productions staged by the Polish Laboratory Theatre of Wroclaw. A leading exponent of audience involvement, he sets up emotional confrontations between a limited group of spectators and the actors; the performers are disciplined masters of bodily and vocal contortions, violent but graceful action, and an almost unintelligible dialogue of howls and groans.

[6] Heckling is a key feature of audience participation at Speakers' Corner.

copeable-with. Boys together don't want to lose face. But the people who were really dangerous were middle-aged women by themselves. It seems their status in society is rated so low that they have nothing to lose. So when assaults on the actors happened, like hot cups of tea being thrown, it was always by middle-aged women.

It's a new way of approaching the business of creating theatre. You're assuming that the audience is an active partner in the business of a performance. And so potentially any given performance would be, by definition, different from any performance that had preceded it and that was going to follow it.

Yes, pretty different.

After *The Speakers*, the second production we did was *Fanshen*.[7] Because it has a political context (it's about life in a Chinese village, and how communism came to it), it politicised the company. So Joint Stock became a co-operative, and indeed did take most decisions collectively; about whether the budget should be spent on the set, or whether the money should be spent on travel, whether the actors should travel in the van – those kinds of questions. So the company at that point got a political agenda that it didn't have when we were doing *The Speakers*, and it got that from the material.

How does the writer fit into all this?

Well, Bill Gaskill comes from the Royal Court, and in those days Royal Court practice was to eschew editing. You rehearsed the script as it was written or you didn't do it at all. Whereas the school that I came from, and which is certainly now current mainstream thinking, is that a script can be workshopped, given new readings, and other kinds of aids, that help the limping text to cross the road! I believe that a script is a starting-point, whereas to Bill it was a kind of inspirational Holy Grail that you either did or you didn't do. So we also came from different points of view, and that was part of the fertility of Joint Stock. But the truth is that both of us have a huge respect for the writer and know the writer is the starting-point. One of the ways in which Joint Stock really succeeded was to hand the material back to the writer. Too many groups were interventionist, jealous of the artistic process, and wanted to take that over from the writer, whereas we researched *Fanshen* endlessly, but finally turned all that research back over to the writer.

---

[7] Two-act play by David Hare, first produced by Joint Stock at the Crucible, Sheffield, 10 March 1975, directed by Bill Gaskill and Max Stafford-Clark. It opened at the ICA Theatre, London, 21 April 1975. Extracts from Stafford-Clark's production notebooks for this play are published in *The Joint Stock Book*, pp. 110–16.

There was a lot of stuff in the workshop about women and bound feet and so on, none of which interested David Hare, so it didn't get into the final version. Similarly, *Cloud Nine*, which was about sexual politics, was researched, and actors chosen for the original workshop were selected not just for their acting skills but because of their own sexual agendas – there was a gay couple, a lesbian, a single parent, a divorced father.[8] But at the end of the workshop the material was very firmly handed to Caryl and it was absolutely her decision that the play would begin in Victorian Africa, and that there'd be a gap of a hundred years, but the characters only aged fifteen years between the first and the second half. So that quite complex scheme was not something that in the workshop we were privy to at all, it was very much her idea. What I'm saying is that respect for the writer, handing the material back to the writer, and the kind of acceptance that the writer is the senior collaborator, is very much part of Joint Stock's success – and Out of Joint's tradition, too.[9]

How does the director fit into all that?

Well, all of you act as a research team during the workshop process. Your role becomes more of a conventional director during the rehearsal process. The roles are much looser in the workshop. Take *Serious Money* which, because it is about a specific subject, is easy to focus on.[10] When we started work on that none of us knew anything about the financial world. The one thing that held us all together at the beginning was mutual ignorance! And whenever we met people – stockbrokers, futures traders, bond traders – they would say, 'Oh, you'll never understand it, of course we'll explain, but you'll never understand it.' In fact, the actors became extremely skilled pretty swiftly. The first job in every workshop session was to read the *Financial Times* and interpret it, and people would follow a story through. One actor was following a story about chocolate futures, and he told us that two-thirds of the world's chocolate was grown in the Côte d'Ivoire, the old French colony. Now the French Transport Ministry had introduced a new policy: their subsidies for transport were to be withdrawn in the year 1989. This meant that chocolate was going to become far more expensive to transport from the Côte d'Ivoire to Belgium and Germany, which were the centres of manufacture of

[8] *Cloud Nine* was first produced by Joint Stock on 14 February 1979, directed by Max Stafford-Clark. Recollections by three of the actors involved are published in *The Joint Stock Book*, pp. 138–42.
[9] Out of Joint was founded by Max Stafford-Clark and Sonia Friedman in 1993. It specialises in the production of new theatre works.
[10] Caryl Churchill's play evolved from a workshop by the English Stage Company and was first performed at the Royal Court on 21 March 1987. Its success, helped by its popularity with those who worked in the city of London, led to a run in the West End. See Brenton's observations on it, p. 37, above.

chocolate. So chocolate futures were going to go up. We should invest in chocolate futures now. And we followed the story and it seemed pretty clear. At the end of the workshop we were talking to a broker who had come in to meet the whole company, and just as he was leaving this actor said, 'Oh listen, there is something I would just like to ask you: what about chocolate? I've been following this story through about chocolate futures in the Côte d'Ivoire.' He explained the whole thing to him, and the man said, 'My God! I must get on my mobile now!' That was how far we'd come – of course, there are a lot of clever people in the financial world, but probably the people who get double Firsts go into diplomacy. It's a world that you can crack once you get into it, and copper futures was terrific, very exciting.

Again, the decision to write the play in bounding verse and buccaneering couplets was entirely Caryl's, and it was one she took once the workshop was over. I suppose the actors become human tape-recorders and researchers. The director, and the writer too, all of us prompt the research in the workshop period.

And is your job to conduct improvisation sessions based on this research during the preparation period? Is that what you do?

I might well do that, yes.

What sorts of other things would you be doing?

Well, some improvisations would simply relay the information somebody had gathered, not all of which they might necessarily understand. Someone would say, 'I had lunch with the stockbroker or I was allowed to sit at his table, and he took a phone call on his mobile and he said, "If Frankfurt goes long get me twenty three at eight." But of course I couldn't hear the conversation at the other end.' It was like a pile of bric-a-brac, a junk shop; and using this method Caryl assembled a body of information.

It's pretty pragmatic. You react to the material that's coming in. There are other times when the writer or one of the actors sets up an exercise. One of the most successful exercises in *Cloud Nine* was set up by Caryl. It was an imposition improvisation whereby somebody would go out of the room and you would impose a quality on them: let's say they were incredibly stupid. They would then come in and enter an improvised situation without knowing what this quality was. And gradually it became self-fulfilling. If you treated this person as if they were deeply stupid – 'Can you make some coffee? It's in the cupboard' – they actually began to fulfil that, which was fascinating. And I might act in an improvisation too. If I'd met a stockbroker or somebody useful that day, I might well be in the improvisation. So the roles become much looser in the workshop and then reformulate and become much tighter in the rehearsal period.

How closely would you work with a writer during that workshop? Would you be setting up improvisations together? Would the writer be involved in acting out the improvisations?

She/he might do. If they'd been to see, let's say, in the case of *Cloud Nine*, an East African expert, and nobody else had, I might well set up an improvisation which placed the writer as an actor.

What I'm getting at is, are we talking about a situation in which everyone is on the same level, everyone is an actor, and everyone is contributing not only to research towards the finished product, but also towards improvisational exercises that are ...?

Yes, that is the case. At the same time, don't forget that people have particular skills. I mean, of course I'm not as good an actor as the real actors. And in the end you're trying to catch the writer's imagination. So if she says, 'Oh look, what really interests me is *that*. Why don't we think of setting up an improvisation about that area?' Then of course that's what you want to do, because in the end the whole purpose of the workshop is to stimulate the writer. And it's no good, as in *Fanshen*, with us becoming fascinated with bound feet and the position of women, if in the end that's of no interest to David Hare.

Is there a value to exploring all kinds of subjects that actually turn out to be dead ends in terms of the finished product, insofar as possibly they're providing background of some kind for everyone concerned?

Yes, absolutely, it's providing a stimulus to the actors. The role of actor is often a passive one: you are summoned to a job, you get it or you don't get it. An actor is rejected more times in a year than most people are in a lifetime. So that to say, 'Look, this is a level playing-field, we're all in this together, and we don't quite know where it's going, and we'd like you to go off and meet these stockbrokers', is perhaps unexpected and stimulating. Two of the actors in *Serious Money* got jobs on the floor of the London International Futures Exchange as runners, so they were earning three times more as that than they were as actors! I remember a workshop where somebody went off and worked in a sweatshop for a day in Kentish Town with largely Asian immigrants. I mean, an actor's job is first of all to observe, and by saying, 'Your observation is very important and could indeed be crucial in the formation of the play', you give the actor an importance and a role that they don't normally have. I remember the second play Joint Stock did was called

Yesterday's News,[11] and it was about a nine-day wonder, a nine-day crisis in Angola in which English mercenaries were involved – do you remember Colonel Callan?

Oh, that was in the Seventies wasn't it?

Yes. He was ex-English Army and was leading this band of mercenaries; they recruited people who were ex-SAS, and ex-Paras from Northern Ireland, and also people who were schoolboys straight out of the East End. It was a real mess – and he shot some of his own men, that's what provoked the scandal. In the end this play turned out to be about that incident. One of the actors, Paul Kember (who later became a playwright and wrote *Not Quite Jerusalem* that was produced at the Royal Court), revealed an extraordinary skill for investigative journalism that was at least as great as his skill as an actor. He tracked down the phone number of the man who'd recruited the mercenaries, and for a moment we were ahead of the press. Indeed, somebody else gave us the numbers of two mercenaries who had been out there and worked for Colonel Callan. It was a very strange situation because they thought we were journalists with huge chequebooks; they didn't realise we were an impoverished fringe theatre company. They were quite keen to meet, but the financial situation wasn't clear. They agreed to meet in this pub very close to the rehearsal room where we were, and I met them with David Rintoul, one of the actors. It turned out later that they suspected we might be IRA: both of them had served in Northern Ireland. Anyway they talked in the pub and they said, yes, they might come and see us, how much money was in it? They said they'd think about it. So David and I went back to the rehearsal room where everybody else was, which was St Gabriel's Parish Hall on the Churchill Estate in Pimlico. It was freezing cold, and there was a boiler, a stove in one corner of the room, and everyone was huddled round that, and I said, 'I just don't know whether they're going to come or not but we had better set up something else in case they don't.' And suddenly they both burst into the room, and one of them came and stood right in the middle of us, and the other one went round the room kicking open with his foot all the exit doors – bang, bang, bang, like that – so all this cold air came in and we were stunned, sitting there. He was just checking the place, that we weren't setting him up in some way, that we weren't IRA or anything like that. They came back, sat down, and one of them said, 'So you want to talk?' It turned out that one of them came from Walthamstow which is where Will Knightley, one of the actors, came from. And they talked for about two hours. They

---

[11] Written by the company and Jeremy Seabrook, first performed at the West End Centre, Aldershot, 6 April 1976. It opened at the Theatre Upstairs, Royal Court Theatre, 11 May 1976.

talked about how to set an electronic ambush, and how to kill somebody with the kind of expertise that other people talk about classic cars or fine wines – exactly the nuance of how to kill the most number of people in an ambush. One of them was a very, very good storyteller, and you couldn't help but become fascinated by that, despite the fact that what he was saying was morally repugnant, and that his political position was completely offensive. I think we learnt something that afternoon, which was that violence is attractive. Of course it's very easy to hold up your hands in horror at things that are happening, then and indeed since, all over the world. But once you understand how exciting it is, then you have learned something quite horrifying but very important, and we learned that that afternoon.

You mean attractive in dramatic terms?

Attractive in dramatic terms, exciting to hear about, and attractive to participate in, I would imagine. Certainly it had been the centre of these young men's lives and they had no other recognisable skills. They were into minor chequebook fraud now they were out – not nearly as thrilling.

Are there disadvantages attached to this way of researching and preparing a play?

Well, in *Yesterday's News*, the second play, we did lose the writer. The writer was Jeremy Seabrook, who is probably better known as a sociologist.[12] He had written a couple of well-regarded plays for the Royal Court. But the areas that interested the group didn't stimulate him. He already had a strong idea of the play he wanted to write and there wasn't really a meeting-point, and so we lost him. That can happen. And I think also Caryl Churchill, who's worked most in this way, would say that she has given up doing it because it had become for her a bit formulaic. She has a great deal of experience with the workshop play. But she would now say she would discover certain facts, there'd be an element of mystery written in, a bit of surrealism – and in the end it was her way of coping with the tremendous bank of information and the very tight timeframe. And finally, far from being a discovery, it became a repetition. So I think it would be difficult to get Caryl to do a workshop again.

You mentioned a timeframe. What would your timeframe have been for something like Fanshen? *If you were putting it together, how long would you allow for the workshop?*

Four weeks. And then there was a gap of up to nine weeks, or maybe a bit longer, ten weeks. But we couldn't pay the actors during the gap. So the

[12] Author of *The Underprivileged* (1967), *Unemployment* (1982) and *Landscapes of Poverty* (1985), among other works.

pressure from the actors was always to make the period as short as possible. The pressure from the writer was to make the gap as long as possible.

And the gap is the writing time, isn't it?

That's right. So we negotiated, and I think it came down to nine weeks or ten from twelve.

So once you've got a text from the writer, do you then put it into production in the usual manner?

Yes.

So we might say that the main difference between this method and the usual one is that you have this workshop period at the beginning during which the actors and the director and the writer all muck in together, intellectually and physically, in a period of investigation?

Yes. And all the results of that investigation are placed at the disposal of the writer, who's free to select or reject whatever they choose. If we were, let's say, a feminist group, or a gay group, or a group with an absolutely rigid Marxist agenda, then we would want the play to be written to that prescription. I would imagine *The Cheviot, the Stag, and the Black Black Oil*, which I think is the most interesting of the plays John McGrath wrote for 7:84,[13] was written in order to expose the exploitation of Scottish resources by England. And that was the clear agenda behind it. We would never place an agenda on the material but would allow the writer to find it. Having said that, of course *Fanshen* was adapted from the book of the same name by William Hinton, so the agenda was probably already placed there by him.

And indeed Hinton had a role in the final work itself.

Yes he did, he was very clear with David. I think David was stimulated by the conversations he had with him about what he thought should be in and what shouldn't.[14]

---

[13] First published 1974, reprinted by Eyre Methuen, 1981.

[14] 'Once the play opened and William Hinton – who assumed that the play would fail, as previous attempts to dramatise the book had – heard that it was doing well, he arrived on a plane from America with a whole series of emendations. The play was therefore rethought over and over again between him and the company and between him and me. The finally agreed text is a compromise between him and us simply because the view he takes of the Chinese Revolution and of events in that village is inevitably a slightly rosier one than that which I and the company took', *File on Hare*, pp. 28–9. Hare comments further in *The Joint Stock Book*, pp. 105–10.

Do you still use this method?

Yes, I've done it quite recently with Rebecca Prichard, who has written a play called *Yardgals*, which was done at the Royal Court. It's quite an ambitious subject. What we've done in the course of the workshop is interview an enormous range of people, to compile an oral history of this century. At one end, there were the oldest people we could find. The earliest memories were effectively post-First World War – an elderly actress remembering her father coming back at the end of the war. It's very moving. And at the other, we interviewed kids on the housing estate across the road from our offices. The idea was to create a millennium play, or a century play – it may be one of many plays that take that as a theme. There's a very good documentary series on television that I caught a bit of, called *Century Road*, have you seen that?

I think I did see a bit of that.

It took a number of roads called Century Road – one in Yarmouth, one in the suburbs of north London, and it traces the people who lived there. Again that leaves itself open to the material you find, as opposed to finding it in order to prove a particular point.

I wonder whether we could turn now to Howard Brenton's Bloody Poetry. *I suppose* Bloody Poetry *differs from some of the other plays you did with him, like* Epsom Downs,[15] *in that it didn't arise from the techniques that you've just been describing.*

No, it absolutely didn't. Not only that, but it had already had a successful production at Hampstead Theatre, which I'd seen there. So the text was absolutely finalised – and I think, looking at my copy of the text, I can see we cut one scene and there's a little bit of a rewrite, but it's tiny. We were working from a printed script.

So how did you begin to approach this?

I suppose you begin with the casting. Byron and Shelley live in the memory, you have an idea of the personalities of those people. Nigel Terry is someone I've worked with before and since – a wonderful actor. He's got a kind of protean personality that seemed right for Byron. And Mark Rylance, who played Shelley – he's also played Ariel, and the kind of parts that you would associate with Shelley – has become an actor-manager since those days. But both those personalities were very apt, so I think that's the starting-point. I'm just showing you the script now at random. As you can see, against the

---

[15] Howard Brenton's play was first performed by Joint Stock at the Roundhouse, 4 August 1977. See *The Joint Stock Book*, pp. 130–3.

speeches I've marked in the intention of each character as they speak.[16] One way of exploring the play it is to read out the action or intention before you speak the line.

What I do first is break the scene into units. What lies behind each speech. It's a matter of analysing the text in terms of motivation and intention. Here's one. I've written, against the text: 'Action: Claire wants to reaffirm their passion.' Her speech reads: 'We are privileged to make this journey. We are privileged to stand on this beach, and see George Byron and Bysshe Shelley meet. It will be history!'[17] So I start like that. The first couple of weeks of rehearsal tend to be discussion and analysis rather than moving it around too much.

With the actors?

Yes.

And would you give your annotations to the actors?

No, no, we would arrive at them together. But I would then ask them to read them out, as part of the speech.

There's a wonderful scene in this play, where the characters are acting out the fable of Plato's Cave. What were the particular challenges or difficulties in setting up a scene like that?

Particular challenges were in understanding Plato's philosophy.

Just to be a bit discursive for a moment, what's exciting about the period, and about Shelley and Byron and so on, was that they were in the age of repression that followed the great revolutionary period in the 1780s. I'm just reading Fintan O'Toole's biography of Sheridan.[18] I'd no idea Sheridan was so closely involved with the Corresponding Societies and toyed with the idea of revolution, because you think of him as a drawing-room, Chichester playwright. There's a lovely bit in it where O'Toole says Byron had dinner with Sheridan, and described him as taciturn, drunk, and so on.[19] But clearly

---

[16] See illustration, p. 66 below.

[17] From Act One, Scene 2; *Brenton Plays: Two*, p. 242.

[18] Fintan O'Toole, *A Traitor's Kiss: the Life of Richard Brinsley Sheridan* (London: Granta Books, 1997).

[19] There are several such letters by Byron, among them one of 31 October 1815, in which he describes a dinner party that 'was first silent, then talky, then argumentative, then disputatious, then unintelligible, then altogethery, then inarticulate, and then drunk ... to crown all, Kinnaird and I had to conduct Sheridan down a d——d corkscrew staircase, which had certainly been constructed before the discovery of fermented liquors, and to which no legs, however crooked, could possibly accommodate themselves' (*Byron's Letters and Journals* ed. Leslie A. Marchand (13 vols, London: John Murray, 1973–94), iv. pp. 326–7).

    O'er the lagoon
We glided, and from that funereal barque
I leaned, and saw the city, and could mark
How from their many isles, in the evening's gleam
Its temples and its palaces did seem
Like fabrics of enchantment — piled to Heaven —

ENCHANT
WARNS

LX 40

BYRON *snorts, raising a glass.*

BYRON. Ha! You poor sod, y'believe in love, y'do, poor bastard.
Yet you harm as many as I, you would-be 'moral immoralist'.
You shred and tear lives around you as much as I, the cynic,
the libertine. Yes, I leave my diseases in married bedrooms,
my children in convents — but you! What have you left?
A wife drowned in the Serpentine? And who was that other
little thing in London, overdosed herself with opium, because
of you? Oh yes, the appropriately named Fanny Godwin, your
second wife's little sister, all of fifteen wasn't she, when you
had her?

ACCUSES *DERIDES GOADS*
CHALLENGE

ATTACKS

BYSSHE. I cannot be —

REBUTS

BYRON. Cannot be what? Responsible? Ha! My darling, darling
hypocrite. What a pity it is that you are not —

PINS
COMFORTS
(much)

Turned the other way too, as I am. We could marry, become
two harmless old men, arm in arm on the sea-shore, writing
verse in peace, retired from this world — soothing, organic
world, of flux, and blood, and manic husbands, and jealousy,
and babies bursting from wombs and aching cocks, eh?

DISGUSTS

He laughs.

D'you know where I found myself, one night last week?
Halfway up a drainpipe to the balcony of an eighteen-year-old
heiress. Dangling in mid-air, d'you know what happened
to me?

GRIPS

BYSSHE. The drainpipe gave way?

HUMOUR

BYRON. Worse!

ENCOURAGES

BYSSHE. Chest pains?

NEEDLE

BYRON. Worse! I looked down into the street and there, dressed
for the opera, was the Venetian correspondent for the London
Daily Mail. Spotted! And then, ah then —

ENTERTAIN
TANTALIZES

A silence.

Figure 1. Facing pages from Max Stafford-Clark's working copy of *Bloody Poetry* (a blurred photocopy of the printed text), with his annotations clearly marked in pencil. For explanation, see preceding pages and pp. 47–8.

BYSSHE. Well, what? Did you go up to love the heiress, or down, to thrash the journalist?

BYRON. For a moment both delights had an equal attraction. / No. I despaired.

BYSSHE. Come, come –

BYRON. No no – despair/ Perhaps it takes a high-blown, high-flown personality, such as I have engineered, ~~to be~~ caught in a scene of outright farce, to feel –

An airy ~~wave~~.

That profound emotion. Up a drainpipe?

BYSSHE. A good story –

BYRON. Is it not, is it not./ Actually, I went down and bribed the spy to silence. Now is *that* within my received character, yes or no?

BYSSHE. No.

He pauses.

No –

BYRON, *angrily.*

BYRON. Then believe what I say, you tight-arsed, 'Libertarian', // 'free-lover', 'free-liver'!

BYRON *looks away, dangling his free hand in the water.*
A silence.

BYSSHE. What are you telling me? You went home, reformed?

~~BYRON, good-humour back at once.~~

BYRON. Not at all – waited 'til the spy was well away – then went to the servants' door – another bribe – and up to her./ Sweet thing. Fair hair. Down on her thighs, unshaved skin – soft, like feathers/I am not telling you that I have reformed, I am telling you that I have despaired.

BYSSHE. What right do you have to do that? You do not have the right./Despair? Easy, George!/Cheap merchandise for a writer. You will end up silent or making a pretty lyric out of the phrase 'I have nothing to say'. /

The people of England – they may well have the right to despair. So would you – if you were a mill-hand in Manchester, or a child down a mine, or a mother to a labourer's children in a filthy hovel –

(margin annotations, top to bottom:)

LIGHTEN

DEMAND
HIT
REJECT

PINS

TAUNTS

DISMISS

~~TEARS~~ SNARES

(REJECTS)

ATTACKS. SCORNS.

CHALLENGE

ENTICES

.CHALLENGE

ATTACK
~~SCORNS~~
ALARMS

SHAME

Byron was fascinated with Sheridan and with the period where revolution was a tangible option. Byron is envious that *he* wasn't alive in the 1780s and 1790s (they're talking, I think, in 1815). Now by that time, after Napoleon had been defeated, it's the time of Castlereagh, isn't it? It's a period of *great* repression in English history, when the establishment is just hanging on, and the industrial revolution is beginning. That's obviously why they leave, because England is untenable. But that correspondence between that period and the grim decade of Mrs Thatcher is obviously one that was very resonant for Howard.

Did Howard bring a lot of research to rehearsals for this play?

I think he'd read one particular book that he recommended: Richard Holmes, *Shelley: The Pursuit.*[20] Obviously we all read that. Actors love reading; particularly if you're playing a character like Byron or Shelley, there is a responsibility to inhabit that person. The women are obviously a bit less public, but not that much, I mean there's lots of information about Claire Clairmont.[21]

Did you do any improvisations for the play?

We probably would have. We might have improvised their offstage life, how they would have coped.

As I recall, the production was anything but realist in terms of its approach to such things as design and lighting and so forth.

Well, there is a theatricality both about their lives and about the situation, and about the cave, and about the end. I see this as being quite important in Howard's work insofar as it's very often about failure, but he's at pains to say it's about magnificent failure.

And that's echoed in the theatricality of it, the sublimity.

Yes. That's quite right.

Given that Howard's propensities are so ordered, do you have to put on a particular hat when you take on his work? Are you thinking in a particular way when you approach the work of someone like this? Are there particular things you have to say to actors?

---

[20] Exemplary one-volume biography of the poet, first published 1974.
[21] Mary Shelley's half-sister, mistress of Byron.

I'm a Royal Court director, so you're trained to be in the service of the writer; they are the banners under which we go to battle. So, yes *of course* you start from sympathising with the writer's point of view, but you also want him to define it in rehearsal.

This production of *Bloody Poetry* was part of a celebration of Howard's work, 3 Plays for Utopia, along with his new play *Greenland*, the revival of *Sore Throats*, and of course *The Genius*. I have great sympathy with his work. I've always thought him a great writer of set-piece scenes and monologues to the audience. In retrospect, I don't understand why we thought Snoo Wilson, Howard Brenton and David Hare all came from the same stable, because they now seem so totally different. With Howard you don't get well-tailored linear narrative, you get great chunks of bloody poetry.

They're intellectual exercises to an extent. Do you have to sit down with the actors and explain some of those intellectual ideas?

Well, he would lead that discussion, yes.

And are actors generally receptive to this sort of thing? I mean Bloody Poetry *is I think quite a demanding play from that point of view.*

Yes, they're very responsive to that because they're playing real people. The ideas that flesh them out are of huge importance to the actors. Howard doesn't lose actors in rehearsal, he's very wise and considerate about what an actor needs in order to play a part. Edward Bond baffles them, and they become resentful and upset. I remember Edward talking to a group of actors in *The Pope's Wedding*, the early play of his I did,[22] and saying, 'You are Rolls Royces, but you are Rolls Royces with weeds growing out of them, Rolls Royces full of weeds!' And this actor, I think it was Mark Wingett, said, 'What are you talking about? How can I be a Rolls Royce with weeds? What're you on about, Eddie?' And Edward became more and more lyrical, elliptical, and confusing. He's the worst director of his own work because he baffles the actors with images. Whereas Howard enjoys rehearsals; he tends if anything to be over-enthusiastic. He'll say, 'That's working terrifically, that's great!' And you'll think, well, it's coming on, but it's not that great yet.

Can I just return to the political agenda attached to Joint Stock when it started? Obviously, recent British history is relevant here.

---

[22] Max Stafford-Clark directed a revival of Bond's play at the Royal Court, 1984.

That's right. To take an example. *Light Shining in Buckinghamshire*, Caryl Churchill's play, and the first of hers in which I was involved, was produced in September 1976.[23] It had been written the year before, so she is using the English Civil War as a parallel to the then Labour Government, and lamenting in both periods the lost opportunities of idealism. The concluding scene of *Light Shining in Buckinghamshire* features a man eating grass alone in a field while somebody else leaves the country and goes to Bermuda. This is an expression of despair both at the cynicism at the Callaghan government and at the situation facing the Puritan extremists at the Restoration. Joint Stock was always responsive and pragmatic, and you certainly should look at the time these plays were written, because the writers were responding to the current social and political situation.

Joint Stock was a co-operative, too.

I don't think we ever defined ourselves as a co-operative although we had a co-operative style of management. I went to the Royal Court in 1979; the first production of *Top Girls* was in 1981, and the revival was in 1991, ten years later.[24] And when I was doing the revival I asked the actors to research their own diaries or to see if they had any magazines like *Cosmopolitan* from ten years previously. We discovered that the whole agenda for magazines had changed. In 1981 it was women in suits, and women as executives, carrying briefcases; the image in 1991 was of sharing, caring, topless men with babies, and the whole emphasis on family images was very strong. The mood was quite different, quite strikingly so. My own diaries of 1981 were full of meetings at the Royal Court in order to plan how to turn what was a hierarchical institutional structure into a co-operative. There were staff meetings and discussions about whether or not salaries should be equal. I had forgotten that completely; it seems quite barmy now! And I think that, having encouraged other people to make the effort, I sat back and watched it fail, and saw how it couldn't work.

But, you see, one forgets that *Time Out*[25] used to have the same structure: everybody was paid the same, from the receptionist down to the chief editor. And then the split between *Time Out* and *City Limits* marked the end of that theory in practice. How to put that theory into practice was very much our concern in 1981, and by 1991 I'd successfully forgotten all about it.

---

[23] Joint Stock first performed this play, which had been workshopped by them, at the Traverse Theatre, Edinburgh, 7 September 1976. Caryl Churchill's comments on the production appear in *The Joint Stock Book*, pp. 118–21.
[24] Max Stafford-Clark directed the first production of Caryl Churchill's play at the Royal Court, 28 August 1982. The same production opened at Joseph Papp's Public Theater in New York the following year.
[25] Magazine featuring a directory of forthcoming events published weekly in London.

And that, in a way, is one of the most deleterious effects of Thatcherism isn't it? Not just in the theatre world but British society at large. It's put us beyond that kind of experiment.

That's right. If you had presented the agenda of today's Labour Party in 1980 or 1981, it would have seemed very right-wing. I remember discussing with Danny Boyle[26] whether or not to produce a Joint Stock investigative play about the unions, and he said, 'No, don't do it, we really shouldn't do it because we'll just end up union-bashing.' And I said, 'No, no, if that's what we find out, that's what we should present.' And he said, 'No, don't do it.' Anyway, we didn't do it, so that was that. Of course, the corruption of the right was visible to us, but the corruption of the left was absolutely *in*visible to us. If you had a play open the night before, you'd go into the *Guardian* offices in Gray's Inn Road at two in the morning to get the first edition and there'd be 200 people with their feet up reading the *Sun* – they weren't even interested in their own newspaper! And you couldn't make a film without five guys holding a boom, and three people to make the tea. This interview, if it was done by the BBC, would have required five people; now it's just one person with a tape recorder. So you have to say, horrible though Mrs Thatcher was, that battle with the unions was probably essential.

Does that make plays like Bloody Poetry *and* Fanshen *less appealing to audiences? Do you think that's a barrier?*

I think all plays are a product of their time, and you have to go back to look at that time. *Cloud Nine* was a difficult play to revive because it was a pre-AIDS play, and it's about sexual politics. So when it was revived last year at the Old Vic that was the first time that play could be revived, because it was so specific to its time.[27] I did a play at the RSC called *A Jovial Crew* which was written in 1639/40 by Richard Brome – and was, records tell us, the last play to be performed before the theatres were shut. Now the text seems pretty baffling, and of course it's not as coherent as the Elizabethan plays. It's about a benign landlord who becomes totally autocratic and insists on benevolence to people, and when you go back and study the period you can see it as a coded message, as a way of criticising Charles I. Once you see that, and you read about what went on during the period, then certain elements of the play become clear. So any barrier to understanding is caused by the time that's passed.

---

[26] Boyle directed a number of productions for Joint Stock before joining the Royal Court. He is best known today as the director of such feature films as *Shallow Grave*, *Trainspotting* and *The Beach*.
[27] Tom Cairns revived the play at the Old Vic, March 1997.

It's easier to think of Fanshen *and* Magnificence *as having more relevance to an age in which people were capable of believing in ideals.*

This discussion goes on all the time. Tomorrow morning I'm in a script meeting at the Royal Court, and the constant reference in conversation and the constant subject is, what do you do now that there are no ideals left? English writing and Irish writing has never been more celebrated abroad than it is at the moment: Sarah Kane, Mark Ravenhill, Martin Crimp, are big names in Germany. I'm regularly invited to conferences in Amsterdam, Copenhagen, Palermo, New York, Berlin, about the new English writing. But in part the new English writing is successful because it no longer has the specific political agenda that occupied Britain during the Eighties. As a director you have to be pragmatic, you have to move on, you have to say, the function of the theatre is to respond to the world we're living in, and it may be a matter of personal regret that plays no longer seek to expound ideals. But it's understandable that a new generation finds it hard to live in a century that has successfully demolished all beliefs – whether it's Christianity, the family, science, feminism, socialism. We're left at the end of the century with very little to believe in.

But there's still a place for the sublime in modern theatre?

Absolutely. Having said that, you hope that it's untrue and you set out to prove it's untrue each time you go out to bat.

It's often occurred to me that Blue Heart *is a kind of sublime.*[28]

Those plays come out of a mood on the part of the author of anger and irritation with the theatre. If you've written *Serious Money*, saying people are greedy, and by doing this play, by exposing this greed, I hope that I may make people change – and what happens is that the play is hugely successful, but people don't change at all, then how successful is the play? Caryl has had a distinguished career as a playwright. Yet at the same time, by the stringent agenda she sets herself, she might well say, 'I failed in my principal objective as a playwright.' One way of looking at *Heart's Desire* and *Blue Kettle* is that they're angry little plays saying, 'Fuck theatre! What does theatre really do? Is it worth doing? Let's send this play backwards and see what happens!' At

---

[28] *Blue Heart* is a double-bill by Caryl Churchill, *Heart's Desire* and *Blue Kettle*, produced by Max Stafford-Clark and his company, Out of Joint, with the Royal Court Theatre, and first performed at Bury St Edmunds on 14 August 1997. It enjoyed a successful tour of England in 1997, and of America in 1998–99.

the same time she has said herself that they're unsuccessful anti-plays, because they celebrate that magic power of theatre.

They're exciting pieces of theatre.

Absolutely. That's the strange ambivalence of those plays, and she said herself once in a moment of insight, 'If I had really wanted to write a successful anti-play I should have gone on for another two scenes with people just saying "b", "k", and that would really have made the audience angry!'[29]

---

[29] This is the point at which the play arrives; see *Blue Heart*, pp. 68–9.

Alan Bennett

Alan Bennett, *The Madness of George III* (1991)

The Madness of George III was first performed at the Royal National Theatre, Lyttelton Theatre, 28 November 1991, directed by Nicholas Hytner. Hytner also directed the film version, *The Madness of King George*, released 1995.

Its roots lie in one of the oldest rituals in the world: a king disempowered, effectively dethroned, and conducted to hell (or, in some versions, killed), then returned to health and sanity (or, in some versions, resurrected). It is extraordinarily powerful, and has remained so for millennia. *The Madness of George III* is seldom discussed in these terms, partly because the mythic elements are so well camouflaged. Bennett's play is meticulously respectful of historical detail, and incorporates many of the words actually spoken, or written, by its characters.[1] And it is, to a large extent, preoccupied with the political consequences of the King's indisposition. Everything about it, in fact, directs us towards its context, painstakingly established both through the twists and turns of the plotting, and Nicholas Hytner's evocative production.

In a speech deleted from an early version, quoted in the introduction to the published text, the King makes an observation which, Bennett says, is 'the nearest I can get to extracting a message from the play':

> The real lesson, if I may say so, is that what makes an illness perilous is celebrity. Or, as in my case, royalty. In the ordinary course of things doctors want their patients to recover; their reputations depend on it. But if the patient is rich or royal, powerful or famous, other considerations enter in. There are many parties interested apart from the interested party. So more doctors are called in and none but the best will do. But the best aren't always very good and they argue, they disagree. They have to because they are after all the best and the world is watching. And who is in the middle? The patient. It happened to me. It happened to Napoleon. It happened to Anthony Eden. It happened to the

---

[1] Burke's speech in the Commons, for instance, incorporates parts of his *Revolutions on the Revolution in France*; see *The Madness of George III*, p. 70.

Shah. The doctors even killed off George V to make the first edition of *The Times*. I tell you, dear people, if you're poorly it's safer to be poor and ordinary.[2]

The King's madness precipitated a power vacuum which had to be filled – and nearly was – by the future Prince Regent. The rapid succession of scenes and characters underlines the fact that the play is in large part a study of those political consequences. From the moment the King becomes ill, 'he is of no dramatic consequence', as Bennett observes,[3] making the machinations of Pitt, Burke, Thurlow, and Fox the necessary focus of our attention. Although power never transfers to his son, it does shift rapidly to other 'parties'. Those fluctuations provide the substance of the plot.

The mythic elements, too, concern power, and are hinted at throughout. As the King observes, 'The father pushed aside, put out, put away. Ruled out. The father not dead even.'[4] In the meantime, his son is impatient to replace him; as he puts it, 'To be heir to the throne is not a position; it is a predicament.'[5] The one has power, but cannot wield it; the other is powerless, and constantly frustrated. The most obvious parallel, as it is invoked within the play, is with Lear – another father displaced by ambitious offspring. During Act Two, Bennett's stage directions explicitly compare the King and his servant Papandiek with Lear and the Fool.[6] And it is a reading of Shakespeare's play that provides a turning-point in the King's story, signalling his return to sanity.[7] Crucially, Bennett subverts the tragic model by restoring the King to power; indeed, that is the point made by Thurlow when he returns to London after having participated in the reading of *Lear*:

> He's actually a damned clever fellow. Had me reading Shakespeare. Have you read *King Lear*? Tragic story. Of course, if that fool of a messenger had just got that little bit more of a move on, Cordelia wouldn't have been hanged, Lear wouldn't have died, and it would all have ended happily ... which I think would have made a much better ending. Because as it is, it's so damned tragic ...[8]

Thurlow's observations are a daring touch, and witty. If the King is a Lear figure, he is one whose story appears to have 'a much better ending' than that of his counterpart in Shakespeare. However, Bennett is equivocal on that point. At the moment at which the play is set, the King achieves a complete recovery, but only for a limited time. The published text includes a scene cut from the Royal National

---

[2] *The Madness of George III*, p. xx.
[3] *The Madness of George III*, pp. xviii–xix.
[4] *The Madness of George III*, p. 77.
[5] *The Madness of George III*, p. 63.
[6] 'Papandiek is sitting hunched up by the King's chair so that the two of them look like Lear and his Fool'; *The Madness of George III*, p. 65.
[7] *The Madness of George III*, pp. 80–2.
[8] *The Madness of George III*, p. 83.

Theatre production, in which a modern doctor explains that the King 'has another attack in 1802 and finally takes leave of his senses in 1810, and dies deaf and blind in 1820'.[9] 'I had an empire once', the King remembers, on the verge of madness, 'There were forests there and lakes and plains and little soft hills.'[10] It is a vision of Arcadia that merges with that of Lady Pembroke, and one to which the King constantly returns as representative of everything he has lost: his sanity, his power, his physical and mental self-determination. Significantly, his references to it cease when at the conclusion of the play he recovers. But Arcadia is no more within his grasp than is complete control of his faculties. Indeed, the loss of the colonies is hopelessly intertwined with his Lear-like failure of vision. His constant references to America suggest that, in his insanity, these connections are somehow evident, and the period of his illness becomes significant as one of expiation:

> I am bound
> Upon a wheel of fire, that mine own tears
> Do scald like molten lead. (Oh, it's so true!)[11]

But if the King's illness is felt to be some kind of punishment, it is out of all proportion to his 'crimes'. And the involvement of politicians ensures that his 'treatment' has little to do with medical need. He becomes a plaything of the interests which surround him. At its height, illness renders him powerless even to retain the company of his wife. The image of the King in the restraining chair as the strains of 'Zadok the Priest' fill the auditorium symbolises everything that has happened. Power has been stripped from the most powerful character in the drama, leaving a void: that, as much as insanity, is his 'wheel of fire' (as it is for Lear).

Bennett is sometimes regarded as an apolitical writer, but his work is profoundly sensitive to the state of the world in which it is created.[12] His introduction to the published text draws a number of comparisons with recent history,[13] but this is not a political work in the same way as, for instance, David Hare's *The Absence of War*, or even Howard Brenton's *Bloody Poetry*. Nonetheless, the hell into which the King descends is that of political disenfranchisement. It may be significant that the closing years of George III's reign, the late 1810s, were a period of intense disquiet generated by the desire of working people to acquire the rights that were denied them. The corruption inherent in the electoral system is vividly illustrated in the play by such characters as Sir Boothby Skrymshir and his idiotic son Ramsden, both candidates in rotten boroughs. Even so, the political focus is less

---

[9] *The Madness of George III*, p. 93. In the revived production (which cut the scene with the doctor), Nigel Hawthorne as the King clutched his temples in the final scene, as if to suggest that his recovery was incomplete.

[10] *The Madness of George III*, p. 58.

[11] *The Madness of George III*, p. 81.

[12] His diaries frequently comment on current affairs.

[13] *The Madness of George III*, pp. xvii–xviii.

on historical context than on the King himself. The point is underlined by comparison with the story of Laius and Oedipus. Just as Laius lived for years with the oracle's information that he would be killed by his son, King George, even before his illness, is aware of the jealousy of the Prince of Wales. The Queen ridicules the Prince's congratulations to the King on his survival of the assassination attempt at the beginning of the play – an exchange designed to illustrate the latent hostility between them.[14] And the Prince's reaction to news of his father's ailment bears out his desperation to assume the throne.[15] The irony is that Oedipus's story culminates with his self-blinding and banishment at the discovery of what he has done; George IV would never need to reproach himself in that way. The course of history was much tougher, much less forgiving, than first appears. Indeed, the fate of George III is very nearly as bad as that of Laius. His son was King-in-waiting from an early stage, primed to assume power at any opportunity. And, despite the cliffhanger resolution, in which news of the King's recovery is delivered to Pitt just in the nick of time, we know that, in due course, by default of illness the King will be supplanted by his heir.

Illness is like accident; it is without meaning. Admittedly, Bennett is preoccupied (at least on a narrative level) with the multiplicity of constructions placed by interested parties on the King's indisposition. At the same time he conducts us on a journey into an underworld of disempowerment that has no significance beyond itself. That the King's predicament is not precipitated by an act of God, envious children, or political machinations is, in a sense, the point of the play. We cannot even argue that it is caused by the failure of a messenger to convey an order with due dispatch. The illness is a force of nature and, like all such things, inscrutable. The meaning of the play, so far as there is one, lies in the journey made by its central character out of the known into the unknown, out of the certain into the chaotic – and back again. That's why the King believes that, even in his madness, his old self remained intact:

> I have always been myself even when I was ill. Only now I seem myself. That's the important thing. I have remembered how to seem. What, what?[16]

The confinement and torture of the restraining chair and other 'medications' echo the detention of the 'sane' King within the semblance of madness. It is a reading that heightens the poignancy of his tale, and underlines the significance of the inner journey from which he returns. Both Nicholas Hytner and Alan Bennett speak of the almost palpable relief in the audience at the King's recovery, and I remember experiencing it myself when I saw the stage production. There are

---

[14] *The Madness of George III*, p. 2.
[15] *The Madness of George III*, p. 16.
[16] *The Madness of George III*, pp. 81–2.

doubtless many reasons for it, but one of them must be the tremendous potency of the myth that provides its model.

I visited Alan Bennett at his home in Camden Town, north London, on 24 March 1999. He had recently concluded work on his new play, *The Lady in the Van*. Prior to our discussion he indicated a desire to speak less about issues of general principle than about specifics, and I geared my questions accordingly. Nonetheless, in the course of our conversation, which lasted nearly two hours, we covered most of the topics which, in one way or another, led me to undertake this study. No student of Bennett's writing can afford to ignore *Writing Home* (London: Faber and Faber, 1997), an engaging collection of journals and articles on theatre, literary affairs, and much else.

Interview

Duncan Wu: *In* A Question of Attribution, *Anthony Blunt says, 'art will always elude exposition'.*[1] *Is that something that you would stand by?*

Alan Bennett: Yes, partly because I'm not very good at exposition, but also because I both envy and distrust writers who can explain themselves. I feel that if you can, to a large extent, explain what you've written or what you've painted, say, there's no point in having written or painted it. I write plays because I'm in two minds about something and can't explain what it is that bothers me, so the way to set my mind at rest is to try and write the play.

The only thing I've ever done in the way of public responsibility is to be a Trustee of the National Gallery, for which my period of office finished in November 1998. I found it immensely enjoyable but I don't think I was any good at it, partly because committees are very strange things to me; I don't quite know how they work and I never knew when to speak. That apart, it brought me into contact with a lot of art history and a lot of exposition. While I found this fascinating and very enjoyable, I felt that whatever one says about a work of art can never outsay what the work of art says about itself. This may just be a defence of being inarticulate or of not being able to express what a picture or play means, but I do feel that at the heart of a work of art there is something that can't be said, or if it can be said clearly, then there's no point in having written the play at all.

For me as a Romanticist that sounds very Romantic.

It probably is, I don't know! I'm sure if I were more articulate, it's not a view I would hold, so it's a kind of rationalisation of my own inadequacies, I

---

[1] *Alan Bennett: Plays 2*, p. 348.

suppose. It may be also to do with my first experience of the theatre. That was with *Beyond the Fringe*, and brought me into contact with Jonathan Miller who's very, very articulate;[2] it might be a reaction against that, in a way. There was a great deal, when we were doing *Beyond the Fringe*, of having to explain the point of what we were doing, and I often felt that the explanation went well beyond the actual stuff that was on the stage.

I was interested in what you said in the introduction to the printed text of The Madness of George III *about Nicholas Hytner's role in helping you write the play. Do you have an ideal view of how the writer–director relationship works?*

No, but there are some directors who are much better at helping you with the writing than others are. Ronald Eyre, who I worked with on *Habeas Corpus*,[3] was good on that, though he was also quite puritanical. He was by nature – and originally by profession – a schoolmaster, but very good at slimming the text down, seeing what one didn't need. It's a skeletal text, so much so that it can only be staged in the way he staged it; there isn't enough dialogue to do it any other way. Richard Eyre is good with the text, particularly with seeing how it can be reconstructed.

Nick Hytner is good with the text too, but he can also instinctively gauge the proportion of encouragement to criticism that you need. If there's too much criticism you're discouraged and feel you've such a long way to go you can't bear to take the text up again; too much enthusiasm and it means you'll be lazy and won't bother. Nick somehow just gets the proportion right. It was the same in *The Wind in the Willows*[4] and *George III* and I found in many ways he was the ideal person to work with. Also he's tireless, he actually works very, very hard, which directors often don't do; often they leave a play to 'settle down', or when it's got to a certain stage they feel that if they tinker with it any more they'll destroy what they've already achieved. Nick goes on after the first night so that even when it's been judged, as it were, he'll still fiddle with it. That's a great compliment, for a start. I don't have that sort of energy myself, so I think it's very much to be valued.

The Wind in the Willows *and* George III *were theatrical* tour de forces *in terms of the staging, sets – just the sheer technicalities to do with getting them on a stage.*

Yes, well, that's more to do with Nick than me. I couldn't see how either of them could be staged. I could see the basic form of the stage on *George III* –

---

[2] Bennett collaborated with Miller, Peter Cook and Dudley Moore on *Beyond the Fringe: A Revue*, which opened in London at the Fortune Theatre, 10 May 1961.
[3] First performed at the Lyric Theatre, 10 May 1973, directed by Ronald Eyre.
[4] First performed at the Royal National Theatre, 12 December 1990, directed by Nicholas Hytner.

the staircase – and specified that in my first draft as I thought that might be a way of doing it. And I could visualise the court appearing over the brow of the hill as they do at the start. That came from Richard Jones' production of *Too Clever by Half*, the Ostrovsky play, where he had a very steeply raked stage. Somehow that stuck in my mind. I could see that, but not how the fairly short, rather cinematic, scenes that I had written could be staged on that set. Nick took that in his stride. With *The Wind in the Willows*, he told me to write it and he would take care of all the problems. These considerations are very much in my mind at the moment because I've just delivered him a stage adaptation of *The Lady in the Van*,[5] and while I can see how to do some things, I am totally baffled by others. I just hope that he'll be able to solve the staging problems as well as he did in the other plays.

It must be quite liberating to just say to yourself, I can do more or less anything I want and just leave the –

Yes, it is, if it's somebody who's not deterred by that and doesn't mind one taking his skill for granted. His sense of theatricality is much, much stronger than mine, and probably stronger than any director I've ever worked with. He's got more flair, I think, and (I mean this as a compliment) more vulgarity.

Those plays exploit the potential of the theatre much more than Forty Years On, The Old Country *and* Enjoy,[6] *which just use one or two sets.*

Yes. Of course one of the reasons for that is that they were in a subsidised theatre, which has got much more resources. *Forty Years On*, though, had quite a complicated setting and probably wouldn't be done now on the commercial stage as being too expensive. The structure of the play was complicated too, partly because it was the first play that I'd ever done. In those days I thought that the staging was part of what a playwright had to do; I didn't know that you could just leave it to somebody else, the designer or the director or whatever. So I did work out how it could be presented, and how back-projections could be fitted in and so on, quite roughly. I don't think I could have written it if I hadn't seen that. On the other hand what I would never do now (which I did do then) is write a play where the structure is so

---

[5] Bennett's account of Miss Shepherd, the lady who lived in a van parked in his driveway, was first published in the *London Review of Books*, 20 October 1989. It appeared in pamphlet form the following year, and was reissued as a book in 1999.
[6] *Forty Years On* was first performed at the Apollo Theatre, London, 31 October 1968, directed by Patrick Garland; *The Old Country* at the Queen's Theatre, 7 September 1977, directed by Clifford Williams; and *Enjoy* at the Vaudeville Theatre, 15 October 1980, directed by Ronald Eyre.

complicated. I wouldn't dare inflict on an audience such a convoluted account of the times as I did then.

Do you have a place in the rehearsal room?

A specific physical place, you mean?

Do you feel you have a role to play?

Oh. I enjoy it very much – *George III* quite definitely and *The Wind in the Willows* the same, because they both evolved a lot in rehearsal and there was quite a lot to do. With other plays, as I've got older, I've attended less than I used to. *Forty Years On* was different because I was in it so had to be there. I didn't go to *Getting On*,[7] and that was probably a mistake because when I did go Kenneth More tended to feel threatened by my presence, though that was only one of the things that went wrong with it. With *Habeas Corpus* I was there all the time, *The Old Country* as well, *Enjoy* I was there but *Kafka's Dick*[8] less. I was in one of the *Single Spies* plays and directed the other.[9]

If a play goes well, and it's a happy set-up, I enjoy it as a social experience. I like being there, and getting to know the actors, and just to actually see it evolving is a pleasure – particularly with *George III*, and Nigel Hawthorne's performance at the centre of it.[10] You felt you had actually written something when you saw him do it.

I get the feeling that you were quite active, because you mention the third rewrite quite close to the end of rehearsals of George III.[11]

Well, there's a photograph of the table in the rehearsal room with all the rewrites hung up, and it looks like a load of laundry hanging up to dry, all these sheets that the poor actors had to take away every day and learn. There was so much rewriting to be done, and so much butting together of the scenes, that you had to be there, really.

---

[7] First performed at the Queens Theatre, 14 October 1971, directed by Patrick Garland. For further discussion see Bennett's introduction to *Alan Bennett: Plays 1*, pp. 14–15.
[8] First performed at the Royal Court Theatre, 23 September 1986, directed by Richard Eyre.
[9] Double-bill of *A Question of Attribution* and *An Englishman Abroad*, directed by Bennett and Simon Callow respectively, first performed on stage at the Royal National Theatre, 1 December 1988.
[10] Nigel Hawthorne played the King in the stage production and film adaptation of *The Madness of George III*.
[11] *The Madness of George III*, p. xi.

Your introduction to the published text describes in very helpful detail what lies behind the play, and the various 'encounters' you had with George III over the years.[12] I'm curious as to what made you realise that his story was dramatically exciting, that it had dramatic potential.

I think it was just the fact that it took place over a relatively short timescale, and that it was self-contained, and that his illness was sudden and his recovery was sudden, so that in itself was dramatic. And there was the fact that his illness brought with it a political crisis. I never felt that I managed to get the sense of political crisis on the stage as sharply as we got it on film. But that's because we had to do the House of Commons in a very impressionistic way with just a couple of spotlights, or whatever, whereas on film you did actually see the whole House.[13]

I think I'd known the historical layout of the crisis ever since I first read about George III when I was an undergraduate, but obviously I didn't think about writing plays then. What happens is I tend to write stuff on cards or whatever, and keep them. I keep things that are current on my desk, and turn them over when I haven't got anything else occupying me, and jot things down on them, so I never have to start with a blank sheet of paper. I work with things and put them on one side. Sometimes these files get quite thick, and that must have been happening for a few years; I think I had a file on George III for four or five years before I actually started to try and put it into a theatrical form.

A file ...?

A folder, you know.

Containing images or lines or ...?

Just thoughts about scenes, and probably notes on stuff I'd read about madness – because I think there's stuff in Foucault about it. I used to read stuff like that, or dip into it, without always finishing the book, seeing what I could glean. Certainly in Foucault there's all this stuff about the execution of Damian, who tried to assassinate Louis XV, and which George III talks about in the first scene, when he says it's not long since somebody had tried to assassinate the King of France.[14] The torture of Damian in the name of justice was a description of exactly what was going to happen to George III

---

[12] *The Madness of George III*, pp. v–ix.
[13] Bennett's script for the film has been published, with photographs from the production (London: Faber and Faber, 1995).
[14] *The Madness of George III*, p. 3.

in the name of medicine. I probably had that thought a year or two before I started building a play around it. Moments like that. And at the end of the first act, when the King says, 'I am the King of England', and Willis says, 'No sir. You are the patient',[15] I probably had that moment but it was made what it was by Nick putting 'Zadok the Priest' underneath it. I didn't know how that would work until I saw it in rehearsal.

And what did you think when you saw it in rehearsal?

I thought that was wonderful, absolutely wonderful, I couldn't get over it. It's a very tense moment in the play, and it was always a tense moment on stage because Charles Kay (playing Willis) had to time his dialogue so exactly with the music, and the music is in its nature very repetitive so it's quite easy to go wrong. He had to come in at exactly the right moment with the beginning of the speech in order to make sure the dialogue ended at the right place in the music for the final line to come out in a silence, and then the music could come in again. I suppose it's like opera, in a way. Sometimes, inevitably, it didn't work, but when it did it was absolutely wonderful.

It's a hell of a scene, I remember it vividly. Is it a sort of hell?

Well, it is a kind of nightmare for somebody who is as powerful as that suddenly to have no power whatsoever, and for nobody to take any notice of what he says, when he's been deferred to all his life. It is a hell, I suppose. Correspondingly the sense of relief when his doctors and his ministers do start to take notice of him and he starts to get better is wonderful. It's almost a sense of redemption. I would hesitate to say I knew these things until I saw them presented. I wouldn't dare to say that I wrote that in; it may have had to be shown to me as much as to anybody else.

I ask because I keep on thinking that there's a mythic dimension to the play. Of course it's grounded, and should be, in what seems to be the realpolitik *of the historical moment, but at the same time there's a mythic dimension. It's about a king figure who goes down to a sort of hell and then is returned to life; however reserved his return is – and the rug is constantly being pulled from under it – nonetheless he does return.*

I think that's true though I would again hesitate to say I knew that. That's the kind of thing which a commentator is allowed to say, but about which the author should be more reserved. Or it's something you can perhaps see once

---

[15] *The Madness of George III*, p. 51.

you've written it, but I wouldn't have wanted to know that before I wrote it. I don't know whether that makes sense.

It touches on something else which came up quite a lot when we were rehearsing. Nick said to me, 'What is the play actually about?' I just said, 'Well, it's about George III and his attack of madness.' It was true, and I did believe that, but at the same time we were both of us anxious during rehearsals, anxious that some larger meaning was eluding us and wasn't being pointed up – though that was partly because a scene at the end was cut. It's where the King sits down on the steps, takes his crown off, steps out of time, discusses with the Queen what it all means, and talks about the problems of the celebrity when it comes to illness.[16] Nigel Hawthorne felt that detracted from the end of the play, and found it very, very difficult to do – which I understood and sympathised with. I was tempted to agree simply on theatrical grounds, because it interrupted the flow of the play towards the end. So it was put in the introduction to the published text. Nevertheless, when you'd taken that speech out I think it raised again the question that there was some large moral that maybe we'd missed. Afterwards I found a quotation I'd copied out from Molière's *La malade imaginaire*:

> To speak frankly, our profession has never struck me as a pleasant one when conducted among the great, and I've always found it better for us to stick to the ordinary public; they're accommodating, you don't have to account to anyone, but what troubles one about the great is that when they fall ill they insist upon their doctors curing them.

Which is virtually what the scene we cut out says. It's said rather better in Molière, but anyway. I think losing that scene maybe robbed the play as we did it of a bit of a dimension, but then there were theatrical compensations for that.

Some commentary remained, most notably in the King Lear *scene, and Thurlow's commentary on tragedy.*[17]

There is comment there, it's quite true. But in the playing of it, the sudden ray of sunshine almost bleaches out what has been said. The audience is just so pleased that the King's coming round that they almost don't listen to it.

This is another point really, but I went through two versions when I first wrote the play, and then in August 1991 we did a reading with any actors who were available at the National at the time. Nigel was playing his part, but nobody else was; it was just anybody who was in the company, and they

---

[16] *The Madness of George III*, p. xx; quoted pp. 75–6, above.
[17] See *The Madness of George III*, pp. 80–2, 83.

came along one morning to the studio and we did it, in order to see how it would work. The text was in a terrible state and I was very self-conscious about some of it, because I'd never exposed anything as early as that to anybody – certainly not to actors, and I was frightened that they would be very sniffy about it. Anyway, it was quite a useful exercise. Simon Russell Beale was in it, this run, and was very encouraging but alas wasn't in it eventually.

Apart from Nigel, the best performance was from Robin Bailey as Thurlow. He was just wonderful – funny, light, but also very worldly. A superb performance. Unfortunately he wasn't available for the production, and was quite frail anyway by that time, but I always missed him. He made it so funny and yet at the same time was a credible politician; I got a real sense of politics from him. I was really sorry that we couldn't have him.

I can imagine what he might have been like.

It was a kind of *dancing* performance. And Thurlow's part wasn't very well written at that time, but Robin Bailey just gave you an insight into what the part could be.

The style of the film was realistic, it was as I imagined the Commons to have been.

It was the Divinity School at Oxford. A lot of the settings were used again in *Shakespeare in Love*. David Parfitt was the producer of both *George III* and *Shakespeare in Love*, you see. So we had Broughton Castle, and they had Broughton Castle, and the courtyard at Eton, which we used too, lots of places. He economised on locations.

The style of the stage production was almost the exact opposite insofar as it was quite stylised, and the audience had to make a bit of an imaginative leap. Do you feel a particular affinity to either one of those two styles?

I find I write naturalistically, while wanting to be much more impressionistic. It's partly through writing so much for television, and also my skills being weighted much more towards dialogue. I long to be more abstract, to play on an empty stage, and not to be trammelled by naturalistic considerations. But it's seldom I can break away from it, so I'm always pleased when I can, or when people push me in that direction.

As with The Old Crowd.[18]

---

[18] Television play transmitted by London Weekend Television, 27 January 1979, directed by Lindsay Anderson.

Yes, absolutely, that's quite right. I hadn't thought of that but that's right. Not being allowed to do it in a naturalistic way.

Was Lindsay Anderson quite important?

Lindsay got some things wrong and was occasionally a bit silly, and of course the play was condemned at the time, but I found the experience of working with him quite liberating.[19] I like the notion of a totally bare room. If I could only write this short story I've written, *The Clothes They Stood Up In*, as a play![20] That's a relic of *The Old Crowd* I think, because it begins with them being absolutely burgled of everything, and so the curtain would go up on a totally bare stage. It's a breath of fresh air.

I remember once we did a terrible production of *Habeas Corpus* for America after it had been in London. I liked the London production because it had been so spare, there were only three chairs on the stage, it was very very plain. And then with the American production all the scenery came back into it, and all sorts of props, the whole stage was absolutely cluttered, no clean lines to it at all! It was really depressing for all sorts of reasons apart from that, Celeste Holm not being the least of them, but I remember when we were in Boston I went one afternoon to the Boston City Ballet. It was *Carmina Burana* adapted as a ballet, and it was absolutely plain, nothing on the stage at all, and it was terrific. Then I went back to the theatre so uplifted by what I'd seen, and then so depressed by what I'd done and all the clutter I was responsible for. I do like a bare-ish stage.

It happens in Enjoy *too at the end.*

That's right. That was Ron's notion about clearing everything up; I instantly embraced that.

What's the appeal of it? What's the appeal of an empty stage?

I don't know really. Of course it's what we started with in *Beyond the Fringe*, the stage was totally empty then, but I don't think it's to do with that. I don't know. Maybe it's more preachy, just you and the audience. I don't know what it is, but the plainer the stage, the more I like it. How we're going to do Miss Shepherd, and *The Lady in the Van*, I don't know – there has to be a van, obviously, but I don't know that there needs to be much more.

---

[19] Bennett discusses this in his introduction to *The Writer in Disguise* (London: Faber and Faber, 1985), reprinted in *Writing Home* (London: Faber and Faber, 1994), pp. 267–81.
[20] First published as an audio cassette read by Bennett, 1997, and published in book form the following year.

I always hated those plays where there are areas marked off and little bits of paling marking where the garden is and the walls of the house. My heart sinks, I don't know why. Because when I was a boy and used to go to the theatre at the Grand in Leeds, all the sets were naturalistic there and I loved all that.

In the case of George III, *were you envisaging the whole thing in naturalistic terms as you wrote it? Were you envisaging it much as we see it in the film?*

No, because I was writing it like a film but not seeing it. I was just writing it jerkily, I think; the cuts, it seemed to me, were cinematic in the stage play. I didn't think about how you got from one scene to another. As I say, I knew what was coming at the end of Act One, and that it had to mount to that. I may have thought of areas of the stage representing one place and other areas being another. Again, that's a relic of naturalism but I never conceived the Brechtian idea about the curtains and all that.

Is that technique Brechtian?

Well I think so, isn't it? Didn't one of the Brechtians do a thing where you drew a curtain across and it cleared the stage? If it isn't then it's what I've always thought of as Brechtian. I saw a review of something quite recently where it said that. What could that have been? Anyway.

I think there are two really important scenes in the play: the big scene at the climax of Act One with the restraining chair, and the Lear scene in Act Two. Is that how you conceived the play?

Yes, the Lear scene is a turning-point, obviously, and the end of Act One hammers something home that's happened in a very theatrical way, quite a shocking way really, people were quite upset when the curtain came down. The Lear scene I wouldn't have been able to invent. I'm quite timid, imaginatively speaking; the fact that Willis did actually read *King Lear* with George III, is actually a fact. If he'd read *Twelfth Night* or something like that, I wouldn't have had the wit to change it to *King Lear*, so I'm glad he got it right. But it is a turning-point. It's like a pause in a symphony when a new theme comes in very sweetly somehow, it's just a very touching moment when suddenly it happens. It's quite a gentle turning-point, really, and it was wonderful to see that for the first time in rehearsal.

I saw Nick just by accident yesterday and we were talking about *Elizabeth*,[21] have you seen that?

---

[21] Film directed by Shekhar Kapur, released in 1998, starring Cate Blanchett as Elizabeth I.

Yes.

Which I hated, I'm afraid, and he hadn't liked it. I was talking about the flippancy with which they discarded historical fact, so that Mary Queen of Scots (as far as I understood the plot) seemed to be poisoned rather than executed, and all the things that happened seemed to be concertina'd to within the first five or six years of Elizabeth's reign, something like that! And Nick was remarking on the timidity with which we tampered with history compared with that! The point in the film of the *Madness* where Nick suggested bringing the King from Kew to Westminster to prove to the MPs that he was well quite shocked me,[22] although I realised it would work. I was certain I'd be hauled over the coals for it, with people pointing out that this never happened – but when you see something like *Elizabeth*, none of which happened like that at all! Anyway, Nick managed my timidity very well, and I'm sure he'd have been much more cavalier than me had the play required it.

There's a slight loss in the film, in that Thurlow doesn't pop up to deliver his comments on tragedy.[23] Thurlow tells us what King Lear *is – it's a tragic story – and how it could have been turned into a comedy: 'Of course, if that damn fool of a messenger had just got that little bit of a move on ...'.*

That was an echo of Nancy Mitford's *The Pursuit of Love*, in which Uncle Matt happens to read *Romeo and Juliet* and is found wreathed in tears. And then he says, 'It was all the fault of that damn Padre!' Thurlow's remark is an echo of that; it's the same sort of thing. I have a feeling Thurlow was a character and would have been quite capable of saying something like that.

It's prompting us to analyse the play in terms of tragic form.

Again, that didn't occur to me at the time so I can't claim credit for that.

But it must have been clear to you as you wrote that Thurlow's prompting us to step back and say, right, well, we're watching a comedy? Or is he?

I don't know. I just thought it was a funny scene, I have to say. He's getting carried away describing the scene to Pitt, who's a cold fish, and Thurlow's got sidetracked into the joys of Shakespeare. I suppose that's what I was thinking of. And that was all true, of course. I hope I'm not torpedoing a theory you have. I can't honestly say I was conscious of any of that. I saw it as a good

---

[22] This episode provides the climax of the film; see *The Madness of King George*, pp. 66–8.
[23] *The Madness of George III*, p. 83.

scene with Thurlow being carried away describing all this, and Pitt just being very anxious to know what had actually happened, and how the King was.

Do you think in terms of tragedy and comedy?

No, I think in terms of the edge of tragedy and the edge of comedy, because I always think that's the best place to be, in everything really – in my television stuff as well, just to tread that line. People mistake extremes for edges. When you get an actor giving an extreme performance like (and this is no criticism) Anthony Sher as Richard III, say, or Daniel Day-Lewis in *My Left Foot*, using all his physical resources in a real bravura acting performance, if that's an extreme, that's something I'm not drawn to at all. I'm more drawn to somebody acting at the edge – like Richardson and Gielgud in *Home*,[24] for instance. That would seem to be treading a very fine line between tragedy and comedy, and I'd want to do that rather than the other. I don't think I've quite expressed it properly, but I know that extremes aren't edges and extremes aren't for me, really.

Nigel's part, particularly the end of the first Act, is an extreme, and that's why, although I'd written it, I felt someone might have given it to me. Somehow they'd added something that I hadn't put there myself. Great acting is thought to be extreme acting and it isn't. I suppose that's partly what I mean. I like something that can just tip over from comedy to tragedy or comedy to sadness.

What is tragedy?

I wouldn't be able to answer that, absolutely not. There's no point in my even starting. I know it when I see it, that's all, and I know it on the few occasions that I have written it, in a scene or whatever. But I wouldn't be able to define it.

Which of your plays do you think are tragic?

I don't think any of them are tragic through and through. I can't answer that. It's like giving yourself an accolade, and I'm reluctant to do it. I think the end of Act One of *George III* is tragic because the King is absolutely powerless. He's the most powerful person in the kingdom and he's rendered utterly helpless. But I wouldn't be able to define what tragedy is. I don't think in those terms. I think in terms of having an idea for a play, I don't really go beyond that. I'm

---

[24] David Storey's play, a quiet, ironic conversation piece set in an insane asylum, was first performed 17 June 1970 at the Royal Court Theatre, directed by Lindsay Anderson.

not boasting about that or taking any pride in it, it's just I don't think in general terms really.

Is George III *comic or tragic?*

It's neither really.

It keeps a foot on both sides of the fence.

I'd have thought you could criticise it on those grounds but ...

Oh, I wouldn't criticise it on those grounds.

I say that only because I have been criticised for that, right from the start – of wanting to have it both ways. *Forty Years On* was criticised for that reason – that it was neither one thing nor the other. I can't resist the comic if there's a possibility of it, but then that's true in life, and is true in most people's lives, I think.

There is some notion that it can't be a tragedy if you leave the jokes in, and I don't agree with that. I think some of the monologues are quite ... I think *Nights in the Gardens of Spain* with Penelope Wilton[25] was a tragedy, but a lot of people didn't!

That was chilling.

I don't enjoy talking in those terms. My opinion of what I've written is not really worth more than anybody else's in that sense. But that was tragic, and I thought the one that Eileen Atkins did, *The Hand of God*. And the one David Haig did as well.[26] Oh, I don't know; it makes me uncomfortable even to talk about it.

Nobody would criticise Shakespeare for having written in Measure for Measure *or* All's Well *or* Troilus and Cressida *plays that were neither one thing nor the other.*

I think people have got used to me, but that was certainly what happened at the start of my career. 'Why can't he make up his mind?'

Or Larkin for writing poems that simultaneously embrace the Romantic sublime and rubbish it.

---

[25] One of the second series of *Talking Heads*, directed by Tristram Powell.
[26] *The Hand of God* and *Playing Sandwiches* were among the second series of *Talking Heads*, directed by Stuart Burge and Udayan Prasad respectively.

It's funny about Larkin, I was just thinking before you came about the business of Nick and I worrying about what *George III* was about, and trying to wind it up into providing some sort of message (for want of a better word – not really a message, some sort of statement). Of course that's exactly what Larkin does, and when he becomes opaque, or when he fails, it's always in that respect – when he's trying to roll it up, going from the particular to the general. That's when he falls down.

Where, for instance?

I only know because of having to read his poems in public and trying to make sense of them to an audience. You realise he's arguing it out with himself but he doesn't always carry his audience with him somehow. From the poetry-reading point of view there are bits where the end is slightly soggy because he's not quite got the argument straight. In 'An Arundel Tomb', for instance, there's the image of

> a trough
> Of smoke in slow suspended skeins
> Above their scrap of history ...

Now what does that mean?

The smoke?

But what smoke? It's a tomb in a church. Then he's on solid ground again: 'Time has transfigured them into / Untruth ...'; it's all fine. Whenever he does go soft, it's always in this windup section. Mind you, by comparison with Auden he's lucidly clear!

Larkin can be obscure. I once had to tell a student that I honestly couldn't work out what one of the High Windows *poems was actually about.*

That's probably more educative that anything you could ever have said, I should have thought. Sometimes he's quite content just to make a poem of an incident, like the racehorses in 'At Grass' – just an account of these racehorses and their past, without drawing any elaborate moral from it. At other times he fears he's required to make the larger statement. At the same time, it's encouraging to find that somebody so good does mess up.

Do you feel any affinity with Larkin in terms of what you're up to in your work?[27]

---

[27] Bennett comments at greater length on Larkin in 'Instead of a Present' and his review of Andrew Motion's biography, 'Alas! Deceived', *Writing Home*, pp. 320–4, 357–78.

To some extent, and I think people think of me as a miserable sod in the same way as they think of him as a miserable sod. I like him being rivetted to fact, I like the poetry coming out of very ordinary things; that I find sympathetic.

I don't like poetry of ideas much really. I don't find him so sympathetic as a man, having read the biography.[28] I had an imaginary notion before which didn't measure up to what he was really like. I met him once and he was so deaf he couldn't hear what I was saying, and we didn't make any sense at all. He wrote something to me, and I wrote back, and I think I said that I did think of him as a light in that corner of England. I said this, and then I thought afterwards, oh, he would have thought me a right fool for saying that. But I did used to think that, and that he was someone with whom one had a private relationship through his work – that he was speaking particularly to me. It's harder to feel that now, but his work does survive everything that has happened since. They now have Larkin trails, and even go round and visit the scenes from the poems. I imagine he would have hated that.

There's an element of Romanticism in poems like 'The Whitsun Weddings', and even in 'Sunny Prestatyn', there's a distant yearning for something else, an escape, something else beyond what there is. Is that something that you feel any kind of affinity for at all?

Yes, and I would have said certainly in terms of the way I grew up. I felt that very strongly when I was in Leeds as a boy, without knowing what it was. It seems ludicrous to say so, but I felt Leeds was a romantic city, and I used to go for long suburban walks in the evening, and find it a very dramatic and beautiful place, and yet long to be away from it. That period in my life is recalled by Larkin. It's not 'up north' in inverted comas, it's nothing to do with that; it's much more suburban, just starting out in life and wondering what's going to happen to you. I'm trying to write about that at the moment, so it's very much in my mind.

Trevor in Me, I'm Afraid of Virginia Woolf;[29] *the Queen in* Single Spies; *the King in* George III – *they're all prisoners, aren't they? And so are Blunt and Guy Burgess.*

I can see that once it's done. Once they're on paper I could see that one could make a connection, but at the same time I wouldn't feel it right to say, I'd seen that beforehand, or that it had occurred to me before they were written. I could see that once they're objectified, then you could compare them, but I don't feel it's something that's come consciously from me – though it has

---

[28] Andrew Motion, *Philip Larkin: A Writer's Life* (London: Faber and Faber, 1993).
[29] Television play transmitted by London Weekend Television, 2 December 1978, directed by Stephen Frears.

come from me, of course, but whether consciously or not I don't know. I don't think so.

Sydney in Kafka's Dick *argues that we expect artists to conform to a myth – that they have to pay for their achievement in some way,[30] and the only person who appreciates Kafka as a human being is Sydney's wife Linda.*

Well I have often found that the people who've got closest to me are the ones who've never read a word I've written. Books are a barrier.

I keep writing a scene in which a character is discovered in front of a bookcase, or as in *Me, I'm Afraid Virginia Woolf* metaphorically in front of a bookcase.[31] Coral Browne's in front of a bookcase in *An Englishman Abroad;*[32] Orton's in front of a bookcase in *Prick Up Your Ears;*[33] in *Getting On* the same scene occurs;[34] in *The Old Country*, right at the end, there's something similar.[35] Very often it's a young man standing there saying, 'How shall I catch up?' or 'How shall I encompass this?' or 'How can I get round this?' That's, I suppose, me and literature, in a very crude way; it's the sense of bafflement, the sense of being outside. I think there's something of that in the Geoffrey Palmer character in *Kafka's Dick*.[36] I'm trying to think where else it occurs. It's even in *Forty Years On*, though in a more dissipated way; the whole play is in a sense about the culture of the last forty or fifty years, and trying to come to terms with it. I think that's to do with starting out in Leeds, and feeling that nobody who came from Leeds ever got anywhere – like Trevor in *Me, I'm Afraid of Virginia Woolf*. But I don't think that's answered your question at all.

There was a speech in *Kafka's Dick* that was taken out which was exactly like the scene in *George III* that was taken out, a speech about biography. I don't know why we took it out:

> I want to hear about the shortcomings of great men, their fears and their failings. I've had enough of their vision, how they altered the landscape (we stand on their shoulders to survey our lives). So. Let's talk about the vanity. Read how this one, the century's seer, increases his stature by lifts

[30] See Sydney's long speech, *Alan Bennett: Plays 2*, pp. 112–13.
[31] 'Hopkins was never without a book. It wasn't that he was particularly fond of reading; he just liked to have somewhere to look'; *The Writer in Disguise*, p. 37.
[32] 'She investigates the bookshelves. Takes a book out. Puts it back'; *Alan Bennett: Plays 2*, p. 291.
[33] Orton is stealing books from a publisher's office; a still from the scene may be found in *Prick Up Your Ears: The Screenplay*, p. 37.
[34] 'George is clearing out his bookshelves, running his finger down the shelves and selecting volumes he doesn't want'; see *Alan Bennett: Plays 1*, p. 129.
[35] See *Alan Bennett: Plays 2*, pp. 268–72.
[36] Geoffrey Palmer played Sydney in the first production of *Kafka's Dick*.

in his shoes. That one, the connoisseur of emptiness, is tipped for the Nobel Prize yet still needs to win at Monopoly. This playwright's skin is so thin he can feel pain on the other side of the world. So why is he deaf to the suffering next door; signs letters to the newspapers but holds his own wife a prisoner of conscience? The slipshod poet keeps immaculate time and expects it of everyone else, but never wears underwear and frequently smells. That's not important, of course, but what is? The gentle novelist's frightful temper, the Christian poet's mad, unvisited wife, the hush in their households where the dog goes on tiptoe, meals on the dot at their ironclad whim? Note with these great men the flight and not infrequent suicide of their children, their brisk remarriage on the deaths of their irreplaceable wives. Proud of his modesty one gives frequent, rare interviews in which he aggregates praise and denudes others of credit. Indifferent to the lives about him he considers his day ruined on finding a slighting reference to himself in a periodical published three years ago in New Zealand. And demands sympathy from his family on that account. And gets it. Our father the novelist, my husband the poet. He belongs to the ages, just don't catch him at breakfast. Artists, celebrated for their humanity, they turn out to be scarcely human at all.[37]

That seemed to be what it was about, that's what Sydney was complaining about in *Kafka*, but we took it out! As we did in *George III*. It was probably right that it should go, because it sounds too zonkingly like a message, but that was what Sydney felt about Kafka and I suppose those are the reservations I have about literature. And that's part of the content of that scene that recurs again and again.

You also dropped Ida McAlpine from George III; *although she pops up in the published text*[38] *she wasn't present in the production I saw at the National.*

It was in the first time round, and when we revived the play the next year, we needed to tighten it up and that was one of the things that went. Again, for the reason that the actors felt that the audience deserted them a bit on that, and were bemused at suddenly being plunged into the present day. Though I liked that side of it. It was partly that you needed a really powerful presence to actually come on at that stage of the play and command a short scene, and there was nobody in the cast who could do that. You needed to explain about the porphyria, and that was the only way we could do it on stage. It really wasn't done at all in the film, because I don't know how you do it without it being anachronistic. It's my historical timidity again.

---

[37] *Alan Bennett: Plays 2*, pp. 21–2.
[38] *The Madness of George III*, pp. 92–3.

It's important, because it's part of the Larkin effect. It's pulling the rug from underneath the optimism of the ending.

Yes, that's right. I hadn't thought about that, but it's true. I like shocking people like that, even though they think, oh you've spoilt yourself, or you're trying to be too clever, or whatever. There's a bit in *The Lady in the Van* where she suddenly sits up in her coffin and starts talking about the kind of play that I might write about her, and actually accusing me of timidity about it, and about what the play's going to say. I suppose that's the same sort of thing.

Accusing you?

Yes, accusing me. Obviously, I appear in the play. She says I'm not good at that sort of thing; it hadn't occurred to me but I suppose that's the same scene, really.

What drew you to The Lady in the Van *as a dramatic subject?*

It would be much easier to do as a film, but I wanted to do it on stage because it would be much harder. Also I wanted to do it in an almost expressionist way, so that the van actually ascends to heaven at the finish. The van is lifted out of the garden but it goes on and on and goes up to heaven with her. And things happen to it: it occasionally is illuminated. At one point it's like a diptych; it splits in two. I wanted to do things like that, in a way that mirrors the fantastic connections of her religious imaginings, and gives them some reality on the stage.

Miss Shepherd was very religious, wasn't she? Your attitude in the prose account is somewhat detached from all that.

She was religious without being charitable or in any sense nice – I don't mean that if you are religious you are nice – but there was no sense of her extending a hand to help anybody else except herself. Had she been more selfless she might not have stayed alive. I haven't softened her on that account. Her brother was the real Samaritan; he was much more Christian than she was. As I say, I've just written the first draft, and I've no idea how it will come out eventually. But it was that non-naturalistic element that I wanted to catch, which you wouldn't get in a film. I don't see how you could do that in a film.

I'm interested to hear about her going up to heaven because it reminds me of the finale of Kafka's Dick, *where Kafka finds himself in heaven.*[39] *Richard Eyre did a great job on that when he directed it at the Royal Court.*

Oh, it was wonderful – the doors opening and the stage being transformed.

Should I think of that as your version of the sublime?

No, I don't think of it as ... oh, I don't know what it is. In Miss Shepherd's case it's her being given her dreams, being given what she wanted. But with Kafka it was the reverse, really, he'd been given exactly what he didn't want. But that was what had always happened to him all through his life. It was the apotheosis of being miserable.

Why do you give Miss Shepherd what she wants?

Because I suppose it was the last thing people would expect, partly. I don't know, I can't answer that.

It just seems so mean to deny Kafka what he wants.

What Kafka wanted would not be at all theatrical, would it? You'd just have a miserable figure in the middle of the stage and nobody else there! Whereas Miss Shepherd ... oh, I'd just like to see it.

I think there's a connection between Kafka and Larkin, I think their lives were alike. Kafka's life – his on–off relationship with his girlfriends, and never daring to get married, and being terrified that his girlfriends would interfere with his work, and so on – it's absolutely like Larkin.

Yes, very bad case. It sounds like Miss Shepherd is different from any other character that you've written about.

Only because she was real. I've been fairly true to what she was like. I've strengthened some elements in it, but I've been quite faithful to the sort of person she was. Whether it will work or not, I don't know; it's in three Acts. In the first Act I can see there's movement in the sense that she's heading for the garden, which is where she ends up at the end of the Act. In the third Act you know she'll die, so there's movement towards death. But the second Act she's in the garden and you know she's not going anywhere: so that's the problem, and I think that's where the rewrites will take place to provide some spurious movement to this stationary van. But anyway.

---

[39] See *Alan Bennett: Plays 2*, pp. 113–16.

Did the Thatcher years alter your vision as a writer in any way?

I didn't care for Mrs Thatcher, and still don't. She enshrined the opposite of so many qualities I value. She was never in two minds, for instance, lacked all magnanimity, and never missed an opportunity of beating the nationalist drum. I've always had an ambiguous attitude to England. It's what *Forty Years On* is about, and Thatcherism confirmed that. I used to go to New York a good deal in the Eighties and was much happier there.

One incident sticks in the mind. In January 1988 the *Sunday Telegraph* ran an article about why intellectuals disliked Mrs Thatcher. I don't think of myself as an intellectual in quite that way but I agreed to be interviewed, as did David Hare and one or two other playwrights. The journalist writing the article, Graham Turner, had got it into his head that writers and playwrights disliked Mrs Thatcher for snobbish reasons because she was a grocer's daughter who took no notice of their opinions. When he interviewed me he put forward this notion and I said it was rubbish: I'm a butcher's son, so why should I dislike her as a grocer's daughter? I also said I'd never aspired to influence or honours, so whether she took any notice of my opinions was of no consequence to me. I then explained why I didn't like her, instancing particularly her policies on education and the National Health Service, privatisation and so on, and also the way she regarded those who did not agree with her, like the miners and the nurses, as having put themselves outside the community of the nation that she was never in any sense Prime Minister of as a whole.

It wasn't startling stuff but it was what I felt and felt very strongly. I talked to other people Turner had interviewed and found they had said much the same. None of it appeared and the only selective quotations Turner used were those which bolstered the idea he'd come along with in the first place. It was a lying piece.

Which, of course, wouldn't have mattered as newspaper articles have short lives. But somehow this piece has gone on record as one of the core documents of the Eighties. Noel Annan drew on it in his book, *Our Age*,[40] and Ian Buruma similarly. I detested Mrs Thatcher for sound reasons and snobbery was not one of them.

Thank you for this interview.

Sorry I've dribbled on. I know David Edgar and he's always so superbly articulate and so wonderfully magisterial, isn't he? I think he's a tremendous figure, and I've sometimes spoken to his playwriting class, and I've always felt they must see me as a big comedown after him, sort of dribbling on.

---

[40] See Noel Annan, *Our Age* (London: HarperCollins, 1990), p. 590.

Nicholas Hytner

Nicholas Hytner

Nicholas Hytner has been Associate Director at the Royal Exchange Theatre, Manchester, 1985–89, and subsequently at the Royal National Theatre, 1989–97. He is the director of many distinguished theatrical productions; for the RSC he was responsible for *The Tempest* (1988) and *King Lear* (1990); at the National he directed Alan Bennett's adaptation of *The Wind in the Willows* (1990) and *The Madness of George III* (1991). In addition, he has directed operas and musicals – notably *Miss Saigon* (Drury Lane, 1989; Broadway, 1991) and *Carousel* (National Theatre, 1992). As a film director he has won plaudits for *The Madness of King George* (1994), *The Crucible* (1997), and *The Object of My Affection* (1998).

I spoke to Hytner at his home in Camden Town, north London, 22 March 1999. He had recently returned from America, where he was discussing future film work. During the preceding days he had read an early draft of Alan Bennett's latest play, *The Lady in the Van*, which he was to direct. We spoke, among other things, about the importance of such scenes as the culminating scene of Part I, in which the King is first placed in the restraining chair to the strains of 'Zadok the Priest' – an unforgettable moment of drama to anyone who saw it, and the 'Lear' scene in Part II, which marks the King's return to sanity.

Interview

Duncan Wu: *Prior to* The Madness of George III *you directed Alan's adaptation of* The Wind in the Willows. *Did it help to have worked together before?*

Nicholas Hytner: Oh very much, very much. It always helps having worked with someone, because you create a working relationship. You start to create a shared language. Also, with a writer, you, as a director, begin to find out in which areas the writer requires collaboration, requires an editorial eye.

With *The Wind in the Willows*, Alan would say to me as he was writing it, 'I don't know how to do such-and-such – I don't know how to bring a barge on the stage', for instance. And I would say to him, 'That's my business, just write it; write it as if you were writing a screenplay.' Because at the time one of the things I was enjoying as a director was finding what were probably over-extravagant scenic solutions to apparently unreasonable demands. I think, to a degree, that liberated Alan and maybe encouraged him simply to write *George III* without any regard to staging solutions whatsoever – none at all. Which was all to its benefit.

Can you tell me in what way?

All I'm talking about here are physical staging solutions. He just wrote it down, as if it was possible – as indeed it is – to get from one place to another, cinematically, without worrying about the limitations of the stage; with *George III*, it immediately became apparent that you could either do everything, and make it the biggest pile of scenery ever seen on the London stage, or do nothing – so we did nothing. That was always clear; it was a play that had to create its own environment.

And from that point of view it was really interesting to see the film version which was –

– which was everything. Yes. Because that's what films are.

Both were equally successful but in very different ways.

Yes.

Academics always talk in terms of realism and non-realism; are those terms that you think in yourself, or do you think in terms of manner, or style when you think about scenery?

I'm not sure that they are terms that usefully apply to the mere presence or lack of presence of scenery. Just because there is not very much scenery doesn't mean that it's not realistic, and of course realism is a loaded word, and an impossible one to define. You don't go into rehearsal with a portmanteau word that describes how everybody's going to act. You *discover* how everybody's going to act during rehearsals. You may have an idea about what style of acting will eventually emerge from six weeks of rehearsal, but you don't go in saying, 'You are required to act in a demonstratively non-naturalistic, presentational style; that's what the play demands.' You find out as you go along.

Funnily enough, I don't think that there was that great a difference between the way the play was acted on stage and on film. Of course it was pulled back, it was scaled down, and the camera discovers much more than a theatre audience can discover without help. A theatre audience needs communicating with; the camera, properly used, is able to find things which I think an actor must actively reveal to a theatre audience. But essentially I think we were dealing with a similar style. There's no word to describe it, but if you take as an analogy the painterly manner of the period, you could put Stubbs at one extreme and Cruikshank at the other. And then somewhere, hovering stylistically somewhere between the two, is Rowlandson – and Rowlandson always seemed to me to be the style that was required for *The Madness of George III*. Sharp outlines, affectionately drawn. The minor characters in particular require sharp outlines: you can't come on as Sir Boothby Skrymshir and start to do method acting, you can't do that. But these things emerge in rehearsal.

So that isn't something you would go to rehearsal with a preconceived notion about, it's something that would develop.

Actually, you've already done it by casting; essentially you've already done it. It's an interesting thing that permanent ensembles of actors (there used to be more of them than there are now) tend to deliver everything they do in a similar fashion. *The Tempest* can seem to be the same kind of a play as *The Caucasian Chalk Circle*, because a permanent group of actors will, however hard they try, project so strong an identity that the differences between writing styles seem to be smoothed out. That is something which, I think, in the academic world, isn't sufficiently recognised. Writers know this, we all know this; an evening in the theatre is as much to do with the identities and characteristics of the actors and of the audience, as it is to do with what the writer is delivering. One knows this because Shakespeare's plays change so much from year to year and from country to country. Once you cast a play like *The Madness of George III* you have, to some extent, established its acting style.

You mentioned earlier the process by which the play was written. You saw it while he was writing it, and indeed advised him on revision. Is that something that you normally do?

Yes, that's completely normal. I'm sure there *are* playwrights who deliver entirely the finished product, and the only job the actors and the directors have is to put it on. But by and large, I think playwrights value feedback from anybody. The first thing, it seems to me, that a director has to do is to identify places where he doesn't quite get what's going on. Sometimes – often – it can be explained to me what's going on, and I realise I'm just being obtuse, and that's fine, and then the job is to make sure that equally obtuse members of the audience won't be as confused as I was. Very often it's simply a matter of: I didn't get it.

But sometimes it is because there are genuine obscurities. Alan tends to write too long, quite deliberately too long. The play that he's just shown me is at least half as long again as it should be. One is being asked to say what, at this moment, as an unbiased observer, one finds superfluous. There was a lot of that in the first draft of *George III*. It was very long indeed, and hadn't quite found a shape. I read it and thought it was fantastic, and I said to him, 'What do you think it's about?' And he said, 'Well, it's about the madness of George III.' He is always reluctant to identify what the central metaphor of his plays might be, but in this case he was being absolutely accurate. It is not a play which would work if there were constant authorial intervention, if there were a big finger wagging at you telling you why it was a useful thing to do to watch the story of the madness of George III. In a sense, it's available and accessible to any amount of interpretation, to any kind of appreciation or enjoyment. It was always hard to pinpoint exactly why it was so resonant to audiences, because the play doesn't explain itself. There are many playwrights who, if they'd written it, would tell you why it was resonant. You wouldn't be in any doubt as to why this story had been chosen.

I suspect that its widespread appeal was to do with being able so easily to identify with the experience of knowing yourself not to be what the world perceives you to be. The King is thought to be mad but knows himself not to be mad. It is through the King, and through Nigel Hawthorne's performance, that most people connected to the play. Beyond that, there were those who were intrigued and interested in all the political machinations (which of course were fascinating and really well-written), and I think there is the primal, traditional appeal of the King at the top of the wheel of fortune tumbling down, which in our voyeuristic way we have always enjoyed watching – always, for centuries. And seeing the King of England's chamberpot still has a kind of potency.

Anyway, to get back to the early part of the process before rehearsal; yes, it's different all the time. I believe Pinter just delivers a finished play with every comma in place, and I know for instance that in Kazan's autobiography[1] he says quite unequivocally that the best plays he directed were those that arrived on his desk requiring little or no work: *Death of a Salesman* and *Streetcar*. Who knows whether that's true? I suspect it is. It may be that works as singularly revolutionary as *Death of a Salesman* and *Streetcar* do just arrive; but it's different every time. The play I did a year or so ago, *The Cripple of*

[1] Elia Kazan, *A Life* (New York: Knopf, 1988).

Inishmaan by Martin McDonagh,[2] was just that: it required nothing, a few little cuts, that was it. In one of his introductions Alan says he wouldn't have much time for anybody who started telling him how to rewrite one of his *Talking Heads* for television, but he enters this process looking for editorial interference. And also, to get right back to where we started, he wants to know, from a physical point of view, how best do we make this a show?

What do you mean by that?

Well, since we'd gone through barges and trains, motor cars and rivers, and all that,[3] he very much delivered this as a series of scenes and expected me to find the best way of staging it. The stage directions in the published text describe the production, which makes me very pleased with myself.

Is that what you started with? Is that exactly what you started with pretty much?

No, that's what hit the stage. And there were no stage directions, virtually no stage directions, in what he gave me.

It must have been one hell of a challenge, because there are times reading it when one thinks this could be a great radio play; sometimes it seems quite speechbound. Of course, that's clearly untrue of the work as a whole – take for instance the scene with the restraining chair.

Well, the chair was a gift. 'Zadok the Priest' was what I brought to it.

You brought 'Zadok'?

I don't think Handel was in the first draft.

'Zadok''s there as a kind of ironic commentary.

Well, the whole of Handel is. Yes, Handel seemed obvious. But you know, I'm always looking for that kind of stuff, I'm always looking, because I think the audience deserves all that. They deserve it. Seriously. You've paid your £25, for your £25 you have to get an awful lot, you get Nigel Hawthorne, you get a terrific play, but you're not getting a big set because we can't afford one, and also we don't want it – so at the very least you can send the audience into the bar at the end of Act One with a blast of Handel! It makes them really

---

[2] First performed 12 October 1996, Cottesloe Theatre, Royal National Theatre, directed by Nicholas Hytner.
[3] That is, in *The Wind in the Willows*, which featured all these things.

feel good – and I'm being facetious – but a play like this needs flourishes of self-conscious theatricality all the way through, it seems to me.

Is it pure theatricality? Perhaps I'm just completely taken in by it. But I go to the theatre exactly for those moments where there's a collision of image and sound, something sublime. It's very hard to verbalise, by definition. Is that sort of experience something you verbalise to yourself? How do you conceive all those moments, those highs and lows?

It's hard. You do develop an instinct as you work, for when you need to pump a bit of that stuff in. But also it's not just that you pump it in, it's that you have to have earned it. You can't just say, 'We've had ten minutes of conversation, we could do with a blast of music.'

When directing the stage production I think I did verbalise and rationalise the way I approached the play. What happens here is that a king obsessed with etiquette and order and formality, and with imposing an air of restraint on his court, is in the end restrained himself. That licenses the use of theatrical images of formality and order and a kind of etiquette *ad absurdum*. So we provided, at the beginning, more of that than you would think was possible if you were operating according to conventional theatrical instinct. What you usually want to do at the beginning is get on with it, get on with it, get the exposition out of the way, get on with it, plunge into the story. Do you remember that opening, where all the characters come thundering over the top of the set? You plunge right in, somebody tries to assassinate the King and we're up and running. Then we had tremendous trouble with the second scene. That's the scene with Sheridan, Fox, Burke, and Mrs Armistead.[4] In the revival, which toured the States, we cut Burke and Mrs Armistead out completely. These are the things that become clear only when you start to perform. It wasn't what was needed. It was very witty but largely expository.

What in fact we needed was a second sequence of Handel, something immensely long in theatrical terms, four pages dressed in bright red, a descending wall, and no talk. Just sending those four pages in very, very, very slowly, delivering dispatch boxes, and Pitt arriving at 90 degrees to them, and the wall flying in. The resources were minimal, absolutely minimal. But music is always overpowering, and in that case it was extraordinarily potent. That must have lasted a minute and a half, and we were only five minutes into the play – and that you don't do. That you're not supposed to do, you're supposed to get on with the play. But somehow what this play required – people walking very slowly forwards and backwards, and a wall that flew out very, very, very slowly, and Handel, because that's the court's rhythm. (It's not the

[4] See *The Madness of George III*, pp. 4–6.

King's rhythm, although the rhythm he wants to impose on everybody else is slow. The King's rhythm is exactly what he chooses it to be at any particular moment.) Minimal resources, no text, but a genuinely theatrical embodiment of order, harmony, decorum and stability. So the descent into madness and chaos had a context, and something to return to. The pity and terror elicited by Nigel's performance required that theatrical bedrock.

The play did change a lot during rehearsal and during its run. There were three separate casts at the National Theatre, and each time it got shorter. I think it was probably twenty minutes shorter when it closed than when it opened.

That's remarkable.

Well, it happens quite a lot.

Is it just because the cast gets better?

No, you cut things. Usually things get longer because people start to indulge.

When Alan was showing you drafts of the play as he went along, were your interventions from the point of view of what he was intending to do as a writer, or were they from the point of view of a director envisaging how you might stage it?

Both. Obviously, different plays, different playwrights, require different collaborations. A play which is three people in a room, there's nothing to say as far as the staging is concerned; it just stages itself. A play like this, which has an epic quality and a cinematic sweep – then yes, sometimes I would say, as at the end of Act One, 'I think I can make something of this if we just fiddle with it a bit.'

A reading, just a single reading, is incredibly instructive. It's dangerous, because what tends to happen at a reading is that the best actors do best – and at a reading you can get anybody to play anything; the best actors in the country will come and take the tiniest part because it's only a day or two, and everybody enjoys themselves. So that you can find yourself thinking that some tiny part is extremely important or hilariously funny, but when you cast the play, you can only get a regular actor to play a tiny part and suddenly it doesn't work at all. So readings can be misleading.

Mostly I think it's about clarity. But Alan presents fewer problems than some writers, because his plays are totally transparent, in that they are always about what they appear to be about.

I know exactly what you mean, that's what makes them so hard to write about! My theory as to why it resonated so much is because this is the oldest story in the world, the story of the king who dies and is resurrected. It is the oldest ritual in the world, and ritual is at the root of drama. At the same time it's set in a particular historical time that is meticulously well accounted for, in scholarly terms. It is as accurate as you can get and yet has all the force of myth.

Yes. That seems absolutely right. Just keep that quiet from German directors because then it'll start getting staged as a myth. There is a mythic quality to it, of course there is.

That's why the sublime quality of the National Theatre production seemed so appropriate. I remember when I saw the restraining chair and Nigel Hawthorne in it at the climax of Act One, it was clear to me that we had been taken on a journey to hell. The whole thing was unspeakable. It was a vision of the exact opposite of what he's come from.

Interestingly, it's one of the things which works better on stage than on film, or certainly it worked better on stage the way I did it. There are born movie directors who maybe would have been able to do that on film in an equivalently powerful fashion, but there is something about an empty stage, a raked wooden platform, nothing else; about being able to put the chair dead centre in a strong white downlight; to be able to arrange a kind of symmetrical stage image; to be able to concentrate the whole power of the stage on the one place where he is, because an empty stage stands for anything, and is in fact the most potent of playing spaces; to have that dramatic image immediately before the interval – structurally it felt like the climax of the first half. All those things fed into the power of that scene on the stage. It was fine in the movie; we did some fantastic stuff leading up to the chair, with him hurtling down the corridor and everybody chasing him and dragging him back whilst the 'Zadok' music built to a climax. But by the time we got to the chair, it was just a chair in a little room, that's what it was.[5] I craned the camera up for a shot from directly above the chair, but in the end a chair in a room is a chair in a room. It doesn't have the resonance of the stage image. There it is at the centre of the stage, at the bottom of a grand staircase, where you can see it's a parody throne. I wonder whether we'd have done better in the film playing that exterior.

To have filmed the restraining chair outside?

But it wouldn't have felt right. There are directors who could do that, but it just felt wrong to me. Film is so literal: he would have had to run out of the

---

[5] There is a photograph of how it appeared in the film in *The Madness of King George*, p. 46.

castle, and you would have been thinking, why have they got the chair outside in the middle of a field? And it would only have worked, it would only have had the equivalent power, if it had been literally just the chair, the earth, and the sky. It wouldn't have worked in Windsor Castle courtyard which would have necessitated an endless chase out beyond the castle walls.

But movies always require a different kind of storytelling. At the end of the play it's Thurlow who brings news to Pitt that the King's better, and in the movie that didn't seem to be good enough. The movie actually warps history a little in that it has a kind of parody chase sequence, as the King is brought in a coach from Kew to London to arrive out at Westminster yard, while the Regency debate is building up to a climax inside the chamber. All the MPs come running out, and there he is.[6] I suggested that when I was location-hunting, and starting to realise how that whole thing might play in movie terms. It's got to be the King himself. He's the guy. You don't want Thurlow being the one who delivers the climax of the movie! The King has to deliver that. There Alan the historian was a little fastidious, and had to have his arm twisted a bit, because it didn't happen, he said. Jesus Christ, have you seen the film *Elizabeth*? Not a single thing in *Elizabeth* seems to bear any relation to historical fact! *The Madness of George III* is essentially, page-by-page, true, including a lot of the dialogue.

The extraordinary thing is after the *King Lear* scene we could have gone on for ever in the theatre. It was like a party. Once he was better, the theatre audience just wanted to see him shit from a great height on absolutely everybody who'd tormented him, one by one, at great length. I think it was twenty-five minutes from the *King Lear* scene to the end of the play – which is extraordinary, because once he's better, he's better: that's the end of the story. It didn't occur to me that the film would be any different, so we shot miles of film we didn't use. All the stuff that's in the play had its equivalent cinematic scene, and we could only put half of it (if that) in, because the movie audience is less patient than the theatre audience.

Is there something inherently undramatic about it as well?

Yes, it's not dramatic at all, but by that time the theatre audience was past caring; they just wanted to see it. We just raked in the laughs.

At the end of the play Alan brings on the historian whose book he was reading and she explains about the illness.[7]

Dr Ida McAlpine. It got cut out halfway through. It was in the first run; never a popular scene.

---

[6] *The Madness of King George*, pp. 67–8.
[7] *The Madness of George III*, pp. 92–3.

Why not?

It's hard to say. It felt like a device from another play, but in a way that scene was a victim of the success of the rest of the play. The rest of the play so convincingly and truthfully appeared to deliver the English court 1788–89, that the appearance of a woman in a white coat was not going to be bought. Alan always regretted losing that scene, because what she says is so interesting. But even that was a substitute for an extended last scene, a ten-page last scene, where they all got to step out of the play and talk about what had happened: Pitt got to talk about his legacy to history; Fox got to talk about his legacy; everybody got to talk. They just chatted on about what you had just seen – which is difficult, because the audience wants to say, 'Yes, I know, I just saw that.'

Can I ask you about your background as a director? I know you came from opera and Shakespeare, and there are echoes of Lear *here, and I suppose* Oedipus. *Was all that classical experience of use to you in creating this production?*

I don't know, really I don't. Shakespeare is useful from all points of view. If you can make Shakespeare work (in some ways Shakespeare always works, but), if you develop a knack for staging a Shakespeare play – firstly so it is intelligible all the way through, secondly so there is a real relish, a communal relish amongst the entire cast for the language that they have to speak, making it simultaneously intelligible and pregnant, and thirdly if you can stage Shakespeare so that it never stops – then clearly you can do this play.

Is it to do with seeing things in operatic terms, seeing things in epic terms?

No, I don't think so. Opera requires a certain degree of shamelessness and flamboyance and bravura, and sometimes the work I do has that to a fault. There *are* directors who are afraid of music, who are afraid of big theatrical flourishes, or just don't like big theatrical flourishes – I'm not one of those. But there are also good directors who cannot move from one thing to the other without a blackout, without keeping you waiting. And you don't necessarily realise that this is why the evening is dragging and feels flat; it's very often because you've spent half the evening sitting in the dark waiting for the next scene to begin. That very often happens. But I often wonder why a play needs a director; there are some plays which probably hardly do.

Are you a facilitator as a director?

In the theatre, yes.

That's essentially what you are.

In the theatre. Sometimes a little bit more, sometimes a little bit less. You do often find yourself thinking, what kind of a job is this? But somebody has to understand what's going on. Somebody has to be sympathetic to the play, and know how it works, and know how to communicate that to everybody else involved – to actors, designer, lighting designer, everyone. Somebody has to be the translator of what's on the page onto the stage. Often the job's done simply by casting, so that in that process you've done your job and done it well, or done it irreversibly badly. Does *George III* get produced? I think I saw that there was one repertory production somewhere. Is this play done anywhere else?

Not that I know of.

It's too big, the reps can't do it, it's too big. There's no rep now that can afford this kind of a cast. Once in a blue moon. Twenty years ago every single rep would have done this play by now, and that, sadly, is a fact.

David Edgar

David Edgar, *Pentecost* (1994)

Pentecost was first produced by the Royal Shakespeare Company at The Other Place, Stratford-on-Avon, 12 October 1994. After some cast changes it opened at the Young Vic in London, 31 May 1995. On both occasions it was directed by Michael Attenborough.

TUNU's *story is initially incomprehensible as no one but her speaks her language. But gradually, through a kind of collective reading of the story, supplemented by* TUNU's *own hints, confirmations, corrections and echoes of the other* STORYTELLERS' *gestural language – for 'king', 'expedition', 'capture', going into a forest, giving a gift and so on – the story emerges and becomes clear.[1]*

Tunu, the Sinhalese refugee among the hostage-takers in David Edgar's *Pentecost*, has been all but silent up to this moment in Scene 6. Her moment in the spotlight is the hinge on which the entire action of the play is to turn. Up to this point, the hostages and their captors have been united only in mutual distrust and ill-disguised hostility. But with the 'collective reading' of her narrative, they are drawn together. Before they realise what has happened, Oliver, one of the hostages, has understood that Tunu's story is a version of the Christian myth and is completing it for her. The scene is a remarkable one in that it contains, in a *coup de théâtre*, the play's entire meaning.

   Edgar's play takes its name from the occasion, after Christ's death, when the apostles were filled with the Holy Spirit and spoke in tongues.[2] It was a moment when mankind was redeemed, at least partly, from the confusion that had reigned since the destruction of the Tower of Babel and the scattering of language. Edgar's play takes its theme and mood from those miraculous events, and stems from a line of thought that has championed the concept of a universal tongue. Monboddo, Hartley, and Coleridge speculated on it, and Esperanto was invented in 1887. For countries under Soviet rule in earlier parts of the twentieth century, Russian was a kind of universal language, imposed by Stalinist dictat. Today,

---

[1] *Pentecost*, p. 86.
[2] Acts 2:1–4.

English as a second language is spoken by nearly 1.5 billion people, and one in ten is learning it; as Edgar writes:

> English is defeating Spanish, French and German not so much via Hollywood, but precisely because it is already a hybrid, it is already massively impure, and thus lends itself effortlessly to the development of those myriad dialects, creoles, pidgins and patois into which it has mutated all over the world ... Contemporary culture, then, is a conversation conducted in broken English. It is mobile, rich, hybrid, mutating and corrupt. Like Greek legend, it is subject to considerable creative misinterpretation, mistranslation, and misuse. But it grows out of a need as ancient and as profound as the desire to belong, which is the urge to travel, and having travelled, to communicate with those amid whom we have come.[3]

Scene 6 of *Pentecost* presents us with a situation in which two groups of people are united by a common act of understanding – the recognition of the common thread of myth that unites alien cultures. The conversation presented to us is, for a moment, unbroken. Oliver reiterates Tunu's story in his own way:

> ... a God forbids his child the forest fruit. The child of disobedience is banished and his children are condemned to wander through the earth. But finally the God in pity sends his only son for their redemption. Who teaches them through parables and tales. Who rides unrecognised into the holy city. Prophecies his capture and his death. But promises his followers that nonetheless, in three days' time he'll prove himself the thing he claims to be.[4]

Recounted by two people, neither of whom speak each other's language, the story is instantly recognisable. It's the oldest in the world – that of the king who dies and returns to life. It focusses our minds firmly on the subject that underscores a profoundly intellectual drama – our responses to a shared myth that binds humanity together. We are not strangers. However 'strange', the need to communicate with those among whom we find ourselves is one of those ineluctable forces that affirms our shared condition. Not that the play goes so far as to argue the existence of a universal culture; on the contrary, its aspirations are informed by an acute and unsentimental analysis of the world. It fully acknowledges the points of separation between people – and doesn't flinch from contemplating the consequences of misunderstanding. In form, it is essentially tragic, for it climaxes with a botched attempt to resolve the hostage situation, in which Oliver is mistakenly shot dead. That climactic sense of waste at the end of

---

[3] David Edgar, 'English in Revolt', *Daily Telegraph*, 15 July 1995.
[4] *Pentecost*, p. 88.

the play re-enacts the Christian myth, which has already informed our reading of the fresco.

Just before he is shot, Oliver has an insight into who painted it, and how. He suggests that the artist was an Arab, who envisaged the nativity with a previously unknown intensity partly because he had only recently heard the story of Christ's life and death, and had crucially misunderstood it:

> OLIVER: An Arab colourist, who learns his fresco in the monasteries of Serbia or Macedonia. Who sees the great mosaics of the mighty churches of Constantinople. And who thinks, like any artist, I could do that too … But his huge advantage over almost everybody else is not just that he has the classic geometry the Arabs kept alive for the best part of 800 years, nor yet again the optics they hypothesised around the first millennium, but the fact that nobody's explained to him that painters aren't supposed to use them. So he has two eyes, and they tell him things have three dimensions, and he paints the world that way. With all that innocence, that freshness and rage, we bring to things when we come up against them for the very first – first time.
> GABRIELLA: Because, for him – it is.
> OLIVER: Exactly.
> GABRIELLA: And so they tell him this strange story.
> OLIVER: Of a woman who has to see her son die on a tree.
> LEO: Shortly after he had told her and his followers –
> GABRIELLA: That he will die –
> OLIVER: But rise again in three days' time.
> LEO: So for him the story's not about her weight of grief –
> GABRIELLA: But actually –
> OLIVER: – her want of faith.
>   *He's at St John.*
> He's not reaching out to comfort her at all. He's reaching out to warn her. It's an act of admonition.[5]

Pentecost is resolved through an imaginative leap resulting from an act of empathy undertaken by Oliver for a stranger who died centuries before. It is not as if his theory can ever be proven, but it is supported by the available evidence. The point of Oliver's explanation is that it takes for granted the central thesis on which the play rests: that the world in which we live is created through what Edgar describes as the 'conversation' of cultures. Though imperfect, riddled with inaccuracies, interpretive errors and misconstructions, it is all there is. The hybrid technique of the Arab artist postulated by Oliver, who combines in his work the influences of Serbia, Macedonia, Constantinople, and his native country, provides the model for it. At the same time, the correct interpretation of the painting – that it concerns

---

[5] *Pentecost*, pp. 98–9.

not grief but faith – directs us again to the thematic core of *Pentecost*. It is by an act of faith that we embark on the perilous journey from one place to the next, without being certain that we will arrive. The Arab colourist was held captive, and painted the fresco as a means of bargaining for his freedom;[6] similarly, the captors are refugees who have fled to the West from all over the world. The play is full of journeys undertaken by an act of blind faith. It is a quality that is seen also to inform the act of creation. The Arab colourist cannot have known that his fresco would survive the centuries, but against the odds, despite having been in a ruined building that has been used as a storehouse for potatoes, a museum, a prison, a mosque, a Catholic church, and a stable,[7] it has. Similarly, the refugees themselves, although they may not think of themselves in that way, embody the means by which the artefact is translated from one context to another. Even those who know no other words of English at least speak the lingua franca of popular culture:

GRIGORI: I think he say –
NICO: – Starship Enterprise.
AMIRA: (*dismissively*) It Starship. Dr Spock. Boldly going where no man is gone before.
NICO: Space – the final frontier.
RAIF: Hey. Beam me up Scotty.[8]

Edgar's use of this set of catchphrases is particularly apposite. The refugees have reached what for them is also the final frontier: that of the cultivated, prosperous West. They too wish to be beamed into safety. And that phrase, 'Boldly going where no man is gone before', as Amira renders it, articulates the sense of risk and uncertainty that accompanies our travels into the unknown.

That insecurity and doubt are defaults in modern life is one of the givens of the play. At times it seems that everything is under threat – most obviously the fresco, which we are told has been buffetted by the elements, whitewashed, and generally maltreated for centuries. Human beings too are at constant risk. The refugees tell stories about their perilous journeys from oppression. The shared myth at the core of the play concerns a life brutally interrupted. And the denouement of the play offers its own wry testimony as to the fragility of life: the fresco is not to survive the end of the play, nor do Yasmin, Raif, Antonio, or (significantly) Tunu and Oliver. It is as if the insights brought to the drama by Tunu and Oliver must, by definition, be placed under threat, presenting survivors with the challenge of preserving them.

---

[6] See *Pentecost*, p. 7.
[7] See *Pentecost*, p. 5.
[8] *Pentecost*, p. 85.

LEO: You must hang on to one thing.
GABRIELLA: ... What?
LEO: That he was right.
   Pause. GABRIELLA *looks up to* LEO.
That basically, we are the sum of all the people who've invaded us. We are, involuntarily, each other's guests.[9]

Why is Oliver's insight important? Because the world-view offered by the play is not detachable from its aesthetics. The Keatsian view of the work of art elevates the Grecian urn, or the song of the nightingale, to the level of the permanent. *Pentecost* apprehends all too clearly the ephemerality of art. But it's not the fresco – despite its obvious significance – that really matters. What is preserved through the play is the insight offered by Oliver into how the fresco got where it did, and why. Art is seen to be the product of migrant agencies, converging on a particular time and place, by accident.

The course of the play may be tragic, but its consolation is an insight that contains the seeds of hope. It is a curiously equivocal play, and the most striking image in it – that of the demolition of the wall carrying the fresco – is double-edged. Its destruction is, on the one hand, an act of violence which echoes the events that have shattered such countries as Chechnya and the former Yugoslavia since the dissolution of the Soviet Union. On the other, it reiterates the image of the crumbling of the Berlin Wall on 9 November 1989, when the German city was reunited. That duality is a clue to the play's perspective, for it finally offers two visions of the future. There is the way of the barbarians, such as Czaba, or there is another. The gap in the wall opens out onto another world, not unlike the fabled Illyria invoked early in the play by Oliver,[10] in which we will be made involuntary guests in someone else's country.

I spoke with Edgar at his house at Balsall Heath, Birmingham, on 9 July 1997. At first glance the preoccupations of *Pentecost* seem distinct from those of his earlier works, and as a means of gaining perspective on his career I set out to discuss issues of general principle; to take a retrospective glance at some of his earlier works, and finally to concentrate on *Pentecost*, and in particular the means by which Act Two, Scene 6 was developed with the cast and Clarissa Brown. Edgar has written in useful detail on the theatre and current affairs in *The Second Time as Farce: Reflections on the Drama of Mean Times* (London: Lawrence and Wishart, 1988).

JAMES: I'd say – primarily – we're right in being internationalists. In ascribing the failure of the Soviet Revolution – and indeed of the other revolutions made in its image – to the Stalinist betrayal, the attempt to build socialism in one country. And we're right too to believe that what is going on today

---

[9] *Pentecost*, p. 104.
[10] 'Because ... because ... This is Illyria, lady'; *Pentecost*, p. 13.

in almost every Western country – what you describe so elegantly in your articles about America – is in many ways a genuinely revolutionary phenomenon.

MARTIN: Well, good.

JAMES: The rejection of the centralised rigidities of old left politics.

MARTIN: I'd go along with that.

JAMES: The creation in their stead of a new left politics in which the means and ends of revolution are the same.

MARTIN: Well, I couldn't put it better my –

JAMES: A politics defined primarily by the belief that it is possible to build the New Jerusalem within the very belly of the monster, not in the future, but in the here-and-now.

David Edgar, Maydays, Act 1, Scene 6[1]

Interview

Duncan Wu: *I love that exchange in* Maydays, *especially James Grain's remarks about building 'the New Jerusalem within the very belly of the monster, not in the future, but in the here-and-now'. I suppose I like that because it plays to so many of the things that draw me to Romanticism.*

David Edgar: That's not, of course, James Grain's view. I can't remember the precise context, but he represents the tension of the late Sixties between the hippy, drug-taking, let-it-all-hang-out, sexual revolution end, and the hard-nosed Marxist, traditional new left end. The question of whether you could build things now was a very crucial division between the two camps. So that wouldn't be something that James Grain would have approved of.

Do you approve of it?

When Trevor Griffiths was asked about *The Party* – his play about thinly disguised versions of various people who were in the ambit of the Workers' Revolutionary Party – his answer was, 'There's a bit of me in all of them – they're all me.' To a certain extent that was a good answer; to a certain extent it was an evasion. I do however think that if, when you are writing, there is not a split between your heart and your head (to put it at its crudest) then probably you should be writing about something else. So I have all kinds of attractions towards that single-minded, non-sentimental, serious

---

[1] Quoted from David Edgar, *Edgar: Plays Three* (London, 1991), p. 219.

revolutionary zeal that James Grain expresses – it *is* romantic in one sense, desperately and fundamentally romantic to its core – as opposed to something much more vague, wishy-washy, half-hearted, and, it seemed to me at the time, not always serious. I was distinctly sceptical about the lifestyle alternative – and, certainly, the idea that you could build a better world through the consumption of narcotic substances seemed pretty unserious to me, and remains so. So there was a bit of a division there, but the argument of the play is that James Grain's kind of politics either turns you into a zealot, or drives you out. And if you leave, you may become a zealot in the other direction. That is what happens to Martin Glass.

So no, I don't approve of the politics and, in a very profound way, I became disillusioned with the peculiar Trotskyist variant of the hard line, by which Eastern Europe was seen as irrelevant to the conversation, and the Soviet Union, Eastern Europe and China as a kind of aberration, a deviation from the norm (as you know, Trotsky believed that you can't build socialism in one country, and therefore any country which attempted to do so somehow was part of this great Stalinist heresy – Martin expressed it in his grand speech at the end of Act Two),[2] and that therefore, because of these aberrations, there must be a non-existent but notional norm, rather like the theories of the universe which hold that anti-matter must exist because there's no other explanation to fill the hole our present theories have in them. It seemed important to me that the left should take on board the Soviet and East European experience. This is the context out of which *The Shape of the Table*[3] and *Pentecost* came.

On the hippy side of the question, I was very emotionally attracted to the idea that politics should start from where people were. Every writer on radical politics from Burke onwards – and no doubt before Burke – has pointed out that love for the whole of humankind often appears to pre-empt caring for people that you actually know. That seems to me to be a well-observed and important argument. You have to admire people who are prepared to sacrifice their personal lives and, indeed, the lives of people around them, for what might seem like abstract ideals; to start with the personal seems like a good approach to politics. On the other hand, it's a politics that becomes very vulnerable; for example, it seemed to me, from the 1960s to the Seventies, that politics became personalised to the point (particularly through the ecology movement and the health movement) that it was virtually a matter of being nice to your own body. Concern for planet earth mutated into the concern for planet body, as the youth of the 1960s jogged slowly but surely to the right. So I suppose that's the fundamental contradiction that the play is looking at – which is a contradiction in me also.

---

[2] It provides the culmination of Act Two, Scene 7 (*Edgar: Plays Three*, pp. 275–7).
[3] *The Shape of the Table* opened at the Royal National Theatre in November 1990.

All your plays seem to be discursive documents, conducting arguments of a kind. What do you see as being the purpose of conducting such arguments in a public forum? Is drama performing an educational function? Or is the act of writing the play the process of developing your own ideas about what you think? And do you feel that the experience of going to see a play is capable of changing someone's political opinions?

Well, when I began writing in the early Seventies as a young socialist – a young Trotskyite, indeed, at that point – I took quite a mechanical view. I thought that plays were there in order to encourage people to go out and man barricades. I did do some plays for a small theatre group, the General Will,[4] which had that intent; in the case of a play about housing, it might even have had that effect.[5] Obviously, that's not the best way of doing things, and I did discover in the late Seventies, when I became actively involved in the Anti-Nazi League in a campaign against the National Front,[6] that there were more effective ways of politically campaigning than writing Plays About Things – although, paradoxically, *Destiny*[7] has probably had the greater political impact than anything I have ever written for the stage or television.

Can you tell me in what way?

It's interesting, because it does go to the heart of your question. It encapsulated, in a *very* clear way, a way of looking at things which made sense of the world, and therefore supported a particular argument. David Mamet's *Oleanna*[8] did the same thing – it was propaganda against political correctness; there's no question about which side it comes down on. The central character is a man much more sinned against than sinning, and seeing it done before you, seeing the process, seeing how it could happen, brought home a particular condition, for better or worse, whatever everyone's view of it. It

---

[4] Four of Edgar's plays were produced by General Will: *The National Interest* (August 1971); *The Rupert Show* (January 1972); *Rent, or Caught in the Act* (May 1972); and *State of Emergency* (August 1972).

[5] *Rent, or Caught in the Act* toured by General Will, May 1972 onwards. It was written specifically as part of the fight against the Housing Finance Act brought in by the Conservative government of the day. Edgar has recalled that it played to no fewer than 30 tenants' groups, and 'was the most successful agitprop play I've ever done' (*File on Edgar*, p. 19).

[6] In 1977 Edgar became a regular contributor to *Searchlight*, writing specifically on anti-Nazi themes. His essay, 'Racism, Fascism, and the Politics of the National Front', is reprinted in his collected essays, *The Second Time as Farce* (London: Lawrence and Wishart, 1988), pp. 68–93.

[7] *Destiny* was first presented by the Royal Shakespeare Company at the Other Place, Stratford-upon-Avon, 22 September 1976. It was produced by BBC TV as a 'Play for Today', 31 January 1978.

[8] Mamet's play was first produced in Britain at the Royal Court Theatre, 24 June 1993.

turned *Oleanna*, certainly in the educational environment, into a code for a certain risk that, for example, a male lecturer would take by being alone in a room with a female student.

The Absence of War[9] is another such play. A lot of people felt that in the General Election campaign of 1992, Neil Kinnock had somehow destroyed something of himself in order to try and achieve an objective which then he didn't achieve, and therefore was left with nothing. David Hare encapsulated that so well that somehow he deepened it, and it would now be difficult to think about Kinnock, if you'd seen the play, without thinking of that extra-ordinary rally scene – or indeed for me that extraordinary last scene with the waitress ticking off the protagonist, George Jones, in the hotel.[10] Certainly it's impossible to think about the Kinnock entourage – and about entourages – without thinking about that play.

Destiny was concerned with something just as distinctive. There was a debate in the mid-Seventies about whether or not the National Front was a fascist organisation or an anti-immigration pressure group. The conventional liberal wisdom, particularly as expressed by Peter Jenkins in the *Guardian*, was that to call them fascists was left-wing paranoia and left-wing grandiosity. He said that in fact they were very small, very insignificant, and were articulat-ing something quite real: peoples' fear and worry about immigration. To call them fascists was to equate Britain in the Seventies with Germany in the Thirties, and that was a typical grandiose left-wing trick, because if that was true then the left becomes much more important thereby, because the left was much more important in the Thirties. One thing pulls up the other.

The National Front *was* a Nazi party. Their leaders were fascists. They had fascist pasts, and pursued a policy of using concern about black immigration to advance a cause indistinguishable from that of the Nazi party in the Thirties in Germany. That was true, and the play articulated that, and did so in a way which showed how people were seduced by that set of beliefs – par-ticularly into the anti-Semitic conspiracy theory. It fitted with what people saw around them, and their responses to what was happening when the play was being performed in 1976–78. It was performed at Stratford in 1976; London in 1977; and was televised in 1978 – the period of the zenith of the National Front's success in local elections, generating a lot of street violence. All of which increasingly fitted with what people were seeing. Indeed, that was how Dennis Potter judged *Destiny* when he wrote about it in the *Observer*, and I was very proud that he said what he did. Clearly he felt he had seen something which made absolute sense and truth.[11]

---

[9] By David Hare, first presented at the Royal National Theatre, 2 October 1993, as part of the Hare Trilogy.

[10] Edgar refers to Act Two, Scenes 8 and 9.

[11] Potter commented: 'A play which astonished me with its intelligence, density, sympathy, and finely controlled anger. For once, too, the compassion was not withheld

But there are limitations, obviously. If you are the National Front you are not going to sit and watch *Destiny* and say, 'Oh, good Lord, I've been wrong!' And indeed, if you're Peter Jenkins, you're not going to sit there and say, 'David Edgar has convinced me of his argument.' Like any – I was about to say 'propaganda project' – but like any project that aimed to persuade anybody of any view about anything at all, 99 per cent of it is supporting what people already think, or is akin to what people already think. If you think that the Soviet Union is paradise on earth, then *Animal Farm* isn't going to change your mind. If you're somebody who supported and believed in and was attracted by the general project of communism but had had serious worries over a number of years, then *Nineteen Eighty-Four* is going to be sufficiently recognisable to underline, to confirm, to embolden what you believe. So that's what I think plays do.

One of the faults of the early Seventies when we were trying to get the fabled working-class audience was that we weren't speaking to the people who were coming to the plays, and were pretending to address the working class. In fact, we did have an audience which was basically the student movement (or the ex-student movement) of the late Sixties. Our audience was us! Which was, of course, a rather large, and quite an important group of people. It basically comprised those who entered the public services – teaching, social work, probation service, journalism, the liberal professions – who were often of working- or lower middle-class family origin, but for whom class conversion was no longer the great trauma it had been for those who came of age in the Fifties. A high proportion of playwrights of that generation were much more middle class than Wesker and Osborne and Arden – be that as it may, we were less obsessed with culture and class, or with class expressed *through* culture. By the Sixties there was a well-established stereotype of the first working-class boy to get to Oxford in forty generations (to quote Neil Kinnock), who can't speak to his father, and can't cut it at the darts board any more; well, I think that people in the Sixties had got beyond that, because the Sixties had opened and collapsed so much of class.

So by the Seventies there was a new audience with new questions, one of the most important of which was: is it possible to be a revolutionary once you've left university? We were asking questions about amelioration and incorporation; for example, is a social worker patching up the system? What do you do if you're a Trotskyite teacher, or a revolutionary social worker, or whatever? Those questions were the really fundamental questions. How do you deal with

from those deemed beyond the pale. Here was an examination of the extreme right in British politics which caught up all the strands which make it function: the nostalgia, the disappointment, the dumbly aching resentments, as well as the psychotic anti-semitism and other such racism that traditionally disfigures these movements' (*File on Edgar*, p. 48).

working-class racism? How do you deal with working-class sexism? Those are the questions that really interested people who'd been at university in the Sixties, and who were now in the NUT or NATFHE or the AUT,[12] or social workers, or working for local government. What they really wanted to know was how they dealt with those issues; they weren't really interested in plays about strikes. They might be quite interested in plays about teachers' strikes, but they weren't so interested in plays about miners' strikes. They were fascinated by plays about racism and sexism, because that's what they dealt with every day, and confronted. They were also interested in plays about being on the left, and the difficulties with that. If you go back to the Elizabethan, Jacobean periods, the Restoration, the Edwardian periods, there are playwrights finding a subject in which they could address a new audience about topics of popular concern. Often, that topic turns out to be the wash, the downside of great national triumphs which had occurred some time before. So you get Shakespeare writing his great plays twenty years after the Armada. Much Restoration drama actually isn't from the Restoration period; it's later than that. It's the moment where the new London emerges as both terrific and scary – you know, sexual dalliance and so forth. Similarly, you can see the same relationship between the zenith of high Victorian capitalism and plays by Wilde, Shaw, (in particular) Granville-Barker, and Galsworthy. Similarly, I think Osborne and onwards is a response to the Second World War.

So in the Seventies there's a new theatre audience whom you're addressing, and in plays like Maydays *and* Destiny *you're presenting to people problems with which they can very clearly identify. I hope it wouldn't be naive to say that* Maydays *might be seen as a kind of justification for Martin Glass. And I hope it's not perverse to suggest that* Destiny *could be read almost as an apology for people like Turner or Rolfe. It's an explanation of some sort. Do you then provide an answer? Or was your aim in those plays in both the late Seventies and early Eighties to hold a mirror up to your audience, clarifying for them the central issues that they themselves had to confront?*

Well, clarifying is only one step down from re-education, isn't it? I think it's much more two-way than that. A conversation took place between the audience and the playwright – not typically a direct conversation, though on occasions it was direct. The reason for *attempting* to make Turner, Rolfe, and Martin Glass three-dimensional characters was precisely in order to say, 'This journey that they have undertaken' – which is a journey that I regret them having made – 'is an understandable one'. And you draw the dramatic dialectic as precisely as you can. Martin Glass is never particularly likeable,

---

[12] In Britain, trades unions for schoolteachers, and lecturers in colleges of further education and universities, respectively.

but you admire him to a certain extent, and he certainly has serious and appealing features. But the course down which he goes is certainly one of which the play does not approve. It would be perverse to say that the course that Turner and Rolfe take is admirable, and it would be pretty perverse to say that of Martin Glass, not least because of the way that the play helpfully provides a conscience in the form of Amanda, the female character, who makes it absolutely clear (probably rather over-clear) where we are.

The National Front – and certainly John Tyndall,[13] on whom the character of Cleaver is closely based – watched the television version and apparently quite liked it. That's because they were presented as fully realised, rather considerable figures, and their counterparts weren't saying anything they'd disagree with. But I wasn't writing it for them. It wasn't a fascist-converting operation – *absolutely* not. It was concerned to present a model that would make sense to people who were *anti*-fascist. The reason for making the fascists recognisable, and treating them seriously as human beings, was precisely in order to say to the anti-fascist movement, 'You've got to understand these people. You've got to understand how it works – and *this* is how it works.' In the same way, with political defection in *Maydays*, I was saying to those on the left, 'You've got to understand how you *yourselves* are driving people over to the right; this has happened before and it'll happen again.' In fact, in this country it's probably happened less – certainly less than in America and France – but nonetheless it has happened. So it certainly wasn't saying to people like Kingsley Amis or Alfred Sherman, 'You've made a terrible mistake; rejoin the Communist Party.'

I suppose what you're saying is that, to an extent, when you were writing plays in the late Seventies and early Eighties, you were writing for the already converted. I hope that doesn't vulgarise what you've just said!

It does, to the extent that the notion of conversion, the notion of that sort of plot-proselytising, was something I gave up in 1975. Preaching to the already converted implies that one's acting like a missionary! What I'm trying to suggest is that one's talking about a conversation with – by and large – like-minded people, in which the notion of conversion is not an appropriate description for the process. Nonetheless, let me put my objections to one side; proceed.

Right, well we've cleared that up. I'm asking how your position changed over the years, from the position you occupied pre-1975, to the work you found yourself producing during the 1980s. Certain changes are in the forefront of my mind: such

---

[13] Leader of the National Front party during the 1970s, now of the British National Party.

matters as the shifting socio-economic profile of your audience, and the interna-
tional success of Nicholas Nickleby,[14] *which went over to the States. How did your*
relationship with your audience change during that time?

Of course, one did carry on talking to an audience of generational peers,
because people of my age still go to the theatre – and that particular generational experience of being twenty in the late 1960s is a very particular one
that will stay with us for the rest of our lives. It was a very intense and exciting
period in which to be a young adult. On the other hand, one hopes that one
is in conversation with a *new* audience. Inevitably, one's less clear as to who
they are. I suppose the nearest I get to thinking about that is to try and keep
up with what people feel to be the prevailing social issues and questions. All
the East European plays – in particular *Pentecost* and the one I'm writing now
– are concerned with the postmodern model; they're concerned with culture.
I'm *much* more concerned with culture than with politics now than I was. A
change in subject-matter and certain changes in form are to do with changes
in fashion. For instance, narrative is more important now than it was in the
Seventies. I think people are, by and large (though there are exceptions to
this), much more impatient with being baffled, with obscurity.

Does that bother you then? Does that change the way you write?

(Pause.)

No–yes. A bit, yes. I'm very struck by the formal conservatism of the plays
written by people under the age of forty. *Goldhawk Road*, for example, by
Simon Bent, a generic young-people-in-flats play: there is a sofa on the front
cover.[15] The banishment of the sofa was the central project of the post-
Osborne era – kitchen-sink drama – get rid of the sofa, bring on the ironing
board! The move out of the drawing-room was the one cohesive factor for
thirty years of British playwriting; now you can't go into the theatre without
the curtain going up (and often, indeed, there *is* a curtain) – and there's the
sofa! It's rather fashionably disguised in art, but if you take *Shopping and
Fucking*,[16] or *Dead Funny*[17] – there it is: the downstage centre sofa. Okay,

[14] Edgar's adaptation of Dickens' novel was first performed by the Royal Shakespeare
Company at the Aldwych Theatre in July 1980, and opened at the Plymouth Theatre,
Broadway, New York, in October 1981. A television version was transmitted by Channel
Four in Britain in November 1982.
[15] *Goldhawk Road* was published with two other plays by Simon Bent, *Wasted* and *Bad
Company*, by Oberon Books in 1997.
[16] Play by Mark Ravenhill about five misfits in an uncertain drug society; a harrowing,
fast, and humorous commentary on London life in the 1990s. It was first produced by
Out of Joint at the Royal Court Theatre, 26 September 1996.
[17] Play by Terry Johnson (1994) inspired by the death of the comic Benny Hill.

Skylight has a kitchenette in which you spend so much of the evening, but it's in a flat too! (And it's in real time.) And along with the sofa comes everything else that one expects of naturalist drama.

I feel ambiguous about that for the same reason that anybody in my neck of the woods feels ambiguous about the claims made by commentators about the need for accessibility in culture. It's the question about popular versus high art. If you're Ken Worpole,[18] you basically believe that there is no difference, and, because more people see it, *Cracker*[19] is better than *Racing Demon*.[20] That argument proposes that the old arts are out of date and that the great achievement of the new, more popular, arts is to collapse this distinction (essentially a class one) between the two. If you're on that side you're fine, and, equally, if you're a cultural elitist you're fine.

However, if you believe, as I do, that accessibility is important, and that we're in the same game – that is to say, that 'high art' (in inverted commas) is playing absolutely the same game as popular storytelling forms – but that 'high art' is in some way *better* than more popular manifestations, then the question of how, and in what way, it is 'better' becomes a much more painful and difficult question. However wonderful I think *Prime Suspect*[21] is, *Boys from the Blackstuff*[22] was better: but the question is why?

Similarly I think that the accessibility of post-war British theatre, as opposed to, say, German theatre, has been a great virtue and a great vice. It's been a great limitation, but it's made theatre accessible to a public and part of a conversation. It hasn't gone up its own bottom. If presented with the proverbial question of being offered a range of doors to go through, but being allowed to pass through only one, I'd probably choose the one marked 'accessibility'. It's very, very important. If the price of that is having to deal within rather narrowly confined notions of storytelling and narrative, then I think it's a price worth paying for being able to address an audience on serious matters.

I take it, from what you've said, that during the Seventies you accepted the notion that it wasn't possible to change the world by writing a play, but it was nonetheless possible to engage in some kind of conversation with your audience. Is that something that has altered?

---

[18] Cultural commentator, known for such works as *Dockers and Detectives: Popular Reading, Popular Writing* (1983) and *Reading by Numbers: Contemporary Publishing and Popular Fiction* (1988).

[19] Television series featuring Robbie Coltrane, popular in the mid-1990s.

[20] Play by David Hare, first performed at the Cottesloe Theatre, London, 8 February 1990.

[21] Television series starring Helen Mirren as a detective, popular during the 1990s.

[22] Television serial written by Alan Bleasdale, made in 1984. A student text, edited by David Self, was published in 1985, and reprinted in 1990.

I think it was a big change to me in the Seventies to shift from the agitprop view of art as propaganda, to the view that starts with the writing of *Destiny* (though *Destiny* is a much more propagandist work than *Maydays*, and is a kind of bridge between one sort of aspiration and another). The difference between 1972 and 1977 is for me so much bigger than the difference between 1977 and 1997, in that, fundamentally, I've been engaged in the same kind of project since 1977. I'd ceased in the mid-Seventies (I hope) to set the work against some kind of abstract yardstick, of asking, 'How much does this further the revolution?' Once you stop doing that and start treating your own artistic development with more seriousness, and start feeling that one can respond to what audiences want, desire and need, then everything becomes so different that any subsequent differences are minute by comparison.

In terms of a career, any playwright will run into crisis when they have written out their early body of work, particularly if it's been successful, and they have to recharge themselves. That crisis almost always coincides with (and it's probably caused, in effect, by) the period when they cease to be fashionable. All kinds of pressures are thrown at them: another generation is coming up behind them; 'Whatever happened to ... ?'; early promises not fulfilled; tired; old – all those criticisms are levelled at writers when they reach their sixth or seventh play. It's a very difficult moment, and there are writers who haven't survived it. I certainly went through it in the late Eighties, when I was trying and failing to break into television. (Although some pieces of work were produced, that project was not achieved.[23]) One of the reasons I started the playwriting MA at Birmingham University in 1989 was that I was feeling a bit low about my own work at that period, and I'd written work in the Eighties (from *Nickleby* on) that didn't have anything like the kind of consistency of approach of what I'd written in the Seventies. *Nickleby*, *Maydays*, *Entertaining Strangers*, and *That Summer*[24] were vastly different from each other. I was concerned that I might have lost touch with the times, and was re-energised by the desire to confront my responses to events in Eastern Europe. Clearly, *The Shape of the Table* was a *succès d'estime*, and *Pentecost* is a *succès d'actualité*. I mean, *Pentecost* did touch a chord. Of the three single-word title plays of mine which have been produced by the RSC, I am less and less able to describe accurately who came to see them and why. I know very well why people came to *Destiny*; I have a general notion of who came to *Maydays*; and I feel much less clear about *Pentecost* (although I can produce elaborate theories about it). In a way, I do feel less in touch because the audience in

[23] Edgar probably has in mind, most notably, *Vote for Them*, co-written with Neil Grant, produced by BBC TV and transmitted in three parts on 2, 9, 16 June 1989.
[24] First productions of these works took place in 1980, 1983, 1985, and 1987, respectively.

the Seventies was an audience I knew; after all, it was very much an audience consisting of people like me.

And you don't know them so well now?

I don't feel I know them so well now. Partly because we're talking about a new generation.

You've mentioned the effect on you of events in Eastern Europe, but during the 1980s were there events at home, in Britain, that changed your vision? Did Thatcherism change the way you looked at society or the way you were relating to theatre audiences?

Although I had my doubts, at the beginning of the Eighties I wanted to assume that Thatcherism was a temporary aberration, and that the 'grand narrative' we had in the Seventies remained valid. The grand narrative I have in mind is the view of things presented in David Hare's *Plenty*[25] – exemplified most of all by the idea that moral authority was gained by being on the right side of the wall. It took a particular view of post-war British history:

> 1945–51: failure to implement socialism properly by the Labour government;
> 1950s-60s: squandered post-imperial riches;
> 1970s: decline – moral, political, economic;

at the end of which: true socialism. That model was clearly wrong. At its simplest. But I think there was a feeling – how could there not have been? – that the left would renew its project, and that the catastrophe of the 1974–79 Labour government would bring about the emergence of a more radical left, that would take into account feminism, ecology, and so on. That was the political significance of the peace movement in Greenham Common, and also that wonderful and very broad alliance that supported the miners in 1984–85. But it became clearer and clearer that the miners' strike was not the beginning of the fightback but the end, and that the world had changed fundamentally and irrevocably – a fact confirmed by the collapse of the Soviet empire. Obviously, that had a *huge* effect on everything.

In terms of the theatre, I think it was very important. Thatcherism's strange combination of populism and philistinism was in one sense a bad thing, but on the other hand we suddenly found ourselves on the same side as the great and the good. Many of us were aware that there were some good things happening – for example, in terms of the opening up of television, with the

---

[25] First produced, Lyttelton Theatre, 7 April 1978.

inception of Channel Four Television.[26] That was a capitalist revolution, a market revolution, and it had various very positive effects. The most abidingly important single thing which happened in the Eighties culturally was the death of the avant-garde in the performing arts (though not in the visual arts), and that was, to a certain extent, a good thing. It did confront practitioners with the need to satisfy the needs of audiences; it did say, 'This is a two-way process'; it did say that work that people can't understand is elitist; it did challenge storytellers to write better. Much though I admire Howard Barker, I think his statement that 'We must respect the audience, we must stop telling them stories they understand', is a terrible thing to say! It has a kind of oriental neatness about it, but seems to me to be utterly misguided. I'm now very chary of such views. I even find myself, on occasion, defending big musicals – though not very often. Certainly I think that a lot of genre television is good on every level; good morally, good politically, good artistically. And that, I think, was a by-product of that movement.

I think there was a kind of indulgence which the Eighties cleared out. But it wasn't a straightforward process. It was both with the grain of Thatcherism and, to a certain extent, against it; with the grain of Thatcherist populism, but absolutely against the grain of Thatcher's conservative traditionalist side – which always said, 'Economics is the means but the end is the revival of nationhood, with its ancient, secure, fixed, social and cultural relations', to which much of what came out of the Eighties was deeply antipathetic. So it was quite complicated, but I think the enduring legacy was to bring the criteria of the market-place from broadcasting and cinema into pre-electronic performance media – both to their benefit and their detriment. And I certainly have responded to that.

I wonder whether we could go on now to discuss Pentecost.

Yes, of course.

I was intrigued by the remark made by Czaba, the Minister for Culture in the unnamed East European country where the play is set. He says that if you want real change you put barbarians in charge.[27] Is the play itself in favour of change? Is it a play that's campaigning for a kind of change? It's not, presumably, the sort of change that the barbarians would bring about.

---

[26] Britain's fourth television channel started transmitting in 1982. It is a public service for information, education and entertainment. The Broadcasting Act 1990 required that Channel Four programmes shall: appeal to tastes and interests not generally catered for by ITV, encourage innovation and experiment, be distinctive, maintain a high general standard and a wide range, include a proportion which are educational, provide high quality news and current affairs, and include proportions which are European and supplied by independent producers.

[27] *Pentecost*, p. 24.

Czaba's a convenient little character because he's only in two scenes.[28] His role is to be another of the interests that are competing for the painting, along with the two different churches, and the three different art historians, and indeed the dreaded Pusbas. They're all attempting to appropriate this work of art for their own ideological, economic and political interests. That's what Czaba's trying to do. The reason why he's attractive, apart from his strange way of speaking, is that he's very honest and he's brighter than you think. So he picks things up that you don't expect him to, and certainly he impresses Oliver by his chutzpah, and by his get-up-and-go. No, I don't approve of what he says; putting barbarians in charge gets you either the Mafia or the Khmer Rouge. But to an extent what he says is true: it is an irony that countries run by secure, civilised, British-type bureaucracies find it very, very difficult to change. And it's certainly true that those economies which have been kick-started successfully have been run by people who are, to a certain extent, acting in a quite blinkered way. That's why the much-fabled Third Way, the Swedish idea, was never a starter: because it's something you can't get if you don't already have it (that is, the background and the other things that social democratic countries have already undergone in order to get to the point of having a liberal welfare state in the first place). To some extent, I enjoy the assumed discomfiture of an audience in finding an attractive barbarian in charge of the country. Anybody who has been to Eastern Europe has met people like Czaba, and they're very engaging guys. But at the end of the play he is the guy who's saying, 'Look, we're going to keep these people out.' So, finally, *Pentecost* does not support him or his position.

What does it support?

The position it supports is a notion of the way that culture develops. The play is supporting the idea that the way for communities of difference to work together is not by pretending differences don't occur (a kind of Utopian Esperanto model), nor by adopting the nationalist model of putting up borders around you (emphasise the difference), nor what I kind of increasingly regard as the postmodern mirror-image of that argument: that we can't communicate; that there is no point of contact between us; that the rejection of universalism has led to a kind of celebration of exclusivity. The way culture happens both in the past (as illustrated by the creation of the painting) and in the present, in terms of the bonding between the captives and captors in Act Two of the play (and, in particular, in Scene 6), is through the conversation of cultural worlds. I've written in the *Daily Telegraph* about how English as a second language is incomplete, corrupt and not nearly as efficient as us

---

[28] Act One, Scene 2; Act Two, Scene 8.

both sitting there and talking in perfect Hungarian.[29] The fact is that talking in perfect Hungarian excludes 99 per cent of the population of the planet, whereas talking in ESL may not be as wonderful, as perfect and as pure as talking in medieval Latin, but it works.

So the play is, I think, an attempt to formulate a view of culture which takes on board the collapse of Esperanto universalism, while challenging the nationalist/postmodernist alternative. The story of the painter coming to a church and being taken captive obviously echoes that of the art historians.

A parallel you draw with *Arcadia* is that, in essence, *Pentecost* is a double timescale play, it's just it doesn't have a double timescale.[30]

On re-reading the play for this interview, it struck me that there was something that wasn't as fully resolved as I'd thought. I'm thinking of the argument concerning high and low culture. At one point Gabriella says that different artworks vary in quality, that there's a distinction to be made between Star Trek *on the one hand and, say,* Twelfth Night *on the other. I wonder whether you'd go along with that, or whether you prefer the idea that culture is a big melting-pot of different things which float around cross-fertilising in an unpredictable manner.*

There is something in the play which I genuinely hadn't resolved in my own mind – and that's the question about restoration. I don't think I've resolved in my own mind whether or not Leo or Oliver are right about that. That's partly because I look at the results of the great acts of restoration and have very mixed feelings about them. So there are debates within the play which *aren't* resolved in my mind.

The one you mention is slightly different. It's to do with what happens when you go to Eastern Europe. Do you know Eastern Europe?

No.

Well this is an assumption. I am now about to make a presumptive assumption about *you*, in the manner of those badges that say things like, 'How dare you assume I'm heterosexual?' I'm going to assume that you're a left-leaning liberal intellectual – and you may be in fact none of these things! (Okay, apart from the last of those!) Those of us who are, go to Eastern Europe and meet people like us – I mean, *absolutely* people like us, who share a love of literature, an open-mindedness, probably attitudes of sexual liberalism, and even liberalism with regard to certain forms of deviant behaviour – but

---

[29] Edgar refers to his important article, 'English in Revolt', *Daily Telegraph* (15 July 1996).
[30] Duncan Wu, *Six Contemporary Dramatists* (2nd edn, Basingstoke: Macmillan, 1996), pp. xvii–xxiv.

who you suddenly scratch and find they're royalists. You know, they want to bring the King back! One of their favourite remarks is, 'How marvellous Margaret Thatcher was. Why don't you like Margaret Thatcher?'

Gabriella's attitude results from my visit to Romania, and a tour of the (then) still semi-gutted Romanian National Museum (which does not possess a distinguished collection of paintings) with the woman who defended it against the people on their side who wanted to burn it down on the night of the Revolution in December 1989, because there were members of the Stasi on the roof; they thought the way to smoke them out was to burn down the building and its collection.[31]

But I was very struck by the fact that for these people the really thorny issue was the quilts. It's not about whether *Star Trek* and *Twelfth Night* are the same thing; instead, it's when Gabriella says 'All of our galleries are now full of quilts and bits of painted cart.'[32] My attitude – naturally, being a good, left-leaning liberal – is that the definition of art should be widened, and should certainly include cultural artefacts which have not generally been regarded as high art, particularly because they tend to be produced collectively, or by women, or whatever. Of which the classic example is quilts! The artification of quilts is one of the great feminist cultural projects, I chose quilts for that reason. Quilts are not an accident in that respect.

Judy Chicago.

Exactly! Judy Chicago. And don't forget the AIDS quilt too. So quilts *in particular* are an example of something which people like me would say should be regarded as art. But if you've spent twenty years converting your National Museum from being the holder of a couple of not terribly wonderful collections formerly belonging to counts and other aristocrats, expropriated in 1945 or even earlier, and are then told that you have to devote half of your museum to pictures of your great Leader blessing tractors, and the other half to childrens' crayon drawings, you come to the argument from a different

---

[31] Nicolae Ceaucescu's regime in Romania collapsed after he ordered his security forces to fire on anti-government demonstrators in the city of Timisoara on 17 December 1989. The demonstrations spread to Bucharest, and on 22 December the Romanian army defected to the demonstrators.

That same day Ceaucescu and his wife fled the capital in a helicopter but were captured and taken into custody by the armed forces. On 25 December the couple were hurriedly tried and convicted by a special military tribunal on charges of mass murder and other crimes. Ceaucescu and his wife were then shot by a firing squad.

[32] 'I mean, during 40 years we are having no great artists and all social and historic context, and this means our museums full of children's crayon drawings and old quilts and bits of painted cart because naturally we must combat petit-bourgeois formalism and acknowledge art of heroic revolutionary masses quite as good as Michelangelo', *Pentecost*, p. 33.

place. In other words, Act One, Scene 3 is meant to explain why Gabriella is Gabriella. It serves partly to explain why her attitude to the refugees is so politically incorrect. I mean, she is hostile to them – 'Do we get rid of Russians to get Russian dregs and scum instead?'[33] Nor does her hostility to the gypsies ever change. Oliver *does* go through an element of conversion, but in fact moves closer to her point of view.

What I tried to do was demonstrate why she thinks as she does. She's been in the middle of the dramatic failure (which has had a terrible effect on her own life) of the experiment which took the ideals in which people like us believe to their logical conclusion. But she also shared many things with it. That's the lesson of *Maydays*. You can't say that social democracy and Soviet communism (although there were various very important differences between them in terms of personal freedom and bureaucracy – and very fundamental differences in the political process in civic society) were really very different in kind. In degree they were very dissimilar, but they had many features in common. Some of those were good, including cultural democracy. So I'm for the quilts, really. But I absolutely understand why Gabriella isn't, and I think it's important that *we* understand that.

It hadn't struck me before but, as well as advocating a conversation between cultures, in which cultures justify themselves to each other, the play itself also consists of that. And in the speech Fatima makes in Act Two, Scene 6,[34] she has a point – Fatima being the most extreme of the hostage-takers, the one who wants to stop people being nice to each other, stop people talking to each other, stop people bonding, and who, very unfairly, is casting the hostages as imperialists and fascist and warmongers (which they are clearly not). She's got a point, and indeed to a certain extent the hole in the solidarity of the hostage-takers made by Scene 6 is the same hole through which the commandoes break. It destroys the solidarity that Yasmin tries and fails to recreate and preserve in Scene 7, when the authorities are clever enough to meet the demands of some but not all the hostage-takers.

Are there any elements in the play as it stands with which you're discontented?

There is an emphasis that I'd quite like to have a go at correcting. I am intrigued by the fact that people who have populist instincts, instincts

---

[33] 'Why should we be world transit camp? Why should we get rid of Russian army and get Russian dregs and scum in place?', *Pentecost*, p. 40.
[34] FATIMA: This is – this must not happen. We are sitting here telling infant's stories, with these people. They are imperialists and torturers. They are our captives and we must keep them secure. We have threatened to kill them. How can we kill them now? What will they think of us?

From *Pentecost*, p. 88; the speech is discussed in my *Six Contemporary Dramatists*, p. xx.

towards accessibility, instincts of wanting to embrace the contemporary and the modern, nonetheless sometimes retain the manner of their class and background. I wanted Oliver to be somebody who favours popular art, and whose desire to restore the painting is partly a desire to make it accessible. His support for the restoration and cleaning of paintings is on the populist side of that argument (there's a conservative and a populist side of that argument). He's written his great book on soap opera or beer mats or pinball-machines, rather than on Brueghel or Rubens. The irony is that his manner is still rather elitist. And that's something which, I think, needs another moment of foregrounding in the play.

So the irony is that Oliver, who ends up being the hero, sort of is the hero. At the beginning, the manner and the matter of what he believes are quite a long way away from each other. Because he begins the play with an act of cowardice.

An act of cowardice?

Well, he spends most of the first scene saying, 'I do not want to get involved with this mad woman; I want to give my lecture, go to my reception, and go home.'

Though he comes very well out of it, because he gives her a chance.

Oh yes. And, in relation to that, there's another aspect of the play that didn't really come out in the British production by virtue of the way we cast it. In both the American productions to date all three of the central trio of characters have been cast younger; if you do that, it does become a love story. It's about a man who's just on the cusp of accepting that his career is never going as far as he wants; he's never going to be Professor, he's always going to be only Doctor, I'm afraid, and he's clearly set in his ways. And a dazzling East European personality says, 'Take the biggest risk in your life and follow me and I'll make all the difference.' He does so, and dies as a consequence.

Painting is something that's rooted in both the temporal and the eternal. And that dualism is something you seem to be very conscious of throughout this play. One sits with the rest of the audience, hoping against hope that the fresco will somehow be saved. It's constantly being threatened.

Yes.

There's an urge to understand this play in terms of the dialectic between the temporal and the permanent. Is there any element of that finally in this play, or is one more correct in reading it more in terms about a debate about cultural and linguistic forces operating in the present?

The way you've just put it is not a way that I've thought about it before, though I have my own strange and difficult relationship with permanence, which may well be there subliminally in the play.

The relationship between the whodunnit (or the who-painted-it?) and the thriller is obviously a relationship between two particular stories of what being European is about. One is the story we were brought up with – the relay-race model of the European spirit undertaking (almost apparently completely self-consciously from the word 'go') the naturalistic project, and that baton being passed from painter to painter until you hit late Rembrandt and the thing's been cracked. That notion of the visual arts is more central and easily assimilable than any other, because the difference between the Gothic view of the relationship from God to man, and the high renaissance view, is so dramatically and vividly presented; it takes you from some very rudimentary representations of God, and culminates with God and Adam on the fabled ceiling. The idea that those Serbians, Croatians, and Lithuanians are unpolluted, pure, consistent peoples seems to me to come from a similar stable as that view of the renaissance.

Against all that I would place the Romanticism of the thriller element of *Pentecost*. It derives ultimately from the stories in Vasari,[35] which are great and exciting and thrilling ones. To think about what it must have been like to have been Giotto, or Masaccio, or Michelangelo, is to think about really attractive lives. There's that remark in Stoppard's *Arcadia* – 'I think you're the first person to think of this'[36] – which sums up the magic of it. The romantic story of Dante visiting Giotto as he painted the Arena chapel,[37] and their little conversation, appeals to all of us as a romantic moment. That, and all the mythologies of the way that Michelangelo painted the ceiling.

So that provides the inspiration for the story of the unknown artist, my invented Arab painter, with his strange history. He comes to this village, where nobody has ever heard of him, and leaves behind this remarkable thing hidden in the corner. It is absolutely a romantic story, if ever there was one.

I love the scene when Oliver finds out the truth of it, or he discovers what he thinks is the truth of it.[38] I love the audience response to that and the pleasure that it gives an audience – and I especially enjoy the pleasure and

[35] Giorgio Vasari, *Le Vite de' più eccellenti architetti, pittori, et scultori italiani* (1550, 2nd edn, 1568; *The Lives of the Most Eminent Italian Architects, Painters and Sculptors*).
[36] *Arcadia*, p. 74; discussed *Six Contemporary Dramatists*, p. xiv.
[37] Giotto's 'Lamentation', the fresco in the Arena chapel, Padua (or Cappella dei Scrovegni), c. 1305–06, is the model for the fresco in *Pentecost*.
[38] See *Pentecost*, pp. 97–9.

surprise, as it has all been recently, carefully, and, I hope, not too visibly set up, so that all the various revelations click and come together.

So yes, I think there are things in there which are probably deeper than the theory of the play, as there always are. They're to do with the fact that it's about a painting and not a piece of music, about which I know less – and like less. I love those paintings, and one walks out of seeing the Sistine Chapel ceiling or the Arena Chapel, Padua, or the Masaccio frescoes in Florence feeling taller for it. The soaring emotion that one gets from those great works of European art, what you might call the 'Ode to Joy Effect', absolutely works, and I think the play probably does touch on that, is informed by that – but not in a way that is nearly so easy to discuss as the things we mentioned earlier.

There's a magic element in this play when it's performed, and performed well. I have in mind that storytelling scene – Act Two, Scene 6. Tunu is telling a story in her native Sinhalese, and in a most peculiar way it suddenly becomes entirely comprehensible. That's a kind of magic, and I don't understand really how it works. I'm curious as to how you came to conceive of it, and I'm curious as to how you pulled it off.

That scene went through a whole number of drafts, and they tell the story more accurately than I could. It all comes back to the concept behind the play, and of course the title. Of course, the title is slightly problematic: it gets misspelled; people's biblical knowledge is not what it used to be; and it's also the title of a play by Stewart Parker, which I'd forgotten, and regret, because he was a great and good writer, and died young.[39]

So why retain the title, if it's so problematic?

The starting-point of the play was the idea of the discovered fresco, and the refugees came very quickly afterwards. Well, the idea originally was that there would be a transformation. A real transformation. My original idea, actually, was that there should be a Royal National Theatre/English National Opera co-production. All the refugees would be played by singers; Scene 6 would be sung, and it would be an opera inside the play.

That's an incredible idea.

It is good.

---

[39] Parker's play was reprinted by Oberon Books in 1995.

Has that ever been done before?

Well, there are plays in which there are singers, like *The Tempest*.

Yes, but that's a different concept.

You're right. Well, no, not quite to that extent, as far as I know. And obviously there are plays with dance – I mean Caryl Churchill's *The Skriker*[40] is a play for actors and dancers. Obviously, one reason against doing it is that it is fantastically expensive, because you're employing the expensive bits of both operations. In the case of the music, you're employing expensive singers and, presumably, an orchestra in order to do a tiny proportion of the overall play.

So the original idea was that it would *not* be naturalistic; there would be something that would happen that would be 'theatrical'. I dispensed with the idea partly because I got very interested in *some* of the naturalistic elements of storytelling – such things as showing off and taking your turn and so on. Singing would have pre-empted that. And I'm always anxious about singing because you can't always hear the words.

I read Vladimir Propp's famous book on Russian folk-tales,[41] which aspires to give you the overall storyline of everything. He was a structuralist writing in the Thirties. I got into the idea that there should be a series of stories, which would be handed on like a relay baton, and which would then turn into one single story. At this stage it wasn't intended to be naturalistic. What I was basically doing was collecting stories. I had charts of the various stories in which fathers and merchants and generals instructed their sons and daughters not to go into rooms, eat apples, read books, and so on. At first it was just folk culture; a bit later I began also to be interested in the way that those stories were reflected in contemporary popular culture too.

At that point there were twenty refugees, not eleven. And the stories were told in English. The assumption was that a magical moment would occur, and we would hear them speaking in English. In other words, something magical would actually be represented. People who didn't speak English would speak English. The idea was that English would become a common language. As you've just detected there's a logical problem in that, which is that English is also the language in which most of the play is written when it's not a common language. So how would you tell what's happened, and, anyway, do we want to say that English is a common language? So should they all start speaking in German? Or should it be different again? And I didn't know the answer to that.

---

[40] Churchill's play was first performed at the Cottesloe Theatre, London, 20 January 1994.
[41] Vladimir Propp (1895–1970), *Morphology of the Folktale* (Austin, Texas: University of Texas Press, 1968).

When I wrote the play, partly because it was very late to be delivered to the Royal National Theatre for whom it was originally written, Scene 6 consisted of (in essence) a summary of what took place in it. It was otherwise a blank. The National turned it down – in inverted commas. There was a dispute about what happened next, which I'd prefer not to discuss. But the upshot was that it ended up being produced not by the National, but by the RSC at The Other Place.

The RSC arranged a reading with the 1993 Stratford Company; that is, the one company of actors in England who, by definition, couldn't do it, because they were by that stage with the RSC company in London. It was a very starry cast with John Carlisle, Michael Feast and Penny Downie playing the three principals. They read the play out in a rehearsal room in Stratford. It lasted four hours and was very exciting to hear. By that stage I had written Scene 6 as a series of paragraphs of a continuous story, which told the Vladimir Propp story in various different ways – sometimes repeated, sometimes consecutively, from the various cultures of the twenty refugees, speaking in English. The whole thing was in English; it was really a holding operation.

When the play had been scheduled for the last slot in Stratford in 1994, we decided that, with a ten-week rehearsal period with the whole company, which you get for that slot in Stratford, we'd work on the scene with the actors. I got the RSC to engage a young director called Clarissa Brown, who had been assistant director on *Entertaining Strangers*[42] and *Dr Jekyll and Mr Hyde*,[43] and who had read drafts of the play. She was involved in community theatre and therefore was aware of various techniques of getting people to engage in what some might dismissively and unfairly call the touchy-feely end of drama. It seemed to be the right end from which to approach Scene 6.

I did another draft of this summary, including the sort of stories that we could use in Scene 6. In essence we had the characters of the (now) eleven refugees; we had what they did in Scene 5 and what they did in Scene 7. That was what we started with. After about a week of sitting around and discussing it, the operation split into two, and Michael Attenborough directed the Act One people in a rather arid rehearsal room in The Other Place building, while me, Clarissa and the refugee actors went off to one of the main rooms in the Shakespeare Institute (a wood-panelled room opening onto a garden), in which for two weeks we told each other jokes, had parties, improvised, and played games. As you can imagine, there was a certain amount of resentment from the people in the arid rehearsal room, who were working away on this intractable series of arguments about art history and art restoration, sensing

---

[42] First produced in Dorchester, 18 November 1985; produced by Peter Hall in London, 9 October 1987.
[43] Edgar's adaptation of Stevenson's novel, *The Strange Case of Dr Jekyll and Mr Hyde*, was produced by the RSC at the Barbican Theatre, 21 November 1991. It was directed by Peter Wood; Michael Attenborough was executive director of the RSC at the time.

that up the road, in possibly one of the most beautiful working environments you could conceive of, the rest of the company were playing games with each other.

I can well understand that; in fact I sympathise with them!

Yes, absolutely. We started off by working on the refugees as characters. It was a very good place to start, and eventually defined what resulted. Some of the actors were more diligent than others, and more interested than others, and more committed than others, and that is reflected in the text. For example, the character Amira ended up being much more prominent than she was before – not as a prize, but because the actress was very committed, and came up with some really interesting things. Some of the boys were less assiduous (though some were very assiduous). To take another, the full extent of the Grigori/Nico relationship, and Grigori's prissiness and distress that he'd been taken for a ride by this crazed, mendacious gypsy, was something that developed through this work. We also worked on everybody's journey across Europe. We had a big map and pens, and we traced everybody's journey to get to the location at which the play takes place. Some of that was already in the text – most notably in Yasmin's long speech in Act One, Scene 5.[44] In fact, some of the stories we had gently to change because they were implausible, or didn't fit with what I thought the characters would be. For example, the gypsies wanted to be more honest than they clearly were in my text; they decided that Nico was a more straightforward character than the plot demands. We don't think he has been ethnically cleansed by Serbs, do we? He's realised that being a Bosnian is a pretty good thing to be if you want to get into the West.

One of Clarissa's improvisatory techniques was to get the actors to bring photographs and tell their lives through them. So that little moment when Amira does that was directly inspired by that improvisation.[45]

We then started playing games – storytelling and joke-telling. A lot of work was done in gobbledygook. We asked the actors if they'd bring along some sort of turn, so everybody told a joke or something of that sort. We then started trying to see whether you could understand things in a foreign language, and how. So we got the Antonio actor,[46] who's a brilliant raconteur, to tell jokes in gobbledygook. Then we told stories in gobbledygook. We began with stories in which it was a matter of *recognising* the story, so you'd have to guess, for instance, that it was *Cinderella*. Sometimes it was a joke, and what we found was that we would get the principle of the joke, the

[44] *Pentecost*, pp. 70–1.
[45] In Act Two, Scene 6; *Pentecost*, p. 81.
[46] Nigel Clauzel.

rhythm of the joke – usually something happening twice the same and once differently – but, unless we knew the milieu, it was incredibly difficult to understand what was actually happening. In other words, we can understand that character A had expected C to occur for a third time, and in fact it was D. But only when it was explained that they're on a train did you have any clue as to the specifics. So you're exploring communications. We did a lot of work on that, and it was very useful.

Simultaneously we were asking people to read folk-tales, and again the more assiduous people were coming back with fairy-tales they particularly liked. I remember someone brought in a book of Turkish folk-tales. We also did collections of universal phrases, of which 'Beam me up, Scotty' was one.[47] The word 'Okay' is obviously another, and lines such as 'Hasta la vista'. Some of them ended up in the play and a lot didn't. I ended up with fantastic lists of things to use. It was all-important because it relates to how people communicate with each other in the play.

There's an interesting story about Michael Crichton, the author of *Jurassic Park*, who was an anthropologist. He was in some very, very obscure Goan community and was told a story by a local chieftain, who clearly realised that the anthropologist wanted to be told stories. It was the story of a man who was frightened of snakes. Well, after a while Crichton realised that it was clearly from *Raiders of the Lost Ark*, because he'd seen it, and so had the local chieftain! That interests me a lot, because it shows that an Indian is probably going to see less difference between an Indian folk-tale and *Star Trek* than we do. For the Indian, the folk-tale is still living; it hasn't been airbrushed by antiquity in the way that *Beowulf* (and indeed the Christian story) has been for us. To a large extent, the play is about transcending those barriers.

So I was beginning to amass a lot of material throughout the rehearsal process. I was also accumulating information about the way people use gesture, which is the clue to the Tunu speeches. By the time she tells her stories we have encoded all the gestures that she uses in the action that precedes them, so that she can communicate with us despite the fact that she's speaking in a language we can't understand. We can work it out from the fact that it has a common plot, or common element of plot, with earlier stories we've heard. For instance, there's the fact that gestures for things like 'king' and 'queen' and 'male' and 'female' have been firmly established in the audience's mind. For my money, I would have liked to have encoded them more contemporaneously; I loved it when she threw a grenade to signify 'battle', and I'd have loved for her to have encoded 'woman' in the same way, irreverent, contemporary, to have been much less traditional in some of her gestures.

---

[47] Used by Raif; see *Pentecost*, p. 85.

I also wanted it to be musical. Ilona Sekacz, who did the music, came to some sessions, and she conducted one session where we all beat drums and made music in order further to annoy the poor actors who were working on Act One in The Other Place! We did a workshop on songs, and talked about universal tunes. We knew that music was going to be crucial to the play in some way; I thought it would start with music, I thought there was going to be humming. In one of the scripts it started with people all very quietly humming.

Then there was a crucial improvisation for which we went into The Other Place. We couldn't do it at night, but we did it with quite a compression chamber feel, so as to try and reproduce the feel of its being in the depths of the night. (Ideally we should have done it at four in the morning, but Equity, the actors' union, quite correctly frowns on such things.) We went in there, sat down, and the improvisation started in darkness, as if it were four in the morning, as it is in the play,[48] and improvised the scene. And nothing happened. People came out with wonderful dialogue; 'Your painting. Look like a window'[49] came out of that. Lots of attempts to make conversation happened, which were very useful. But nothing happened. Ilona said, 'What were you trying to do?' I said, 'We were trying to get them to the point where they'd start singing.' And she said, 'People don't sing in order to make themselves feel together, they sing when they *are* together. You've got it the wrong way round.' That was a really profound insight and, of course, absolutely true. So from that, really, I got the structure, but I did gain from that the idea that it would start quite edgily and painfully if it started at all.

The final thing that was good about starting with the characters was that it did open up the possibility of doing it naturalistically – in the sense that they wouldn't speak English if they didn't already, and that we would represent it as it could have happened in real life. In other words, there wouldn't be any theatrical magic. I realised in retrospect that the only way to make it work was to make it a story of the interrelations within the group. That became my foremost concern.

I was about to write Scene 6 when we had a fantastic crisis over Scene 7. The problem here was a more mechanical one. It was to do with the fact that, in the middle of a scene about whether the refugees are going to go to West Germany, Oliver gets inspired and starts talking about the painting in a way that didn't connect with the hostage story at all! It was just unfeasible, it was unfeasible that the hostage-takers would listen to him! We had an evening – me, Clarissa and Michael – where the agenda was to discuss the Scene 6 script, and in fact turned into a demolition of Scene 7, leaving me totally depressed.

---

[48] The stage directions of the published text specify that Act Two, Scene 6 takes place 'Shortly before dawn' (*Pentecost*, p. 80).
[49] Amira's comment; see *Pentecost*, p. 81.

But gradually, as the evening wore on, it became clear that there was an available storyline by which the painting suddenly became important again, because there was a moment of crisis when it could be used as a lever by the refugees. (The course the finished play actually takes.) At the moment Yasmin realises that the authorities are trying to divide them, she says, 'No, we will go together as a block and we're not going to accept some of us going. All of us will go to the German border – if not, we will burn the painting.' The priest says, 'But the painting isn't valuable any more.' In response to which they say, 'Okay, we'll kill Leo, who lied to us.' And then, at that point, Oliver has a reason for intervening, which is to say 'Don't kill him, the painting is valuable again.'[50]

It's very clever.

It's now a really good piece of writing; it wasn't very good before, so that was all very pleasing.

All of that reminded me of the fact that Scene 5 contained growing factional tensions among the silent, secret community of refugees in the play – caused most notably by the fact that Yasmin as leader had lieutenants who were male. And she was female. In other words, I realised that the flow of action from Scene 5 through to Scene 7 should be constructed in terms of the relationships *among* the asylum-seekers, as well as *between* them and the hostages. There was already a bonding operation between the two, but there should be a dispute within the group of asylum-seekers about the fate of their hostages.

So you effectively reconstructed the entire scene from the ground up.

The fundamental dramatic thrust of Scene 6 is as follows: a meal has been had, somebody comes over to the hostages, the hostages say, tell us the time; Yasmin says, don't tell them the time, Amira thinks that is bad, Amira goes over, bonds with the hostages, shows them the photographs. Yasmin says, what's going on, and then she tells them the time. A little act of revolution by Amira against Yasmin's leadership. Yasmin, angry, then turns on two of the boys for telling each other dirty jokes, and Antonio then thinks actually jokes aren't a bad idea. So he 'gives permission' to Grigori and Amira to tell stories, and indeed encourages them by example through his little quip about the violin growing up to be a double-bass. Gradually people are incorporated. Antonio at one point tells his own joke, and that finally brings in the boys, who are sitting at the back like some of the boys often do (and indeed some of our male actors did during our improvisations, saying, I'm not going to be

---

[50] See *Pentecost*, pp. 95–7.

f***ing bothered with all this sissy stuff). But Antonio, deliberately as an act of leadership, decides that it's important that people do bond one with another – not particularly anti-Yasmin but *de facto* anti-Yasmin because Yasmin's not of that view. Antonio's intervention gives permission for enough people to join in for the music to begin, and for that little dance to occur. Out of which comes the confirmation that he was right, which is that the second most silent and backgrounded person, Tunu, is foregrounded, by doing something she's never done in her life, which is to give her great speech to a group of complete strangers. It works for them and for us in the audience, at which point the act of bonding occurs, with Oliver bringing in the connections with the Christian story. Amira invites him to continue, and one of the only two people left on the outside, Fatima, comes forward and says we shouldn't be bonding with these people. Then it is Yasmin who, very reluctantly, follows Amira in saying that the reason why she behaves like this is because of the dreadful thing that's happened to her. The turning-point in Yasmin's character development was the business of her still having her Kuwait City keys, which was an invention by the actress in rehearsal.[51]

You can chart the scene in terms of interrelations between those groups within the asylum seekers. Having rewritten Scene 6 along those lines, I rewrote Scene 7 and then did the final version of Scene 6 on the back of that. On that last rewrite I did make a number of changes. I changed Antonio's story – the earlier one was a much more folksy one about why pigs are black or white. It was quite a funny story, but I decided to do the much more hard-nosed cannibalism joke, which is in the published text.[52] But fundamentally it stayed the same. It certainly wasn't an improvised scene, but it did draw very much on work with the actors.

How do you work with the actors? What are the protocols that are operating when you're working with them in this way? I mean, for instance, when you change someone's story, do you tell them that you want to change their story?

In this case we were *very* conscious of the actors' possession of that scene. For example, I am still of the view that there's one atrocity too many, and I think there should be one less horror story. The two options are either to take Raif's story away from him, or to take Amira's. I was rather inclined to take Amira's story away from her, but you just knew that wasn't right any more, because it was hers, it wasn't my story. She had invented the trip to Prague with the orchestra, and all kinds of other things.

The protocol has changed dramatically over the years. It used to be a rule that if you were in rehearsal you weren't supposed to talk with actors, you

---

[51] Yasmin was played by Katharine Rogers. Edgar refers to her line, 'It is – my house keys. From Kuwait City. It is crazy that I keep them'; *Pentecost*, p. 89.
[52] *Pentecost*, p. 85.

should go through the director always. But that really has gone away now. By and large the general rule is that one should be sensitive to the process. The reason why writers are badly regarded in the rehearsal room (or have been), is that writers tend to demand the final product at the beginning. They tend not to understand how actors work – the necessity of going down blind alleys, and so on; they can be insensitive to actors' egos (not that all actors have particularly large egos, though of course some of them do, as do writers!).

I think there are different protocols, depending to some extent on the director. For example, giving notes to actors. The general rule is that towards the end of the process you become less vocal. If a director spends the first week sitting down and reading through with the actors (as most do), the writer's very active around that period. I use that period to sort out bugs that need to be dealt with in the script. But by the end of the process you're very much working through the director, and certainly when you get onto late runs and previews some directors allow you to give, or encourage you to give, line notes. I mean notes when lines have been delivered wrongly. Another way of doing that is to give them to the deputy stage manager, who's in charge of the book (it's their responsibility to keep the text). So that's sort of encouraging him or her to do what he or she should be doing anyway, which is gently acquainting actors with deviations from the text.

Towards the end, you by and large become more of a ceremonial figure for the actors, though with the director one hopes that one will be able to talk to them after every run and every preview, and that what one says will be incorporated into their notes. Sometimes that works well, sometimes less well. It has always worked very well between me and Michael on the two occasions we worked together.

One of the things that strikes me is that the process was a collaborative one between you and the actors. What do you do when you try and generate another production of Pentecost *with different actors?*

Well, in this case, the process of generation was a mutual one of discovery, by all of us, about people who weren't very much like us. It was a process of character-creation in which I was using the actors' perceptions in order to build characters in collaboration with those actors. I don't think anybody among the actors was ethnically the same as the refugees, with the exception of the actress who played Tunu, Thusitha Jayasundera, who was Sri Lankan; that, in fact, was why we chose Sinhalese. Apart from that, the Antonio actor wasn't Mozambican and the Raif actor wasn't Azeri, and so on. It wasn't like they were playing themselves, nor was it (as with the Mike Leigh method) that they had created characters by going away for many weeks and researching them; they weren't their own creation. In fact, two-thirds of all of the parts were there already. To that extent they were being fantastically helpful, but they weren't producing something which was exclusively theirs – so in this case I didn't see it as a problem. There are certain moral issues about things being created, but artistically I didn't regard that as a problem.

The thing is, the printed text, which anyone can buy for £6.99, is the distilled essence of a great deal of research, and a vast amount of rehearsal activity. What I'm really asking is how one would go about the business of producing something with such a weight of knowledge – both intellectual and practical – behind it.

It has been done three times: twice in America and once in Australia.

And each time you were there weren't you, you were involved?

And there were three cast changes between Stratford and London.

The Stratford/London production was in many respects the best. Inevitably there would be performances containing insights that we didn't have in the original production, and many things which the original production did which have never been done so well again.

I think what I'm saying is, I don't think there's anything specific about that work process which would make this peculiarly difficult to realise. Of course, it is difficult to produce because it's very complicated physically. You've got a lot to do and work out. But there isn't an exclusivism that arises out of the particular way we did Scene 6.

You've played down the notion of what I'd call magic, but at the heart of this play there does seem to be a kind of theatrical magic. The very concept of Pentecost is recreated by the breaking down of language barriers.

Yes, we certainly wanted it to be magical in the sense that we wanted for the characters not to speak in English, but for you to think that they were in a funny way. The fact that you would be dazzled shows how much it clearly worked for you, though it didn't work for everybody! The point about the Tunu speech is that you are suddenly persuaded that you appear to understand more than you think you're going to: it's real magic. I absolutely wanted it to be magical in both that quite literal sense, and a sense that something on human terms was occurring that was unexpected, the result of processes one didn't completely understand.

What do you mean by that?

The model of the play is the Shakespearean Arcadian comedy, in that you have the big shift from a basically urban environment into an Arcadian environment, in which there is either literal magic (as in *A Midsummer Night's*

Dream or *The Tempest*), or the circumstances force characters to behave so unlike themselves (as in dressing up as people of the opposite sex) that it is magical in its effect on others. In this case, instead of shifting from the city to the countryside, what I've done is take an environment which changes its nature very radically. It begins as a place where urban people come to contest a very urban thing – ownership of a painting – and then, just before the interval, it is invaded by the Third World, who turn it into a kind of Arcadia.

My observation of Shakespeare is that the Arcadian element in the comedies is rhymed by an equivalent role of the outdoors in tragedy: the blasted heath, the field of battle, the graveyard in *Hamlet*. Somehow Shakespeare always takes his protagonist outside for the rites of passage to occur: in the case of the comedies, it's usually the rites of passage from childhood to adulthood through to romantic love; in the case of the tragedies it's a preparation for death of some sort. From the moment he leaves Cornwall's castle, King Lear is dying, and coming to terms with it. It's almost as if he's in a zone between life and death. That's true of Timon of Athens, and in a different way of the outdoors in *Macbeth* and *Richard III* and *Hamlet*.

I wanted the shift that takes place just before the Interval to be as dangerous, as big a rupture, as when the location shifts from the court to the countryside in Shakespeare's Arcadian comedies, or between the court and the blasted heath in *King Lear*. By a convenient dramaturgical trick we didn't need a set change because that invaded and transformed the space. Scene 6 echoes the celebrations and festivities found most obviously in *The Winter's Tale*, which occur within the Arcadian space – namely, the party in Act IV of *The Winter's Tale* when Autolycus does his comic turn in the middle of a festive party.

In other respects the structure of *Pentecost* resembles *The Winter's Tale*. The first half is a triangle between two men and a woman, which culminates in a trial in which one man is humiliated and the woman betrayed. There is then a huge shift and a different environment in which festivities of a communal nature take place. Then the two plots come back together again and the second plot solves the problem of the first. Perdita's reappearance solves the problem of Leontes' grief; in the same way, the refugees solve the problem of the painting. So it's actually got the same underlying structure, although I wouldn't claim any other comparisons along the lines of quality or profundity. What was the question again?

I was asking you about idealism in the play.

Oh yes. Now, the meaning of the play is exemplified (and I use the verb with care) in Scene 6. What happened in Scene 6 is that a group of people communicate inadequately, but they go from a situation of not communicating with antagonism to a situation where they're communicating with each other inadequately, but nonetheless quite profoundly. Which is what we were saying about English as a second language: it's not perfect as a means of communication for people who don't speak it as a first language, but it's a great deal better than nothing. It's the way communication actually happens. It's cultures conducting a conversation. That's what the painting's about: a conversation between various influences – Arabic optics and geometry, Byzantine fresco techniques and iconography, the Christian story, and to a certain extent implied Western humanism come together in that work of art. The implication is that that confidence could have inspired Giotto to do what he did. That theory is seen in practice in Scene 6, but what it *isn't* saying is, there is one universal story if we could only find it. It isn't cultural Esperanto: it's not saying, there is one story underlying everything; just find it, and peace, love and beauty will eternal reign (to quote the last line of Nahum Tate's happy ending of *King Lear*). Rather it's saying, there is an inadequate conversation going on, but it is a conversation, and out of it things will come. It's about hybridity and the celebration of hybridity. And yes, that scene contains the play's meaning. Absolutely.

Michael Attenborough

Michael Attenborough

Michael Attenborough is Principal Associate Director at the RSC. He began his career as Associate Director at the Mercury Theatre, Colchester, 1972–74, and went from there to the Leeds Playhouse, 1974–79. During his time there he directed new works by Willy Russell, Alan Bleasdale, James Robson and Arnold Wesker, as well as classics by Chekhov, Shaw and Shakespeare. He has been Associate Director at the Palace Theatre, Watford, 1980–84, and Artistic Director at the Hampstead Theatre, 1984–89. Since 1989 he has been with the RSC.

I visited Attenborough at his office in Stratford-on-Avon, 28 April 1998, to discuss his role in the first production of *Pentecost*. Our conversation covered general issues related to the director's task, as well as his contribution to the final version of Act Two, Scene 6.

Interview

Duncan Wu: *Did you see the printed text of* Pentecost *after the production had already opened?*

Michael Attenborough: Yes – it wasn't actually printed until we came to London. When we started rehearsals there was a whole scene yet to be written which David probably told you about.[1] The text was so mutable at that point that it would have been impossible to try and get a printed text out for the first performance. Instead we used the rehearsal and pre-rehearsal periods to shape the text, and it went into print for the London run.[2]

What sort of changes did you make to the play?

---

[1] Scene 6, which is discussed in detail later on.
[2] *Pentecost* was first performed at The Other Place, Stratford, 12 October 1994, and opened at the Young Vic, London, 31 May 1995.

They were mainly cuts, but the biggest change was that Antonio's story[3] was completely different. In the Stratford production it was a story about a panther, and in London it became a story about cannibals in the jungle.

That's right, cooking the two white men!

Much to Nigel's[4] chagrin; he loved his panther story and was a bit sad to lose it. But it was a trifle flabby, rather cosy, and David and I were worried that there was an air of sentimentality creeping into the whole of that scene. If such a politicised figure as Antonio was going to tell a story in that context, it had to be one that maintained the tension between the captors and the hostages. That's why we changed the story.

That's really interesting – one of the things that came out of my talk with David was his observation of what he described as a 'power shift' away from him while working on Scene 6 (not written when you began rehearsals), insofar as, to some extent, it evolved out of improvisations with the actors. When you make that kind of decision about changing someone's story, is that a factor that you have to think about even at that very late stage? Or was that a fairly straightforward alteration to make?

I think it's a very simple pragmatic problem: by the time you get in front of an audience, if you've done your job properly, every actor has a reason for what he's doing, and the whole experience links together. With any luck, the production is seamless. If you whip something away, it's a bit like taking a peg off the mountainside that you're asking them to climb; you try and reassure them that you're putting a different peg in there which will hold them just as firmly – but it doesn't feel like that to begin with. We did have the freedom (thank goodness!) of another rehearsal period when we took *Pentecost* to London, because I had to re-work it. After all, the Young Vic is a very different performing area from The Other Place. More crucially, there were changes – both to text and cast. There was a new Anna Jedlikova, a new Fatima, and one or two other new actors. So that automatically threw up a series of consequential alterations.

Once we'd opened in Stratford, and watched the run, and identified what we thought worked and what we thought didn't, we sat down and made a shopping-list of things we wanted to change. David then went away and worked on them, and brought them back to me. We looked through them, refined them, and then gave them to the cast at the re-rehearsal stage for London.

---

[3] Scene 6; *Pentecost*, p. 85.
[4] Nigel Clauzel, who played Antonio.

It's very important that you don't let a cast know you're going to do that until they've finished performing, otherwise you dismantle their confidence. It's not easy; I mean, making a change in rehearsal is twenty times easier because they haven't gone so far with the process, and therefore aren't so wedded to what they're doing.

One of the things that was weird about not having written Scene 6 was knowing that in a finite rehearsal period you had to reserve a period of time, in the very final lap, that would have to be devoted to a scene you'd never seen before. And therefore you'd have to take your eye off everything else simply because there are only so many hours in the day. So there we were with the rest of the play virtually at performance standard, and we sat down ten days before we opened and read a new scene! No one had yet learnt the lines; there were bits in foreign languages (which, as you can imagine, is *incredibly* hard to master quickly); and so forth. David sensibly kept the complexities to a minimum, but it was necessary to edit what he had written. One of the qualities of his writing is that he often deliberately overwrites. So you can absolutely bet your bottom dollar that when he hands you a piece of script he expects it to end up with the blue pencil going through sections – cuts, indeed, usually initiated by him. I remember one large section of the first draft of Scene 6 featuring a minor character who had hardly said a word – a very shy, nervous Russian lady (the actress who played Anna Jedlikova doubling) and another character. She suddenly got intimately involved in this last section of this scene, and we ended up cutting the whole exchange. I thought this actress would be mortified but in fact she wasn't at all, she was quite happy to see it go. There we were, a week away from opening, working on a new scene, chopping bits out of it!

What I'm saying is that at that stage you can actually be quite savage; if you want to make equally savage alterations in performance, that's much harder.

Can I go back for a moment to a very basic, fundamental question? I'm just wondering how you'd describe the process of direction to someone who didn't know very much about it, who wanted to know more about your part in the putting on of this play.

I suppose the thing people don't understand is the scale of responsibility. Everything, absolutely everything, is my responsibility. If a prop is wrong, if a costume doesn't look right, if a performance isn't happening correctly, if a lighting cue looks ridiculous – whatever – it's my responsibility, and I wouldn't have it any other way, speaking personally. It's very difficult in any walk of life (and certainly in artistic terms) to have *partial* responsibility for something, and the hallmark of the director's job is to take complete responsibility. In a theatrical production, everything impinges on everything else;

only if something's wrong would a director, for some curious reason, have partial responsibility. When I started as a director, I was occasionally disenfranchised (if that's the word), if I felt a particular actor was beyond my reach, or if I worked with a designer who would stubbornly go his or her way. That happened only rarely, and wouldn't happen now, because (a) I'm obviously older, wiser, more experienced, and probably tougher; and (b) I wouldn't choose those people; I choose very carefully who I work with.

It's a very odd feeling when you have an element in your show which you don't really feel is under your influence. It's nothing to do with power, it's simply to do with the desire that everything should meld and co-ordinate.

So that would be my account of the director's job. It's all down to me: everything that you look at and listen to on that stage is my responsibility. That said, one has to relate that to the strange moment in the director's life when you cut the umbilical cord and walk away. And there's always a ridiculous part of you that thinks, 'How can I walk away? The show will stop!' And of course it doesn't, thank God!

For that moment to happen, and happen creatively, everything on that stage has to have a life independent of you. Most particularly in relation to the actors. It's no use an actor doing something simply because you've asked them to do it. They have to understand *why* they're doing it, and, more crucially, make it their own.

So I would say that the first part of the job is to take responsibility for the whole. The second is to know how to release the creative energies of other people.

One of the aspects of your job that I must say intrigues me a great deal, is the part of it by which you're obliged to interact with a writer. Would I be right in thinking that you are (and in the case of Pentecost, *were) a* collaborator *with the writer?*

Enormously. Since taking over Hampstead in 1984,[5] I've worked almost exclusively on new plays. In fact the Shakespeare I directed here last year was only my second in eighteen years – which shows how rarely I touch the classics! I tend to feel that if I can't collaborate with a writer I'm not the right director for the job. I once worked with a writer who's very talented but whom I didn't feel really collaborated with *me*; this particular playwright was probably happiest when there was conflict – if you suggested a change it was like taking a scalpel to their baby! I can't work like that. Initially, theatre is a series of practical issues. In the end, something happens on stage which transcends that; something like a spirit rises out of the theatrical event which just sweeps everybody along. But you can't get to that stage until you've made a series of fundamental, creative, practical decisions. This section of the play

---

[5] Attenborough was Artistic Director of the Hampstead Theatre 1984–89.

is too long, this section unclear, it needs that kind of set, this kind of cast, or whatever: they're practical decisions. If you can't collaborate, making those practical decisions, I don't think you get to the higher plane, you don't get to that subsequent transcendent stage. The vast majority of the writers with whom I've worked have been fantastically collaborative. I really enjoy collaboration. I have ideas about how it should happen – do you want me to talk a bit about that?

Please do.

On the whole good writers enjoy it too. As long as they know you respect and are truly committed to their play, they'll let you suggest anything. *Pentecost* was actually commissioned by the Royal National Theatre – I don't know whether David told you?

He did mention it.[6]

We were old mates from Hampstead, and were meeting for lunch. Well, he rang me about twenty-four hours beforehand and said, 'Before we meet, could you just have a look at a play I've written? Because I'd love to know what you think of it.' And he sent me this work the size of *War and Peace*! He arrived for lunch and I'd already got a bottle of wine, and I said, 'Have a glass. This is to toast your wonderful play; I would walk across broken glass – (a) to have it done at the RSC; and (b) to direct it.' His face lit up, because he'd just devoted two years of his life to this play.

Once that moment had happened, I could say anything about it (within reason). Because he knew that I loved his play. We fairly hacked into it. He probably told you that we did a reading up in Stratford with a group of actors who, by definition, were the one set of people in England who couldn't possibly be in it, because they would be performing with our company in London – a very good company they were too. It was very instructive, and on the basis of that reading we eliminated a whole sub-plot from the play.

I try to sort out as much of the text as I can pre-rehearsal, because I don't like rewriting during rehearsal. With someone who writes as much as David does, you have no choice but to rewrite some during rehearsal, because he'll only chop away a certain amount beforehand. He adheres to the view (which I support) that, having cut or changed as much as he can, he has to hear and see it performed before he does any more. He has to have the chance to hear what works and what doesn't. And I understand that. He's putting it into a sort of laboratory situation in rehearsal. Some writers aren't like that, but most

[6] See p. 137.

will get to a point when they say, 'You may be right, that section may be too long, but let me hear it.'

Can I ask a question about this? You talk about rewriting – would you actually pencil in a line yourself and take it to David for his approval?

No, I think that's fatal. It's a bit like getting an actor to do something a particular way by saying the line for them. They feel immediately subverted.

So how would you go about it? Would you say take a section, a piece of dialogue, and go to David and say –

And say, 'I think the problem here is "x"'. And I may well suggest a possible solution; he might be grateful for one. Sometimes, when you present the solution, you clarify the problem; and while he may not accept your solution, he will understand better what the problem is. He may say, 'I know what you're getting at, but I don't like your solution, I'll find a better one.'

Very occasionally I have said, 'Look, what about this line instead of that line?' Frankly, that's not a process I enjoy. Sometimes you do get into a situation in rehearsal when something's not clear. So we'll sit down and talk to the writer about it, and perhaps three or four people will suggest alternatives – 'What about if we said this, or that?' I have a rule that, unless a solution is found quickly, I say, 'Let's stop this now, we cannot write by committee, and it's not fair on the writer to expect him or her to come up with an instant solution. So let's explain the problem, they'll come back to us later, and they'll have a much more elegant solution to the problem than we'll ever be able to cook up.' Plays written by committee are fatal.

I try and sort out as much of the text as I can before I go into rehearsal because I think we've got other things to do in rehearsal which are more pressing. But inevitably you still find yourself doing it. I like to take writers with me, particularly if they're that way inclined, through all the pre-rehearsal stages – like casting and design. David's especially interested in that process; for example, he likes to be consulted on who the lighting designer is. He's been in the theatre for as long as I have, and he's got views. Sometimes you have to convince him of your own opinions. For instance, he didn't really know my designer terribly well, and now he's a complete fan!

The lighting in the production was beautifully done.

Thank you. I like to take writers with me, if for no other reason than that if they were party to the initial decision and it doesn't work out in the end at least they were complicit in it! I enjoy that dialogue; I'm happy for writers to come to as many auditions as they want to.

However, I'm a great believer in the view that a writer should also go away for a period of rehearsals. For two reasons: firstly, because I think it releases the actors. Most writers (and this is a sweeping generalisation) in my view are not terribly interested in process; they are interested in results. Sometimes a process entails being utterly perverse with the text. Not necessarily intentionally, but sometimes you know that the way in which a particular actor (or actors) are trying a scene is probably the precise opposite of the way it should be done. But you think, 'I am going to let them pursue this, just to find out how wrong it is. So they will then embrace what's right, fully understanding the trap of doing it the other way.' That's agony for a writer, who might think, 'Why are they doing it like that? It's so obvious! It should be like this!' I think actors sense that and can be inhibited by it, so I tend to like writers to go away for a while. The second is that they shouldn't really be party to the whole process if they're to retain their objectivity in their assessment of the result. What can often happen is that you like a result because the process of getting there was so exciting – but an exciting process doesn't *necessarily* mean the right result. It can sometimes be useful for a writer to come in and say, 'Why is that actor not doing this, or that?' And you say, 'Because we arrived at it through this particular process.' And they reply, 'Your process may have been thorough, but all I'm telling you is, what I'm looking at doesn't work!' So I appreciate their objectivity, and I like their surprise as well – the fact that they will also come in and say, 'I hadn't envisaged that scene in that way but I absolutely prefer it.'

Perhaps we could turn now from general principles to Scene 6, which as we've observed was unwritten when you began rehearsals and evolved out of a collaborative process between David and the company. What did you know about it before you began work on it?

Well it was clear from the start that the scene would have to deal with some thematic issues that were central to *Pentecost*. It would need to investigate topics related to language. The way in which cultures can overlap and cross-fertilise. Basically, what they improvised was storytelling, and means of communication. We were just waiting for that moment when David would say 'Okay, I've got enough in my head. Now I'll go away and write the scene.' Of course, one of the difficult things about this (and you have to break it to the actors) is that what comes back is not their scene. They *think* they have created it – and of course they feel proprietorial to a degree – but what they did was *enable* David to write it, and it is *his* scene. And there was, to a degree, an element of 'But when we improvised we did this, this and this'; and he had to say, 'Yes you did, but that isn't how I've written it; I've written it differently.' He had to be very sensitive to that, as indeed he was.

When he made changes he explained why he had made them, but finally it was not open to discussion. He was saying, 'That is how I want my play. That's the text I want.'

But he approached changes to Scene 6 slightly differently, because he was aware that they had participated in its creation. I thought he did so with great tact and respect.

Once he brought it back to you, did you then take the text over?

Yes.

That must have been quite a challenge given that there had been a gap there, and that you now had to make it connect with the end of Scene 5 and the beginning of 7.

Actually what I did was very instructive. My initial instinct was that, since Clarissa[7] had worked so closely with David and the cast on the improvisations, the best thing to do would be to get her to rehearse the scene. In this way, we would be inverting the relationship we had everywhere else – that is, I was the director and she would come and have a word in my ear if she had an idea about something. She was my assistant, in effect. I suggested to her, 'Let's reverse this process: *you* rehearse the scene and I'll hover over *your* shoulder.'

Well, after just half a session it was clear that it was not going to work. This was nothing to do with Clarissa's ability. It was that we now had a text, and it had become essential for us to make a clean break from the process that had enabled us to reach this point. The moment we put it into production it had to be me doing the work – as it had been elsewhere.

An added advantage was that I in no way deferred to what had happened in the improvisations because on the whole I hadn't been there (as I'd been simultaneously rehearsing the first half).

What happens in Scene 6 is magical. You have a Sinhalese girl telling a story in her native tongue, which gradually becomes comprehensible even though nobody in the audience speaks the language! How do you approach something like that? I ask because the text as printed is terribly inscrutable,[8] and I think it would be hard to stage if one hadn't first seen your production.

Well, the point about those stories is what they share in common. And we tried to use the physicality of the storytelling – that is, non-linguistic narrative techniques – as the central means by which the tales are told. What Tunu is

---

[7] Clarissa Brown, credited as Research and Production Associate.
[8] See p. 112.

doing is telling her story by means of various physical signals and elements of other peoples' stories that we've already seen. She brings them together, showing that they all apply to her story. Thusitha[9] and I worked on her story with Emma Rice – a very skilled woman who came in and helped us with movement, the physical nuts and bolts of the storytelling process. We took every single gesture that Thusitha would have to use in her story, and introduced them earlier in the scene. All the gestures used in Tunu's story have been seen *prior* to the relation of her narrative. So Tunu herself was using what she'd seen. Do you see what I mean?

That's very clever, and as someone who saw the play several times I have to admit that I didn't notice that.

It was very difficult – and not just physically. The story itself wasn't particularly clear. On several occasions I asked David to simplify it. 'Let's not get over-complex; it's going to be hard enough as it is to make the story clear, without it being a complicated narrative.' So we edited out quite a bit. Also Thusitha had to translate it from English (as David had written it) into Sinhalese. So she had to learn the English, the translation, and the movement, and blend the three in her head – which was very tricky for her.

Everybody in the rehearsal room (although they never, or rarely say it) is aware of a ticking clock. Everyone is aware of it as you draw towards the end of rehearsals. To be working on something like this when the rest of the play is almost at performance pitch, was quite unnerving. You think, 'Is this going to come out like a pig's ear?' Indeed, I think it's true to say that this particular story and that particular scene were different from night to night. Some nights it went like a dream, and others it didn't work so well. And that was the risk we took with it.

Why do you think it varied so much?

Well, sometimes we just didn't perform it as well. You needed to have worked the audience up to such a pitch at the end of Scene 5 that they were with you at the beginning of Scene 6, and so embarked on that strange journey. If they weren't absolutely with you at the end of Scene 5, it was hard to hold on to them through Scene 6; so the success of Scene 6 was dictated, to some extent, by the rest of Act Two.

We often blame audiences too much. But actually the personalities of audiences aren't *that* different, sometimes evenings go better simply because we perform better.

---

[9] Thusitha Jayasundera, who played the part of Tunu.

Scene 6 was very like a relay race; it really was handing the baton over. People had to take responsibility for their section of the scene. It's a very special scene, because it consists of long speeches delivered by successive characters. First it's Grigori and Nico, then Antonio, and then that wonderful character, Amira.[10] It's a relay, and no one could afford to drop the baton.

When actors deliver quick one-liners to each other they *share* the responsibility; they build up an energy, a momentum. But with a series of long speeches, the spotlight is firmly on each character, and if anyone drops the baton, the scene dies. Equally, of course, you need the audience to be good listeners; if they weren't, that created problems too.

Something we did in the Tunu story was to have characters amongst the refugees who found it harder to understand what she was doing, so that one character would explain parts of the story to another – a good way of keeping the audience enlightened. That was fair enough; there were bits of the story she needed help with. If we had managed to do the entire thing in mime, I don't think it would have been believable – rather too 'clever'.

Well it worked beautifully on the occasions I saw it – as well as one could have imagined. Of course, there's something inherently undramatic about Scene 6; the stories are fascinating, but there's not an awful lot happening on stage. And yet Tunu's story was one of those special moments in the theatre where something very strange happened, something that happens only in the theatre. I'm thinking of David Hare's observation that theatre's the closest thing there is to religious communion in a secular society.

I think that Scene 6 is particularly interesting because it almost threatens to unbalance the entire play, structurally. From the moment the refugees arrive the play becomes a kind of thriller – it could be a movie – it *is* a hostage drama. And yet, for both the friction of ideas and the atmosphere of Scene 6 to work, you have to take a detour from that for a while. That's quite tough, both for an audience and, more particularly, for the actors – because a situation of immense tension has to be established through a series of well-understood dramatic rules. By rules I mean such things as the fact that hostages can't move in a particular way or they'll get shot. In other words, there are certain naturalistic rules as to how people behave. Inevitably, there were stretches during which it was necessary for us to believe that the hostage-takers had taken their eyes off the hostages. Actors would ask, 'Why have I allowed him to stand up and say that?' It was a question of finding the right balance, you had to allow a degree of flexibility because that *would* happen

---

[10] All the characters mentioned here are refugees – captors, in terms of the dramatic situation. Grigori and Nico were played by Sean O'Callaghan and Steven Elliott; Antonio by Nigel Clauzel; and Amira by Catherine Kanter.

in life. Of course, in a one-and-a-half hour movie you can't afford to let a frame go out of tension, but in life things don't work quite like that. In life we *do* relax a bit, and David would tell you that the nature of most hostage situations is that fascinating and developing relationship between the hostage-taker and the captive. That was one of the things he wanted to explore – and, while we didn't want to sentimentalise it, one of the most compelling elements of Scene 6 is how the Western Europeans (the hostages) begin to get more and more involved with their captors.

One of the interesting things about David's writing is that you could argue that, although he has a very distinctive voice, the architecture of his plays is *relatively* conventional. He follows surveyors' rules. He isn't, in formal terms, a groundbreaker – though, as I say, he is incredibly distinctive. For all that, there are times when he takes big risks. He has a kind of inquisitive desire to see whether he can make something work. He loves challenges. Having worked with him now on two plays – particularly *Pentecost* – I would say that you have to be rigorous about making sure that you take the audience through every complex step he takes (and his texts are more complex than any other contemporary ones I've worked on), but you have equally to be wary of rationalising him out of existence. What I mean by that is that, because he deals with ideas, you could be fooled into regarding him as a highly rational writer. But for much of the time he works on an instinctive basis, a suggestive basis, even when dealing with intellectual notions. In one's desire to clarify the concepts in the play, both for actors and audience, one must be careful not to over-explain him, and so lose that sense of suggestion and implication and mood. For example, one would be tempted to over-explain the last scene – even the last twenty lines.[11] And sometimes you just have to leave those things open and let them sit. Do you understand what I mean by that?

You're warning against the directorial temptation of providing too many signposts to the audience.

On almost every page of his script there'll be three or four things that will make you think, 'I wonder if that's clear to an audience? Is it clear? Is it interesting? Is it dramatic?' All the questions that you *always* ask yourself as Director, but particularly with David's work. Such anxieties can get you into a mode of directing in which you almost *over*-explain it – and sometimes he is a much more risk-taking writer than you would expect. In terms of form you have to allow him to take those risks. Of course, if you think the risk is not paying off you have to say so.

---

[11] Attenborough refers to the exchange between Gabriella and Leo in the closing moments of the play (*Pentecost*, pp. 104–5).

So you as Director would take a step back from the desire to give an explanation to the audience?

I work in painstaking detail, and that sometimes prevents one from seeing the work as a whole. One of the fascinating things that happens when you run a play for the first time is that a whole series of things that you thought were obscure become clear, and things that you assumed were obvious are dimmed. By that, I mean that the play has a cumulative effect – not just intellectually, but emotionally. So that there are certain things you don't need to explain, because actually something bigger is happening, or something else takes care of what you thought was the problem. And then other problems arise. So as you rehearse, you have to discipline yourself to say, 'Let's step right back, let's stop picking away at it, and let's just run it, two or three times if necessary, just to see what might be the *cumulative* effect of this scene, or this section, or this character.' Rather than, moment by moment, thinking about it close up, in minute detail.

It's interesting that you pick the final scene as a point where the audience might expect explanations, but perhaps it's more appropriate not to. After all, it's one of the most impressive pieces of pure theatre I've ever seen, and leaves the audience in a state of shock. You talk about the cumulative effect of a piece of theatre. Is that something you have in your head from the time you first read the play to the end, or is it something you become aware of as you go along?

I think it's both. Actually, I don't think you should ever direct a play unless you have a 'hunch' as to how it would work. The reason why it's a hunch is that you can't quite articulate it, but you have this sense in the back of your mind of the kind of event that you want and expect it to be. If you don't have that you really are walking in the dark. You can articulate that hunch to a degree, but you can't *over*-articulate it, because you have to let the play take you by surprise. And that's what I suppose I mean by just pulling back and letting things cook – finding that the mixture, the recipe, is producing a taste you didn't quite expect. You've put the ingredients in but the final taste is slightly different. It's what I was saying earlier – it's a matter of solving practical problems and then, having put that brew together, letting it just roll and see what happens, because if you *over*-engineer it, *over*-control it, you could reduce it. In any good production, in my experience, there's a wonderful moment where things just take off in a way you hadn't expected. And that is *so* exciting, and you hope that the whole play will do that in the end.

Certainly, with a 2 hour 50 minute dramatic story behind it, the final ten minutes of *Pentecost* should have tremendous emotional and intellectual power behind them. Almost everything on the set has an emblematic value to it; any given prop has a history; even certain words have resonances they didn't have before. If you over-explained all that, you'd strip it of its magic, and if you *under*-explained it, became *too* allusive, you'd risk leaving the audience behind. So it's a very delicate balance, not least because the margin for error is slightly different for each person in the audience. Some people are more with you than others.

I think David's a fascinating writer because people think of him as the great rationalist, the great intellectual – and he *is* formidable. But don't be fooled: there's another dimension to his writing as well.

Actually, the inspiration for Scene 6 was an event in his own home, I think it was at a New Year's Eve party. He said, 'It sounds incredibly soppy to relate, but at this party we were all sharing stories and singing songs, and somehow we almost lost ourselves in time – and had this *fantastic* experience together.' And he had a hunch that that was possible to recreate within this completely different context. When he told me this, I said, 'Don't tell me any more about it, I don't want to be burdened with trying to replicate something that happened in your life at which I wasn't present anyway. I have to just work with what I've got.' The point is that a director has sometimes to trust that the souffle will rise without constantly trying to inflate it.

You're talking about something I find fascinating: it's that element that keeps me going to the theatre. It's the thing that, for me at least, enables the dramatic experience to transcend any other. It's very hard to describe in words; 'transcendence' and 'metaphysical' don't do it justice. But it's related to the fact that the audience occupies the same physical space as the performers, and engages emotionally and psychically, and in other intangible ways, in a shared experience. The thing is, that experience, however one describes it, is exhilarating in a way that is unique to the form. And that, I suppose, is why the practicalities fascinate me as much as the ideas behind a play.

What I want to ask is this. When you first read a play – I mean any play, not just this one – is that something you're looking out for, is it something you want to find? Or is it something you don't want to see?

I would say that it is actually to do with the hunch that I was talking about. I have to turn the final page of the script and have a hunch, a feeling in my guts, that I know what sort of an event it will be. You can sometimes read a play and admire it, but not have that hunch, in which case you should hand it to another director. But if you read a play and admire it *and* have that hunch, it's as if an irresistible urge to create that event is instinctively in your head. I always had a very clear hunch as to what I wanted *Pentecost* to be like; even in its massive five-hour version I had a sense of where its power would be, what sort of power it would have. And I think if you don't have that, you shouldn't really embark on it.

How would you talk about that impact that Pentecost *ultimately has at the very end?*

Basically, what excited me about the play was the convergence of race – that's what inspired me most. I mean, the art history is fascinating and, indeed, the whole question of the demolition of the eastern borders of Europe – that too is fascinating. But in a sense it's all political detail, if you like. In terms of how the dramatic temperature would be raised, *Pentecost* was to do with the clash (or otherwise) of people from different lands and different cultures and different languages: that was what I found absolutely fascinating. And as these characters came together, both in unity and in conflict, I hoped that cumulatively the temperature in the theatre would be very high. I can't put it any other way. I knew it would be very loaded. Because the play would have taken the audience on a journey the like of which they had never had before. And therefore the audience would – you know, on a Wednesday, or a Thursday or a Friday, whenever – on that day, at that moment, *possess* that journey. They would be *part* of that journey. They would be integral to it. You can run a film and if the cinema empties it'll still keep running; if a theatre empties then we all go home and get an early dinner. What I'm saying is: we *share* the theatrical experience, whatever it may be, with an audience. And I thought the whole cumulative effect of what those people went through could be – and should be – very powerful. And on the whole it was.

One of the finest moments in the Stratford production was provided by the actress who played Anna Jedlikova.[12] She was deeply moving at the end. I have in mind the speech on the last page, which begins: 'Look. I know how it appear. What happen in this country since great turnaround.'[13] When she looked at the devastation and the destruction of the fresco caused by the commandoes and said, 'It is, apparently, the weakest wall', people were so affected. There was another great moment, when the Catholic priest, Father Karolyi, entered as the naked Christ.[14] There were many extraordinary moments in the play – like the arrival of the refugees.[15] But Jedlikova's speech in that last scene was where everything was stacked up behind it.

I'll give you another example, a practical example, of where you work in detail and something takes off. I remember working for something like three hours, a whole morning, on the section between the arrival of the refugees and the end of the first half,[16] and it was *incredibly* difficult. Suddenly you've got twelve new characters bursting in, their physical lives taking over this

---

[12] This part was played in the Stratford production by Janice McKenzie.
[13] *Pentecost*, p. 104.
[14] Act Two, Scene 7 (*Pentecost*, p. 90).
[15] Act One, Scene 4 (*Pentecost*, p. 48).
[16] Attenborough refers to a section of four pages in the published text; see *Pentecost*, pp. 48–52.

new space, barking orders in different languages, taking the art experts hostage, locking the door, setting up home quickly – and I had to work on this in immense detail. And I remember, having reached the end of the first half for the first time, having given some shape to it, I said, 'Okay, let's try running it.' I couldn't *believe* how short it was. It was something like two and a half minutes. I had spent a whole morning on two and a half minutes! But the *pleasure* was in all those little details, seeing them come together to make a whole scene.

It's a bit like when you look at an impressionist, or pointillist painting. You look at it closely, and it doesn't make any sense at all; but when you step back, all those little details suddenly make sense as a whole. That's what it feels like. You have to keep your nerve, you have to keep saying, 'Let's sort this little detail out because in the big scheme of things it's going to be crucial. If I skip this, if I muddy this, or skate past it, it will show.' And so you hopefully get all those little details right, and you run it, and what you get is something much bigger than anything you could have imagined. When you do run, you can't say, 'Now this has got to be *really* exciting.' It just becomes exciting, and then the actors find that inspiring. It's a fusion of the practical and the non-practical.

Even something as simple as safety comes into it. If people are running in, hurling oil cans around, running up and down steps to a platform, pushing people over, wrestling with them – all these things have to be done carefully for safety. It's as if you were winding film through the projector, very, very slowly, just to check that everything's right. If it isn't, you've got to stop the action and sort it out. So that when things are *really* motoring and the adrenaline is high, people are still safe.

That must have been a real worry with the final scene!

Very worrying. I mean, what happened to those great chunks of rock had to be done very very carefully.[17]

Just to take a step back – was that all in place by the time you were able to slot Scene 6 in? Did you know pretty well what was going on in the last couple of scenes? Was that all worked out?

You mean, had we rehearsed it?

Right. Am I right in thinking that all the play was pretty much in place while Scene 6 was still in preparation? Still evolving?

---

[17] Attenborough refers to the partial demolition of the back wall of the set; see *Pentecost*, p. 101.

Had to be. Because I knew we'd need time to spend on Scene 6. Having said that, you learn a phenomenal amount from running the whole play, and we couldn't do that until we had Scene 6 in place. So there were still big journeys to be undertaken, but the elements were fundamentally there.

The atmosphere in The Other Place[18] was most extraordinary during performances. People were very affected by it when it transferred to the Young Vic in London – but that was a much more epic space. In The Other Place it was just extraordinary: I mean, this tiny space was housing this *massive* play. You felt sometimes that there were more people on the stage than in the audience (of course there weren't!) – people would be sitting on the front row and the hostages would be right by their feet. That was something we knew would happen. We debated for a long time, David and I, about whether we should do the play in The Other Place or The Swan,[19] and for better or for worse we decided that we should do it in The Other Place because we felt that there was something safe about The Swan – and the one thing I didn't want this play to be was safe. I wanted it to be dangerous and rough, and I don't regret that decision. The only thing that I do regret is that a new play of such ambition and scale wasn't seen on one of our bigger stages. I think that's a shame for the RSC and for David – but artistically I think it was better off in The Other Place.

What advice would you give to anyone who is intending to direct this play?

Of all the plays I've ever directed, it's the one I would least like to pick up and direct after the first production, because, as you so rightly said, there are no two ways about it: there's a lot that you simply can't write down. And, to be absolutely frank about it, I was also phenomenally dependent upon David's meticulous research. He came with newspapers, videos, articles, photocopies – you name it, there it all was. We probably wouldn't have had so much time for that in a three- or four-week rehearsal period, but in a seven-week period you *must* make the time. Now, if I was in a conventional four-week rehearsal period, and somebody said, 'Well, there you are, do this play', my feeling would be, 'My God, there's a mountain behind this play that I just don't know about.' Funnily enough, I've just been in New York and a friend of mine out there has been asked to be Dramaturge on the play for an American production –

What's a dramaturge?

---

[18] Studio space in the Royal Shakespeare Company's complex of theatres at Stratford-on-Avon.
[19] Medium-sized theatre at Stratford-on-Avon, modelled on Elizabethan theatres.

It's like a literary manager – it's a word they use almost exclusively on the continent, but we use it very rarely here. The nearest thing we have to it in the RSC is our literary manager. Every German theatre has a dramaturge. They basically play-doctor; they're like script editors, and will do everything from research into the text, to finding material for the programme, to sitting around in rehearsal saying 'I don't think that scene works'! We don't tend to have that in this country; here it's simply a two-way conversation between writer and director.

My friend had been appointed Dramaturge to a production of *Pentecost* in America, and she was asking me about it, and I just didn't know where to start. There's such a monumental amount! And if you ask me now, 'How is a fresco painted? How do they do it?', I couldn't tell you in detail. I've forgotten a fair amount of it! I'm sure David hasn't because he has this fantastic ability to retain things, but I would have to go back and remind myself of how the fresco would originally have been painted, and of all those wonderful technical Italian terms, in which I became so fluent, and impressed people at dinner parties! – they've gone from my mind. (*Laughs.*) But you do need to know all that. You simply have to learn.

I think of you and David as having worked so closely on evolving this piece of theatre that, to some extent, it is not creatable again – except perhaps in a very different form. If anybody did attempt to direct it they would either have to have David there, or, if not, they'd have to contribute an awful lot on their own to make it work as a dramatic piece.

That's right. It has of course been done elsewhere. David has seen a couple of productions in America and, I think, one in Australia. Funnily enough, when I was holding auditions for *The Herbal Bed*, which I've just been directing in New York,[20] I auditioned both the guys who played Oliver and Leo in the first American production. And both absolutely loved the play.

The whole question of casting is fascinating, isn't it? That's why I like to take the writer with me – because the casting of a new play is a defining moment in its history. If I decide to cast a particular girl as Juliet, who has a particular quality, I am nudging Juliet in that particular direction for my production, and in twelve months' time my direction will have gone. Irrespective of the success or otherwise of what I've done, someone somewhere else will produce Shakespeare's play again. However, if I'm choosing a particular Leo, that decision will affect whether this play will succeed or not, and whether anybody will *want* to do it in twelve months' time. So it is *much* more crucial for a new play than for a classic. Casting at the RSC is very difficult because you're casting for a company, and not for a play. All the

---

[20] Play by Peter Whelan.

people in this show had to be in other plays – otherwise we'd have a company of 300. We are, after all, a repertoire company. Because they have to be in other plays, you have to find other parts that they will want to accept. The flipside of that coin is that you have to persuade the directors of those other plays to cast the people that you want.

I went through a nightmare casting some of the parts in *Pentecost*. Some of the actors that we wanted didn't want to play the other parts they were being offered; or they weren't right for the parts that other directors were considering them for. As it happens, we wound up with an excellent cast in every respect. Generous-hearted and talented.

David Hare

David Hare, *Amy's View* (1997)

Amy's View **was first performed at the Royal National Theatre's Lyttelton Theatre, 13 June 1997, in a production directed by Richard Eyre. David Hare directed Shaw's** *Heartbreak House* **at the Almeida Theatre, London, in a production that opened on 14 August 1997.**

TOBY: Oh, by the way, the director's not coming.

ESME: Oh really?

TOBY: No, he's changed his mind. He's off angling for a big new musical. So he's not coming.

He has taken off his trousers. He has just a strip of cloth round his middle, barely covering him, and he looks pitiful, like Poor Tom in King Lear. *She pours the rest of the water from the jug over him, and he shivers. She hands the jug to a stage manager. Then they stand together a moment, he blue with cold, she already focused on the task ahead, both of them curiously innocent in the silence.*

ESME: Fair enough then. So we're alone.

The light begins to go down, until it is only on the two of them, glazed, nervous, full of fear.

Suddenly there is the overwhelming sound of a string orchestra and the light goes down to near-blackness. Then they turn towards us, and the curtain goes up.[1]

The play's title suggests that *Amy's View* is about Esme's daughter, Amy; in fact, the protagonist is Esme. By the final moments of the play, she has lost almost everything – her husband, her daughter, her worldly possessions, everything but her livelihood. Even the director of the play in which she is appearing has deserted his cast for more lucrative employment on a musical. Her horizons have narrowed until she is focussed solely on the act of performance: 'Fair enough then. So we're alone.' In the midst of this understanding, on a bare stage, something extraordinary happens. For the purposes of the play in which she is about to appear, it is necessary for her to pour a jug of water over her colleague Toby. He has already been compared, in the stage directions, with Poor Tom in *Lear*, so that intimations

---

[1] *Amy's View*, p. 127.

of loss and tragedy are in the air, resonating with the knowledge of Amy's own sudden, meaningless death.

As she pours the water, Esme performs an act rich in spiritual significance, toward which the entire play seems to have been heading. Within the fiction of the drama it is something that must be repeated night after night, as Toby and Esme prepare to appear in that unnamed West End hit; within *Amy's View* itself, the act is repeated on a daily basis, as those playing Toby and Esme act out their roles. It is repetitive, an important feature of ritualistic behaviour. It is also profoundly nonrational, delivering a shift of vision to the audience that propels the play beyond the realm of the material world.

In the Royal National Theatre production of *Amy's View*, directed by Richard Eyre, the moments following the pouring of water were more striking than the published text would indicate. The action was taken to be immediately behind the curtain of the main stage of the theatre in which the fictional play was about to begin. Esme and Toby thus turned *upstage* (rather than downstage, as the published text indicates) to face the fictive audience, with their backs to us, as the curtain lifted. It comprised layers of silk that rippled out before them, billowing up like some enormous sail, finally lifting up to reveal darkness beyond. As this dream-like image filled the stage of the Lyttelton Theatre, the players walked away from the real audience, into the black. The two figures, dwarfed by the swirling clouds of silk unravelling before them, seemed for a moment to recall those of Adam and Eve as they wandered out of Eden at the end of *Paradise Lost*.

Everything in what is barely a minute of real time is the sum total of the two-hour journey that leads up to it. The four Acts of the play span the years 1979 to 1995. During that period we witness breakdown and disintegration. At the outset, Esme is a confident, successful West End actress, secure enough to dismiss the incompetence of her less able colleagues. She lives near Pangbourne with her mother-in-law, partly on her earnings, partly on the money she has inherited from her husband Bernard. Her daughter Amy has lately taken up with Dominic, and is pregnant by him. The narrative strips Esme of everything, leaving her enslaved to her work. The certain world of the English country house, an idealised place in which everything can be relied on, is progressively undermined, until nothing remains, except two characters alone, on a bare stage, walking into darkness.

'It is only now ... that I realize, almost without noticing, that for some time my subject as a playwright has been faith', Hare has written.[2] That observation was published shortly after my first interview with him, but it underlies the approach I have taken to his work. The tragedy of Esme's story is that the spiritual centre of her life has been in a past that never really existed, one she shared with her husband, and which has led her to abrogate responsibility for living fully in the present. 'Frank is my saviour', she tells Amy, discussing her use of her next-door-neighbour as a financial agent, 'He allows me to ignore all that nonsense. I never

---

[2] *Via Dolorosa*, p. 6.

read any of that stuff myself.'[3] And it licenses her rejection of Dominic, by dint of the fact that he works in television, a medium she regards as vulgar. 'You've never understood', Amy tells her, 'You know that I love him. You never see the man who I love.'[4] Esme's blindness is that of someone who cannot see beyond a set of assumptions rooted in an unreal past.

In an interview dating from 1987, Dennis Potter described nostalgia as

> a very second-order emotion. It's not a real emotion. What nostalgia does is what the realist in a sense does with what is in front of him; the nostalgiac looks at the past and keeps it there, which is what is dangerous about nostalgia, which is why it's a very English disease in a way – inevitable, given our decline, Imperial decline, if you like ...[5]

Esme's disease is nostalgia. It has supplanted everything else in her belief-system, destroying her relationship with her daughter, and precipitating her financial ruin. It is often suggested that Hare's female protagonists are driven, often by some unshakeable ideal or aspiration. In this case, the experience that compels Esme is not attached to a political principle; it is personal, and was, at some point in the past, fresh and vital:

> Life with Bernard wasn't actually spectacular. It wasn't as if we were always in each other's arms. It was just calm. And we laughed at everything. That's all. Nothing crazy. But always with him, I felt whole.[6]

That intensity has gone stale, producing a second-order emotion that at once insulates Esme from the world around her, and prevents her from engaging completely with it. It is a kind of soured, degraded romanticism that, instead of energising her, has left her crippled. The parallel drawn in the final moments of the play with Lear is apposite. Like Shakespeare's king, Esme is deluded. The source of her troubles is a failure to perceive things as they are. And as with Lear, that failure leads her to reject her daughter. The two figures who walk into darkness at the end of Hare's play are not unlike Lear and the Fool on the heath, for Esme has by that time been reduced to much the same level as the destitute king. But for all that, *Amy's View* cannot finally be said to be tragic. There are too many consolations, all of them lightly touched in, but nonetheless present. The act of purification in the final moments is, implicitly, one of absolution; the similarity of the two characters to Adam and Eve refers back to a postlapsarian

---

[3] *Amy's View*, p. 57.
[4] *Amy's View*, p. 72.
[5] Dennis Potter, *Seeing the Blossom: Two Interviews and a Lecture* (London: Faber and Faber, 1994), p. 67.
[6] *Amy's View*, p. 125.

innocence; and the billowing-out of the curtains in the fictional play-within-a-play speaks not of despair but of hope. In fact, that final image, which appeals to the nonrational, is affirmative. It suggests that Esme is in the process of remaking herself, of re-establishing contact with the world about her – and of living according to Amy's view.

I conducted two interviews with David Hare. The first was recorded on 10 July 1997 at his studio in Hampstead. I began by asking about general principles, took a retrospective glance at the shape of his career, and then turned to *Amy's View*. In August 1997 Hare's production of Shaw's *Heartbreak House* opened at the Almeida Theatre, London. As this volume is preoccupied with the practicalities of direction, I wanted to ask him about the experience of working on that play, and spoke to him a second time, on 28 November 1997. His concluding remarks contain valuable observations about *Amy's View*. Hare has written compellingly about his work, most notably in *Writing Left-Handed* (London: Faber and Faber, 1991), *Asking Around: Background to the David Hare Trilogy* ed. Lyn Haill (London: Faber and Faber, 1993), and *Platform Papers 9. David Hare* (London: Royal National Theatre in association with the Almeida Theatre, 1997).

Interview 1

Duncan Wu: *I'd like to begin by asking what function you think theatre performs. Some of your plays take situations that are current and dramatise them. Do you think that it's possible for theatre to actually change the way people think, or to change society? Is theatre an instrument of change?*

David Hare: Well I don't quite take situations that really exist, because I fictionalise them. I don't like documentary drama, I distrust it. Indeed, I can't see the point of reproducing on the stage something which will fail or succeed by its similarity to something which is already in the audience's mind. How can that be creative? To write a play about Kennedy, of which the audience's judgement will be 'Yes, that was like Kennedy' or 'No, that wasn't like Kennedy', seems to me to be completely pointless. We're into the theatre of Madame Tussaud's that way. I'm writing fictional stories which people recognise as belonging to the public domain or their own lives. Now occasionally I've gone too close, I think, and *The Absence of War* plainly did.[1] For some people it was impossible to disentangle the fiction from the real story

---

[1] The third in a trilogy of plays about the state of England in the 1980s and 1990s, *The Absence of War* is based on Hare's observation of the 1992 General Election. The documentary materials he gathered for all three plays are published as *Asking Around: Background to the David Hare Trilogy* (London: Faber and Faber, 1993).

of Neil Kinnock – which is a failing of mine; that is, I hoped that I'd taken it far enough away from Neil Kinnock for it to read principally as fiction, but I obviously didn't take it as far as I'd hoped. So, there's that caveat.

But on the larger question, I suppose that I don't know if it does change the way people think, but the illusion that it does is essential to keep me going. When I work I have to be clear about what the politics of the piece are. It may be that they only become clear to me as I write. But I can always analyse my plays in political terms. Yes, I would hope people might be moved to change sometimes by what they see in my plays.

Is it just people like critics who think that theatre should have a function? Or is it enough to see Anthony Hopkins in Pravda[2] *and go away thinking it was just a wonderful theatrical experience?*

No, I don't think that. I'm not against theatre being entertaining, I'm all for it, but good drama is meant to send your head and your heart spinning. I'll give you a very simple example, and it's not at all a didactic play. There was a wonderful television drama by Trevor Griffiths called *Through the Night*, which was about breast cancer. It was about somebody who goes into a hospital for a biopsy, and wakes up to find that her whole breast has been removed. She doesn't realise she's signed a consent form. And the woman says, 'Why can't the doctor speak to me? Why doesn't the doctor ever explain anything to me?' And Trevor shows that the reason doctors don't speak to patients is because it fills them with a sense of their own inadequacy; given that they're facing mortality, over which they have remarkably little power, doctors hate to talk to patients – not because they hate patients, but they hate their own impotence in the face of death. This is his explanation for that age-old question, 'Why can't a doctor talk to you properly?'

Now to me this was a revelation! It had never occurred to me this was why my doctor couldn't speak to me. When I've been in hospitals I've since seen doctors through the eyes that Trevor gave me. An area of life makes more sense because of a work of art that was made about that area of life. And that is a wonderful thing.

At another trivial level, I was nearly the victim of a street scam in New York where somebody pretended to drop a coin on the floor. Because I'd seen the plays of David Mamet they didn't succeed in their scam, but they would have succeeded if I hadn't! At some very basic level that's what art's doing for you.

It's educating you.

---

[2] *Pravda: A Fleet Street Comedy*, by Hare and Howard Brenton, was first performed at the Olivier Theatre, 2 May 1985. A revised version of the play opened at the same venue on 2 May 1986.

Yes. It is.

Do you feel that you've changed in that view at all, or do you think that's remained pretty constant throughout your career?

Yes, I can see that the *way* in which I've written has changed a great deal. There's a point of view which says that the politics in my plays are now much less overt than they used to be. The earlier plays were written not so much in anger but in scorn; they're written dismissively with a young man's arrogance – they're saying, 'This isn't how we should be living, we should live like this.' I think that the preachiness to which people objected in those earlier plays probably has been replaced by a different tone, but I haven't done that in order to conciliate my critics, I've done it because *I've* changed.

Do you think that one of the elements that has changed you as a writer has been Thatcherism?

Yes. Oh yes. I think you can see quite plainly that all socialist writers of the 1970s were thrown for a loop by Thatcherism – partly because we were arguing for a change which didn't happen. I was one of many socialist writers who wanted society to change in a particular direction. It changed in the opposite direction, and the result was that silence came down – snow-like silence in the early 1980s from socialist writers! I wrote *Plenty* in 1978.[3] Okay, the following years coincided with all sorts of troubles in my own life, but I didn't get together a play about the way in which England had changed until Howard Brenton and I wrote *Pravda* six years later. It took me six years to work out this change of direction! To you, *Pravda* may be a piece of entertainment, but to me it's the play in which we formulate this idea that the man who believes in nothing but who *knows* what he believes in – even if it's nothing – will always conquer people who don't know what they believe. So the journalists who saw the play quite rightly intuited that the villain of the play is not Lambert Le Roux: the villains of the play are the journalists, because the journalists don't organise, the journalists don't fight. Rupert Murdoch can't help being Rupert Murdoch. The culpable people are the people who ought to know better, who fail to fight Rupert Murdoch. Why do they fail to fight? Because, as Lambert Le Roux says, 'You are all weak because you do not know what you believe.' And because they don't know what they believe, they can't organise. Now once one had that analysis, which was about how, when Thatcherism arrived, nobody knew how to respond to it – because liberals actually thought they had values in common and found, in the event, that they didn't – one also had the story of Thatcherism at large. Once you

[3] First performed at the Lyttelton Theatre, 7 April 1978.

know what you're fighting for, then you can fight – and, gradually, as we got towards the end of the 1980s, better work appeared about Thatcherism.

I'm interested in the ways in which Thatcherism changed the way you saw the world. I mean, it obviously led to an analysis on your part of the way in which British society functioned.

Yes. That's the sense in which I am a political writer. Most writers say, 'I don't really know what I'm doing', or, 'I've just got this sense ...', or, 'I can't really explain' – but after the event I sometimes *can* explain. I need to explain to be at peace – and then move on. But the moving on in my case was going to the Synod, which I think is the thing that has released a whole wash of work – that is, the Trilogy,[4] and the three plays that I have since written.[5] Every one of them came out of going to the Synod, and understanding that there were all these people whose job was to clear up the mess of Thatcherism. In other words, instead of railing against the ideology, I suddenly found myself in the company of a whole lot of well-intentioned people – sometimes ridiculous people, people who believed things I didn't believe, but who were more or less saying, 'The mess has been made and we're the poor sods who are going to have to clear it up.' And since they became my subjects I've been a very, very happy writer. They *are* my subject, these people: obviously, Kyra in *Skylight* is a prime example. They're the people who work on the front line – in schools and hospitals and so on.

The damage that was done in Britain in the 1980s was done by intellectuals. It was done by a lot of people in Downing Street who were right-wing intellectuals, who said, 'Oh, wouldn't it be fun if we put into practice this mad monetarist theory, or this welfare dependency theory!' Intellectuals were allowed to run riot in Downing Street, and the poor sods who had to deal with the results of what the intellectuals had done were the people on the ground – the doctors and the nurses and the Police. The Police were the most interesting because they were politicised, and they said to me: 'Margaret Thatcher's created the divisions in society, but it's us, the Police, who have to deal with the practical, day-to-day effect of those divisions.'[6] So you had the most conservative body of men and women in the country who had turned anti-Thatcher because of the results of dealing with the divide between the council estates and the private houses!

---

[4] *Racing Demon, Mumuring Judges* and *The Absence of War.*
[5] *Skylight, The Judas Kiss* and *Amy's View.* Since recording this interview, *The Blue Room* and *Via Dolorosa* have also been produced.
[6] For further detail, see *Asking Around*, pp. 61–117.

How should we regard those characters you've just been mentioning? Characters such as Kyra in Skylight, *like Isobel in* The Secret Rapture?[7] *Should we think of them as having a saint-like quality, a religious quality, a Romantic quality? Are they idealists? Should one think them purely in political terms? Is there a way you verbalise to yourself what those people are and what they represent to you?*

They all represent an honest endeavour to live a good life.

It's as practical as that?

Yes, don't they? Isobel in *The Secret Rapture* is a little bit of an exception, so to speak. But everybody in *Racing Demon* is doing their best. I suppose you could say the Bishop of Southwark's a villain, but he actually has an extremely powerful defence of his point of view, and he is by his own lights doing his best. These are portraits of people who are trying to make sense of a struggle for some sort of good life – not just on behalf of themselves but on behalf of other people on a day-to-day basis. They are people I admire, and I hope my admiration for them comes through.

   You know, when I saw the priests I did *not* want to satirise them. And it makes me very annoyed when people say these plays are about the bankruptcy of institutions: that's absolute nonsense! They're about good people within those institutions trying to make them work in very difficult circumstances – that's not bankruptcy. The Labour Party group in *The Absence of War* are very well-meaning people; they mean well, they want to do good. It's just that in order to do good they have to jump through a ridiculous series of hoops which are not helpful to them.

But is there not an absolutist element to these characters? Am I wrong in thinking that when Kyra speaks in Skylight *about the 'purest kind of love',[8] that there's an absolutist or an idealist element to her?*

No, there is undoubtedly a religious ... well, Romanticism is your subject, isn't it? It's very hard to talk about it!

I'm sorry, I didn't mean to ... It's not a trap!

I can see where you're driving! If you're saying that these characters are charged with values beyond the day-to-day, yes, I think they are – plainly. So, if you say Kyra's idea of the good life has a Romantic and self-sacrificial element to it, it does. I'm proud of the fact that Kyra doesn't get up people's

---

[7] First performed Lyttelton Theatre, 4 October 1988.
[8] See *Skylight*, p. 38.

noses, whereas actors didn't enjoy playing the part of Isobel in *The Secret Rapture*. Everybody who plays Isobel is left unhappy, because they think there's an element of passivity in her, that she just allows herself to be beaten up on. Actors who play the part say you don't feel great at the end of the evening because, basically, everyone's just horrible to you, and then you get shot – and that's not their idea of goodness! Whereas with Kyra I do feel that it's a credible portrait of a much more active kind of goodness. One of the things that pleases me about it is that nobody's ever said to me that that's not what a schoolteacher's daily life is like; no schoolteacher has ever said to me, 'You've got it all wrong.'

Do you think that, when actresses say that to you about Isobel, they're right?

Well, I think that as a playwright you're an idiot not to listen if enough people tell you the same thing over and over again. I mean, I've made a mistake, or whatever, with *Amy's View*. These are very early days, and it takes months to see things clearly, but enough people have said to me that, when Amy says of Dominic to her mother, 'You don't see the good side of him',[9] nor do we, the audience, see the good side of Dominic – for me to know by now that I can't blame that on an imperceptive audience. Plainly there is a problem and I will later do some work on it. Some criticism is what I call apples and oranges criticism, meaning: you make an apple and people complain it isn't an orange. That criticism you can do nothing about. But people who say, 'This is only three-quarters of an apple, because that bit's missing' – those are the ones you should be listening to.

One way of looking at the play is to say it's about a clash between two different attitudes towards culture.

Yes.

Do you feel equally sympathetic towards both views?

I feel very sympathetic to Amy when she says, 'I went with him because he was the future, and I'm frightened of you because you're the past.'[10] To me it is not so much an argument about culture, as an argument about living in the past and living in the present. Dominic is basically someone who says, 'Look around you, this is how things now are; you may not like it, but this is the way what you call culture is now seen in society at large', whereas Esme is someone who's clinging to how culture was seen when she was young, and

[9] 'There's a side of Dominic that you never saw', *Amy's View*, p. 105.
[10] *Amy's View*, p. 109.

for whom culture is a sort of enclave. And indeed, beyond culture, the whole subject of the play is a woman who lives in the past because of an accident of her emotional life – which is that her husband dies when she is thirty-six or thirty-seven, and she is never able to move on. She cannot live in the present, and I think a lot of people in Britain have a great deal of difficulty living in the present, and seeing Britain as it is now, and realising what it is now, rather than the almost fictional idea of what it once was. And so it's that; it's an argument between the present and the past.

Esme is very self-aware in that sense, though.

Yes, oh yes. She makes comments about theme parks and all that stuff.[11]

All that sort of stuff. She says, 'Why invite an actress to open a fete? Because it's fake.'[12]

You see, the only thing she has in her life is her love of her daughter, and that's the thing that tethers her to the ground. And yet, out of what I think is stubbornness, she's truer to an idea of honesty to her daughter at the expense of losing her daughter's closeness, so that she says, 'You're making a mistake, you're going off with the wrong man.' It's more important to her to say that than it is to hold on to her daughter. As a result she loses the one thing that might pull her into the present day. Her life becomes more and more madly rooted in the past as the play goes on.

How does her financial ruin fit into that? Should we see that in some sense as her being ruined by the present?

Yes, it's the thing that she's lived on – what one might call a wing or a prayer, or hope! She's lived on not looking reality in the face. I mean, I didn't think these Lloyd's victims were ridiculous, spoilt people;[13] they seemed to me very moving, in the sense that they did what we all do, which is say, 'Well I don't know what I'm doing here, but it seems to be alright so I'll stick with it!' Now this is what we all do in all areas of our lives. We all have relationships where we say, 'Well, I know that person's in pain but I can't really deal with this at

---

[11] 'Miss Marple! Thatched cottages! "Congratulations to Mr Cox on the size of his enormous courgettes …" It's Heritage England. It's some sort of fantasy theme park, but don't tell me it actually still makes any sense', *Amy's View*, p. 45.

[12] Ibid.

[13] During the late 1980s and early 1990s, record losses bankrupted a number of 'names' – that is, syndicate members of Lloyd's international insurance corporation of London, who do not underwrite personally, but who are represented by underwriting agents. Esme, in *Amy's View*, is one such 'name'.

the moment, so I think I'll just ignore this.' But then we get our comeuppance, to use that wonderful phrase. And so Esme gets hers. Because, after all, you can't just open an envelope full of cash and stick it in the bank and never think about it.[14] You will one day pay for that attitude to life. And yet we're all guilty of that attitude to life in large, aren't we? Or do you not recognise it?

I do, I recognise it very much; what strikes me about it is that it's a very moralistic attitude to have.

Mine, you mean?

Well, yes – it seems quite cruel to say she can't just have the money coming through the letterbox every other week!

What I also am after, which is a subtler thing, and which I'm delighted some people have noted, is that ridiculous arbitrariness about people who we judge by what they are and people who we judge by what they do. Do you remember Amy's line: 'We are what we do'? Now there's a completely double standard most of us have in how we judge actions. So this mother (Esme), who is relentlessly cruel to her daughter about this wrong turn that she believes she has taken in her emotional life by marrying Dominic, is completely forgiving to the man who has financially ruined her! She says, 'Oh, but Frank's such a nice man!' And, not unnaturally, Amy becomes furious and says, 'He's a nice man who's ruined your life', and, 'He may be nice, but it's not who we are, it's what we do.'[15] That's at the centre of the play, that argument about whether we are what we do, or whether there is some essential 'us'. And then, if we *are* what we do, how do we make judgements about each other? All of us have areas that we are ... slippery about. We might say, 'I'm the nice person who left my wife', or, 'I'm the nice person who hit my child – but I'm still basically nice. I just happen to have hit my child.' Well, I'm not sure; I think, maybe, if you hit your child you're not a nice person.

It's very biblical, all this.

Well, there's an Old Testament element here.

Precisely. Is that something of which you're conscious?

---

[14] See *Amy's View*, p. 89.
[15] *Amy's View*, pp. 101–2.

Just as I believe that this whole idea that politics is finished because there aren't two systems any more is nonsense, I don't believe that the death of socialism means that the question of social justice goes away. The debate about how society should be fair will go on forever. People will continue to discuss it in Socratic terms just as it has been discussed for thousands of years. Factions will continue to argue about ideas of justice in society. Just because certain religions have lost their hold, questions of morality about how people should behave – what is right and wrong in behaviour – will not go away. In some way moral discussion about behaviour goes on, and I try to show in my later plays that it goes on in a most curious, confused, emotional, bizarre way – but it goes on. And anyone who says it doesn't just isn't looking and listening. People still judge people, they still judge each other by their private actions. And they still say, about certain things, 'Hang on, it isn't right to do that.' Of course right and wrong can't be codified, there isn't a book we can look at any longer and say, 'John, chapter 3, verse 9, you're not meant to do that' – but the book's in our head.

Are there absolute judgements of right or wrong in your plays, or is it all relative?

Well, plainly I love drawing characters who march to some private drum. The early play of mine I like best by miles and miles, to the exclusion of all others, is *Plenty*, and so I do love that character.[16] It was clear to me that I loved her more than the audience did, and the audience was slightly horrified by her. And yet plainly that's the portrait of a woman who is living by some absolute standard and who is angry at society for not coming up to her standards.

She doesn't come terribly well out of the play, does she? Kate Nelligan herself said that she withdrew her sympathy from her half way through it.[17]

Yes, she did.

It's a very difficult play to watch while trying to feel any kind of sympathy for her; there comes a point where it is very difficult.

Yes. If you say, 'Am I drawn to that?', the answer is yes, I like that. I like watching it and I do, to a degree, admire it in people.

---

[16] Susan Traherne, the protagonist, was played first in London by Kate Nelligan.
[17] 'I stopped admiring the woman. I really wanted to pummel her. I would come to the middle of the second act, and I would just withdraw my consent from that woman. I don't think the audience ever knew, but I was very worried about it' (Kate Nelligan on Susan, as quoted in *File on Hare*, compiled by Malcolm Page (London: Methuen Drama, 1990), p. 44.

To return to Amy's View. *I was interested in the relationship between Amy and Dominic, particularly as it seems comparable to that of Irwin and Isobel in* The Secret Rapture.

Yes, it's better drawn. Again, this is a judgement where you have to listen to what people are telling you. Everyone tells me the film of *The Secret Rapture* doesn't work, and that the play does work – and I assume they're right because enough clever people have told me this is so. In some way the act of violence that Irwin committed against Isobel at the end was theatrically acceptable, and convincing. Nobody ever said, 'I don't believe he'd shoot her.' The audience understood the play retrospectively to be about one of those disastrous relationships, and they knew enough about him; it didn't worry them. When the film came along they just didn't believe it or accept it at all. I didn't quite know what had happened to make it credible in one medium and incredible in another! It set me thinking about the two media, and the difference between what is convincing in one or another. But Irwin was always the least satisfactorily drawn part in *The Secret Rapture*, and that was accentuated by the film, plainly. Dominic is, I think, more multi-faceted. Irwin was nothing but his craving for Isobel, he barely existed beyond it, whereas Dominic hints at all sorts of life away from Amy.

What's wrong with the way he comes in in that last scene with a shoebox full of money?

What's wrong with it? What do you mean?

Well there's obviously something wrong with it, isn't there?

Why?

Well Esme's comment on it, 'Those are my daughter's ashes',[18] is chilling in some way.

Well, all she has left, apart from her love of the theatre, is her refusal to let go of her judgement of Dominic's behaviour, and she feels that if she lets go of that then she truly has nothing. He's saying, basically, 'Why can't we be friends?' – which is what people always say after they've behaved appallingly – and she says, 'We can't because at least I have my hatred of what you did to my daughter, and, if I let go of that, I'll have nothing.' It's just like when you see those terrible people on television who want the murderer of their children to be hanged, and you sense that if they forgave they would just

---

[18] *Amy's View*, p. 126.

crumple because there wouldn't be anything. She has that left, she's reluctant to let go of it. But I hope you sense that she might one day.

Yes, I do. And following on from that, I'm very intrigued by the relation of that conversation to the finale of the play. Those final moments are very moving.[19] Am I right in feeling that it is an act of purification, when they pour the water over each other?

Oh yes. That's the killer.

That does seem to hint not just at the possibility of forgiveness, but also something else.

Oh yes. Someone told me, 'I was absolutely fine until they poured the water!', and then she said, 'Why is it so powerful? Why is it so powerful, the idea of them pouring water over each other?' Because it's what everybody wants in response to the mess that they've made of their lives, isn't it?

In the text of the play you make an explicit comparison with King Lear and the Fool.[20]

Yes. One of the artistic problems of Act Four is the degree to which you do or don't show or hint at the fictional work. Within *Amy's View*, in Act Four, there's this play that's become a West End hit, and so, at a certain point in the first draft, we went into that play-within-a-play. We were planning to go a little bit into it; I wrote the first lines of it, and then we decided to leave it suggested. For the actors' sake I wrote a description of the play – they asked for a description of what this play was, and what it was about, and so I invented this play. They now know what they're playing, but I don't want to tell the audience. It was a matter of getting the right balance of suggestiveness.

On the practical side, Richard[21] was very worried about it seeming to be a director's effect. Because he so rigorously belongs to that school of director who believes that their job is to realise the play, rather than to set it in some flashy diadem that the director has created, he was concerned that it would seem like a piece of directorial show-off, if we'd done everything I wanted – which was a stage full of ropes and shipwrecks. He quite rightly calmed it down to just one or two very powerful images. But *he* did it out of a sense of

---

[19] See *Amy's View*, p. 127. That final stage direction in the printed text gives little clue as to the impact of the image.

[20] Hare's description of Toby, one of the actors: 'He has taken off his trousers. He has just a strip of cloth round his middle, barely covering him, and he looks pitiful, like Poor Tom in *King Lear*' (*Amy's View*, p. 127).

[21] Richard Eyre, the director.

modesty; he didn't want to appear to set himself up as Strehler[22] or Brook or some maestro coming along and doing all this theatrical *woop de woop*.

Can I take that further? In your text the final moments of the play are played upstage, whereas in the production the whole thing is turned round and played downstage.

Yes, it is.

Could I just ask what Richard Eyre's role in all that was – was he the one who suggested it should be played that way?

Yes, he and Bob.[23]

What is your place in all of that, are you party to these discussions?

Yes.

And you are making suggestions as well as you go along?

Well, I think in certain ways Richard is often ahead of me. He never wanted to go into that play (the play-within-the-play). In the first draft, the first line of the play (the last line of *Amy's View*) was, 'Who's there, tell me who's there?' It was the boy, Toby, calling out to Judi[24] to see who'd survived the shipwreck. And Richard said, quite rightly, 'I'm not quite sure how I'm going to do the shipwreck, I'll just leave this for now.' Then, at a run-through I said, 'I don't think we need to go into this shipwreck, you know.' And he said, 'I've been waiting for two months for you to say that.' He was just relieved. He works with writers in the same way as with actors: he prefers you to find your own way there. And he recognises that I'm often very keen on things which have helped me write the play but which turn out not to be necessary to the play in the performance. Many times in the last five or six years I have said, 'Oh, I've just realised we have to cut such-and-such', and he'll say, 'Well, I've been telling you that for three months, why do you not listen when I tell you?' And it's very hard for you to say, 'Well, you don't see the damage something is doing until you really experience it yourself.'

[22] Italian theatre director and actor who was a pre-eminent figure in post-World War II European theatre as co-founder and artistic director (1947–68, 1972–97) of the Piccolo Teatro di Milano, Italy's first important modern regional theatre; founding director (1968–72) of the Gruppo Teatro e Azione; and artistic director (1983–90) of the Paris-based Théâtre de l'Europe.
[23] Bob Crowley, the designer.
[24] Dame Judi Dench, who played Esme.

I do remember discussing with Richard the question, do you think it's a weakness that we only see Dominic from Amy's point of view? And that we never see the relationship with Amy when Esme's not there, except in the first five minutes. I can't remember what we decided but plainly we were wrong.

There's something very Shakespearean about the shipwreck. Is Shakespeare important to you?

Yes, incredibly.

You directed King Lear *just before* The Secret Rapture, *didn't you? Are you specifically preoccupied with Shakespearean tragedy?*

Well, as I've said before, I like him because he puts the events on the stage. The claim of Chekhov seems to me a corrupting one in twentieth-century drama: that is, if you put a group of people in a room, the whole of history will seem to flow through that room through that representative group of people. Shakespeare doesn't say that; Shakespeare says, 'If there's a battle, I'll put the battle on the stage; if two people are in love, I'll put the love scene on the stage; if the court meets, the court will meet on stage.' Chekhov moves the angle of view, and says, 'History flows through this room.' Now Chekhov does it because he's a great writer, but a lot of very lazy playwriting has resulted from his influence, and that's why for years I resisted what Howard and I called 'plays in rooms'. We always wouldn't set plays in rooms, we always set plays in public places, and in fact *Skylight* is the first play of mine that has one set – I've always changed the set, changed the place. The only way I always said life flowed through a stage was by putting life *on* a stage, not reflected *off*. There's a remark of Fiona Shaw's which is very brilliant but with which I *wholly* disagree; she said, 'Theatre works by reflection not by representation.' I believe theatre works by representation not reflection. Showing is what the playwright does, and Shakespeare's the greatest show-er of all; if he wants a mass murder he puts it *on*stage. He does it, and he doesn't brook any challenge to his vision. His theatre is the place where everything happens, not where everything's reflected – and that includes a sense of the heavens (which I love in him), and a sense of the epic of history going by (which I adore). So that we're not just individuals; he shows the whole society here, it's a wonderful thing.

What about the tendency of the dead to come back to life? Dead people seem to come back to life in Shakespeare. I remember, in Howard Davies' first stage production of The Secret Rapture, *the figure of Isobel seemed to appear diaphanously at the rear of the stage. And there's a sense in which Amy goes on being present in the play even after the moment of her death.*

Oh yes. Sure.

Is that something that you take from Shakespeare?

Oh yes, but I wish that Edward Bond and Howard Brenton hadn't done it so brilliantly before me. Ghosts were one of the first things Howard played with in the theatre. In those Portable Theatre[25] days he did a lot of ghost scenes, and Edward Bond did brilliant ghost scenes in those early plays, so unfortunately ghosts have always been knocked out for me. Otherwise I'd be doing them all the time, I'm sure.

Do you believe in ghosts?

No, but I can see that people ... One of the things is, when you get to my age a lot of people die, and people that you hadn't realised were important to you become absolutely crucial to you – and the death which you had not expected to knock you sideways devastates you, and the death of somebody else who you thought you were close to barely turns a hair. There is a curious completion, when death comes and you see who the person was by the story being finished, and by them being completed. If their story is a resonant story, they become incredibly real to you, don't they?

Yes.

And certain friends of mine are with me all the time because their stories are so powerful. The shape of their lives turns out to have been so powerful.

I suppose I keep thinking about the emotional impact of these productions after I've seen them, and I wonder if it's to do with this business of peoples' continuing presences. Amy's view is that you are what you do, and what you leave behind is what you have done, and the relationships in which you've been engaged. And that is what Esme still has at the end of Amy's View; *it's what Marion in* The Secret Rapture *is trying to seize hold of.*

Her tribute to Amy is to try and live as Amy would have wished her to. And she makes that speech at the end of the play, do you remember? She's been in this ridiculous relationship with Frank, who had nothing to offer her except

---

[25] Theatre company co-founded by Hare with Tony Bicât in 1968. Hare resigned as artistic director of the company in 1971, and the company itself was disbanded in 1973.

contingency – the fact that he happened to live next door was his *only* virtue. He's the kind of person who gets into all our lives, and makes you think, 'Why am I spending all this time with this person?' – and you realise it's just because their life happens to have bumped into yours. In Act Three, Amy says, 'Take your life in your hands'; Esme says, 'There's no such thing as taking your life in your hands.' And then, in Act Four, a line I personally find incredibly moving is when she says, 'I did what Amy told me. I decided to take my life in my hands. So I didn't make the ridiculous marriage to Frank, I sold the house, I faced my bankruptcy, I've been sensible about it, I live in a sensible place, I live in the real world as I best can now.'[26] That's what she says.

Yes.

That's the tribute you can pay to the dead, isn't it?

And in that sense I suppose you could say Amy does live on – she lives on in that sense.

That's right. I think that if you say, 'What is the reason that people are emotionally affected by this?' – and I know that they are very affected by these later plays – the answer is because they're full of honest searching. I've got unembarrassed about writing plays in which people are genuinely searching for some meanings to their lives beyond the material. And people are completely astonished, these days, to see work that has that dimension; that treat the real world on its own terms, as if it's completely real.

Why do you think people are astonished?

Because there's so little work like that now.

Why do you think that is?

Because film used to provide the ability to dream and it doesn't any more. The cinema, which used to be a place of dream, is now a place of debased reality; television is no longer stimulating to the imagination in the way it was for years. The stories that society is telling itself are sullen little stories mostly, and that's why the theatre is so important.

What you're saying sounds so much like a defensive Esme; it's a defensive Esme's point of view, isn't it? I happen to agree with what you're saying, I can see exactly

---

[26] Hare refers to a brief exchange between Dominic and Esme, *Amy's View*, p. 119.

what you're saying. Partly what you're talking about is a general cultural debasement, a general lowering of the cultural currency.

Well, I'm reluctant to call it a debasement because I can see that you get these occasional points of light where something wonderful comes along, and you discover that the thirst is as real as it's ever been. The audience still wants the serious stuff, and when the serious stuff appears, a part of the audience still responds to it in exactly the same way. A good play still gets exactly the same quality of response from the audience that's there at the time. It doesn't get written about at the same level of excitement that it was written about in the 1960s. And a good film still moves people in the same way, but there do appear to be fewer of them.

I think this is why, in my rather crude and vulgar way, I've cast you as a Romantic, because you seem to me to be writing about subject-matter that seems to me to be quite old-fashioned.

Yes, it is. I wouldn't use the word 'old-fashioned'; I'd prefer to say that it's eternal. Richard has had to work out what theatre is for in the last ten years because he is the person who has got delegated, on behalf of the whole theatre, to defend the medium itself. It's a ridiculous position! In the Sixties, the theatre was confident enough that we didn't all have to turn to Laurence Olivier, and say, 'Laurence, will you please explain to us why we're still doing this thing?' Now, because there've been so many attacks on the form itself, Richard's had to become spokesman for the defence of the form, and he would say that because it's based on the human figure, and because it's based on something real which is actually happening in front of you, far from making it outdated, that makes it eternal, because people will always gather together for some communal enactment of stories that they recognise. And I think that's true. It'll go through periods where it looks more or less commercially possible, but that's to do with it as a profession. In a way, what the theatre is as a profession is far less important than its ability to feed people's imaginations. And that will never go.

I've been told that if you were to go up to Oxford now, as an undergraduate, you'd find that people are expected to work harder than ever before. It's been turned into a sort of Massachusetts Institute of Technology, or whatever – it's no longer an easy ride academically. But there were 145 productions of plays in a single term in Oxford a year ago. Well, something's going on here. Why do students need to enact fictions to each other? What are they doing? It must come out of some real need. Even if the professional network is enfeebled, the desire to sit in a darkened room and watch each other tell stories doesn't go away.

Do you ever think it's the closest thing to going to church in a secular society?

Well we've been discouraged from thinking this, we've been told it's wrong to think this. But Brian Friel said a wonderful thing when he came to *Racing Demon*; he said, 'To be honest, I spent more time looking at the audience than I did at the stage, because, coming from Ireland, I'd been told that Britain was a secular society. But if Britain's a secular society, why is everyone *drinking in* this play about spiritual questions?'

That's exactly how I felt at the end of Amy's View, *and looked round and saw the audience in tears.*

So what are you saying? Human beings have *not* lost their capacity for wonder or awe or whatever this stuff is; they haven't lost the capacity to be profoundly moved by their own condition. It's just that they're not offered a great deal of the work that does that any more, because they've become blasé. And they've been made blasé by mass media. So there's an attack in *Amy's View* on that degraded work; the work in which death is not death and murder is not murder. You look at the old gangster pictures, and murder's murder, and corpses looked murdered, but now it's aesthetics, isn't it?

Interview 2

Many commentators have rightly drawn attention to the zaniness of Shaw's humour. His playfulness with the form of theatre itself is taken to prefigure the arrival of absurdists like Beckett and Ionesco. But less noticed, it seems, is Shaw's underlying steel. Under the surface of the whole enterprise lies the extraordinary contention that it is not anyone's business to try and be happy; that happiness, indeed, may only be a failure and a lure. Using a method of reversal which is notably Brechtian – strong characters turn out to be weak, rich characters turn out to be poor – Shaw explains with remorseless clarity how easily the wish to enjoy life turns into a hopeless infatuation with dreams. He shows how each of us drifts off from the world into which we are born to dream far too lazily of a world in which things might be different.

David Hare, programme note to *Heartbreak House*[1]

---

[1] The complete text of this note is reprinted in Appendix II, by kind permission of David Hare, pp. 253–5, below.

I was intrigued by your programme note to Heartbreak House,[2] *in which you point out that Shaw uses a Brechtian method of reversal in order to create the feeling of decline and indeed apocalypse. It's towards the end of your programme note, where you're talking about character reversal. You mentioned to me Chekhov last time I spoke to you, and obviously there are Brechtian elements in some of your plays. I was wondering how you see Shaw as fitting into that pantheon of precursors.*

Let me say what I meant by the thing about strong and weak first – strong characters turning out to be weak. Actually, there was a terribly accurate review of this. It's very rarely that a critic writes a review where you actually think, '*Yes*, that is exactly *it.*' John Peter in the *Sunday Times* pointed out that the actors and director have taken a very high-risk strategy with this play, which is to pretend that it *isn't* Victorian and rhetorical, but that it's real, psychological, and post-Freudian. Plainly it's actually a pre-Freudian play, but the feeling I had was that Shaw was trying to burst out of conventions of Victorian or Edwardian theatre into a new kind of modern psychological play. It's all about repression, it's all about a family in which nobody can say the truth to each other, and in which the central character, Shotover,[3] has got this mask of behaviour that is all to do with what's being repressed psychologically. I thought the critic was absolutely right. He went on to say that 95 per cent of the play works by the cast actually trying to prove it's a modern play, but certain parts of it just can't work. And he's right again, because certain of them are written for old-fashioned theatrical effect; melodrama and reversal are the bits of the play that won't yield to a truthful psychological approach.

The central example for me, and the most radical treatment of the play in the production (which is also the scene that I thought was most successful), was the scene where Hesione and Hector Hushabye[4] are left alone. It's normally played as a piece of drawing-room romance.[5] She says to him, 'Oh, you really must meet the most attractive women', and he says, 'Oh no, you mustn't do that'; she says, 'You really must be careful or else he's going to fall in love, and you know what happens when you fall in love', and then they get together, and he says, 'You know these women, they flash at me and there's nothing I can do.' And she says, 'Oh well, you know really', and, 'Oh yes, you and I really were frightfully in love.' And it's all normally played as *la de dah*, you know, all that stuff.

---

[2] David Hare directed Shaw's *Heartbreak House* at the Almeida Theatre in a production that opened on 14 August 1997.
[3] Captain Shotover was played in Hare's production by Richard Griffiths.
[4] Played in Hare's production by Penelope Wilton and Peter McEnery.
[5] Hare refers to the exchange in Act I; see Bernard Shaw, *Heartbreak House* (London, 1964), pp. 84–5.

I said that we should try playing this as if it's *Les liaisons dangereuses*, as if they're articulating the very, very deepest feelings in their hearts. And for me the best thing in the production was that bit where Penelope said, 'You and I were frightfully in love with one another, weren't we?',[6] as if it were the most real thing in their lives, and with *no* artificiality or manners – Shavian manner – at all, but completely real. And it proved to me that underneath the conventions of the Edwardian theatre there was a deeply wounded psychological mind at work. That's what appealed to me about it. That's why I really wanted to do it – to prove that. As John Peter says, it doesn't work in the whole play, so for me the burglar scene was particularly difficult, because, if you play the rest of the play as real, at what level of reality is that burglar scene happening?[7] Do you see?

Yes.

That's Brechtian, the burglar scene is Brechtian.

Why do you say that?

Because it's point-making, isn't it? It's political point-making. Outside this circle of comfortable people, here is the smaller fish that's feeding off the bigger fish. It's to make a political point. And then the point about burglary being a racket – it's *The Threepenny Opera* isn't it? It's the whole idea of *The Threepenny Opera*. And Brecht admired Shaw; he said that Shaw's a terrorist, but a terrorist who uses the most unusual weapon – humour.[8] Never a weapon too strong in Brecht's armoury. (*Laughs.*)

Do you feel yourself to have a pantheon of precursors – people like Shaw, Brecht, Chekhov?

When I was young, and Christopher Hampton was adapting Ibsen and Chekhov, I didn't know why he was doing it, and I said to him, 'There's so much to write about in the real world, what on *earth* are you doing with these plays?' Now I do find myself in a dialogue with these writers, and it's happened to me in the last five or six years, and it's partly out of ignorance that I don't actually know the canon terribly well. When I was asked to adapt *Ivanov*, I'd seen it once in my life, thirty years earlier, so I didn't know the

---

[6] 'We were frightfully in love with one another, Hector', p. 84.
[7] Hare refers to the scene in Act Two, pp. 116–21.
[8] 'It should be clear by now that Shaw is a terrorist. The Shavian terror is an unusual one and he employs an unusual weapon – that of humour'; this quotation appeared in the programme of Hare's production.

play.[9] Obviously I'm the junior partner in the dialogue, but nevertheless it is a dialogue based on twenty-five years of my having written plays, and I do want to explore how they solved some of the same problems that I'm interested in. And, obviously, *Amy's View* uses the four-act structure. I don't think I'd have tried to write a four-act play if I hadn't worked on *Ivanov*. The four-act play was the favoured structure of a lot of the writers I most admire.

I know there are things in Chekhov that you reject, that you're not happy with. You point out that the idea of history running through a room is a common theme in Chekhov; I take it that's not something you would try to imitate? Or is it?

Well, this is very, very complicated; I don't know how to talk about these questions because they're *so* complicated. My slight distrust about Chekhov stems from my doubts about whether the scientific method works in the theatre. What I mean by that – and you know more about this than I do – is that *Ivanov* and *The Seagull* are what one might call Romantic plays. They are plays which dramatise a dilemma which is of urgent importance to the person who writes the play. I regard *Ivanov* as the least disguised of Chekhov's works. *He* is there. It's about a man who, at the age of only thirty-five, wants to kill himself, can't see any purpose to life, and feels burnt out at a singularly early age; and it is written by a man who is twenty-six, wants to kill himself, and feels that he's burnt out at a singularly early age. So there is a Romantic iden- tification between the writer and the subject-matter. And the fact that his passion and agony is showing on the stage does not worry the writer. Fair enough, it's there. This is, you might say, a Romantic work of art in that sense, and so is *The Seagull*.

Then he moves to a position which I don't actually believe is achievable in the theatre. I believe Flaubert achieved it in *Madame Bovary*: it is, if you like, scientific absence – the idea that the writer is not present in the work, but that it is presented, as Flaubert would say, medically, almost as a case-history, so that he's *not* there. Now I think *Madame Bovary* is one of the greatest books ever written by this technique of absence. I'm not sure that that is achievable in the theatre, I become impatient with Chekhov deliberately withholding himself in what are called the masterpieces – that is, *The Cherry Orchard*, *The Three Sisters* and, to some extent, *Uncle Vanya* (though much less so in that case – *Vanya*'s transitional). I find those plays irritating, because I long to say, 'Come out from behind the trellis, man, and say what you're thinking!' But he won't, and I think that creates a listlessness in the audience, who know it's

---

[9] Hare discusses his adaptation of Chekhov's *Ivanov* further in *Platform Papers: 9. David Hare*, published by the Royal National Theatre in association with the Almeida Theatre (London, 1997), in his conversation with Michael Ratcliffe (pp. 31–44). His adaptation was first performed at the Almeida Theatre, London, 7 February 1997, and is published by Methuen.

been written by someone, and yet can't understand why that someone doesn't want to show his hand on the stage. Do you know what I'm talking about?

I think so. You're saying that Chekhov, in at least three of his works, is objective almost to the point of absence. They're plays without heart.

And I don't think the theatre's a very good place for that. In McLuhanite terms, it's a 'warmer' medium. It wants a warm presence; you want to *feel* the person behind it. In Ibsen you feel Ibsen, in O'Neill you feel O'Neill. But in Chekhov there's a sort of fake modesty in the author that I find very unattractive! It's a kind of, 'Shucks – what, *me*? You don't really want to know what I think, do you?' That, to me, is a sort of abdication. I prefer a more Romantic commitment from a writer, and I think it's there in Brecht; whatever you feel about him, there's a Romantic commitment to it – 'This is what I'm saying.' And that's why I chose to adapt the early Chekhov rather than the late Chekhov.

To take the point about history running through a room: I think I've lately given in with *Skylight* and *Amy's View*. They are clearly plays that do claim to show history in a room. I felt that the method was over-subtle in *Amy's View* – that is, I don't think the critics have understood it because, if you don't spell it out, they don't get it.

When you refer to the Romantic elements in early Chekhov – is that an element that drew you to Heartbreak House?

Yes. I think Holroyd's biography is absolutely magnificent,[10] you learn a lot by reading it. Plainly, Shaw was in terrible difficulty with women, and in agony about these questions of repression and the impossibility of Romantic action – about doing anything with all this feeling that he was awash with. I'm not saying plays exist as illustrations of their author's psyche, and that you *need* to read Michael Holroyd's biography in order to enjoy the play – you don't. But, on the other hand, the play, in my view, is hot, not cold; it's *hot*, it's full of the torture of having a lot of feeling, and not knowing what to do with it. In the production, we tried to avoid bored, listless sitting around, which all means nothing, and which can happen too easily in Shaw. Instead we played them as very fired up by feelings which were taking them over; they had an excess of feeling that had no conduit, had no exit. We played it at quite a high emotional pitch because of that, and I think that that was successful.

---

[10] Michael Holroyd's biography, *Bernard Shaw*, was published in two volumes, 1988–92, and reissued as a single volume in 1997.

It came over very strongly in all of the performances. Is that an approach that you arrived at before rehearsals started?

Yes.

And is it something that you had to rediscover with your cast?

Yes, you have to have the cast on your side. From the very beginning I said to Penelope Wilton, 'I'm doing this play so that you can say the line, "We were frightfully in love with one another".' And she said, 'I know exactly what you mean, I know what you want.' I wouldn't have done it without Penelope. Not only was she remarkable in her role, but she was the keystone of the style. The production would not have worked if there had been simply a director telling the actors what to do; it needed at least one actor to intuit that style and demonstrate it to the other actors. She was the standard of comparison by which the other actors knew where we were going. It was an incredibly happy period of work, because everybody was working to a common aim. They could all turn round and look at Penelope and know what style we were trying to work in. She just has that gift, she is a remarkable actress.

It was a strong cast.[11] Are there problems associated with working with strong casts?

Not on that occasion. There's nothing magical about ensemble. It's obviously a wonderful thing that there are ten parts all worth playing, so all the actors are happy. They said to me afterwards, 'Can you write a play for this group?', and I said, 'I wouldn't know how to write a play in which there were ten parts, each of which the actors would be happy playing.' It's impossible – it's a brilliant thing to have pulled off. But, having said that, an excessive intelligence and an excessive talent is not a great problem, frankly.

I just wondered whether there had been times when you had to say rein it back slightly – contain it more. I marvelled at the way they brought out things in the text that I'd never suspected were there. Richard Griffiths' performance was full of rage – full of pent-up rage that was surprising but very persuasive.

To be fair, it's the nature of the play; I think, every time you see it, the play is completely different. The only time I'd seen it before was at the Old Vic in

---

[11] Emma Fielding (Ellie Dunn); Carmel McSharry (Nurse Guinness); Richard Griffiths (Captain Shotover); Patricia Hodge (Lady Utterword); Penelope Wilton (Hesione Hushabye); Malcolm Sinclair (Mazzini Dunn); Peter McEnery (Hector Hushabye); John Bowe (Boss Mangan); Simon Dutton (Randall Utterword); Harry Landis (The Burglar).

1974, with Colin Blakely, Kate Nelligan played Ellie Dunn, Eileen Atkins, and Anna Massey. And there were some very, very good performances. It's a play that just is different every time you see it. There was a man who came who'd seen twelve different productions, and he said, 'Every time I've seen it, I go – hang on, I didn't remember *that* bit.' It's one of those plays where you are surprised to find what's in it. For instance, I used to listen to a tape in the car to familiarise myself with the play. It was a good production – Jessica Tandy in a Canadian production – and yet, I'd listened to it quite well and thought I knew it, and then two weeks into my own rehearsals I put their tape on and it didn't seem to be the same play at all! It really takes on more colour according to the actors than any play I've ever worked with.

How do you approach a play like that as a director? Do you plan things like movements, all the technical details before you start or do they just emerge?

Well, Shaw is very specific. Again, Penelope has played a lot of Shaw and warned me of something that actually I'd spotted for myself, which is that everything's in a puppet-theatre in his mind, and that if you don't crudely obey his instructions, which are very, very detailed, about the physical layout, you get yourself into terrible trouble. You have to put the parlour door on the side he wants it, you have to put the main entrance on the side he wants it. And if you don't, it's like trying to play cricket on a rugby pitch – you just can't do it, the game won't play. So there's freedom but there's only freedom if you accept his rules. I don't know another writer so resistant to directorial adaptation; I believe people have tried to do *Pygmalion* with abstract sets, but it just doesn't work, he does want it a certain way. You can be free within it, but he's a director in his own mind. In those days the profession of director didn't exist – or it only existed through Granville-Barker beginning to define it. When you read Shaw's own notes to the actors (because he directed it himself at the Royal Court in 1921), they are incredibly crude and very disappointing, he's not saying anything very interesting. In a way he'd already done his work on the page, in his mind, in the set, and it's all done. This modern journey that a director believes he's going to undertake with a cast is post-Freudian, it's a new invention, isn't it? And it crucially depends on the idea of subtext and psychological exploration – and even Shaw, who is as modern as a writer can be in 1920, even he is not directing actors in terms we would recognise.

But the interior journey is terribly important, certainly to your own plays.

Oh yes.

So you would have assumed that it was there, directing Shaw.

Oh yes, I couldn't do it any other way. When John Peter said, 'They have taken a high-risk strategy', I can't direct the other way. I can't direct by effect. In fact, once when I was young I rather disastrously – or rather semi-disastrously – did Vanbrugh's *The Provoked Wife*. Half of that is realistic. The half about John Brute and his wife, you can do about the terrible cruelty of a failed marriage – and you can make it both modern and cruel. The other half is Restoration *la de dah* – characters called Lady Fanciful, or whatever they're called! I just couldn't do that half of the play *at all*, because it doesn't yield to any interpretative talent. It just doesn't give anything, there's nothing to look for in it, you just have to do it. And so I was completely useless, I didn't know what to say to the people in the camp part of the play, so to speak, but the people in the real part of the play were having a wonderful time.

One of the trickier parts of directing Heartbreak House *must have been the climax, which is in some sense a* coup de théâtre. *Was that a challenge technically, or was that something that just arranged itself?*

I think it felt organic. I was just very concerned not to turn it into a fireworks display, which is usually what it turns out to be. The expectation is that bits of set fall down, and there's a lot of dry ice, and flashes and stuff. I really wanted to cut it right back, because it isn't really about all that – in fact, it's about a house *not* being bombed; it's not about a house being bombed. So that stuff doesn't seem to get you anywhere. But I wanted to do it by noise – and I'm not sure how successful it is. I can't say it was the part of the evening to which I most looked forward.

It's an impossible play in a sense, because, as you point out in your programme note, it's a comedy of manners grafted onto an apocalypse.[12]

Yes.

And one wants the apocalypse to grow out of the psychological drama, out of the dynamics between the characters – but it doesn't!

It doesn't. I went to Ayot St Lawrence.[13] If you go to there, you find it to be a very, very cold house, and you go, 'Oh my God! This is like the worst kind of Edwardian villa where a very repressed couple live.' The worst room is the

---

[12] 'From the outset, Shaw's attempts to mix high farce with divine tragedy, and to marble an apparent comedy of manners with grave presentiments of impending catastrophe have brought out an anger and exasperation in some spectators which has never truly abated', Hare, programme note to *Heartbreak House*.
[13] Shaw's country home at Ayot St Lawrence, Hertfordshire, where he lived from 1906 until his death in 1950.

room where Mrs Shaw put chintz in to warm it up, which seemed to me to have the effect of making it even worse! However, you go outside and you think, 'My God! Hitchin and Hatfield are only eight miles away, and yet the garden is incredibly uplifting and inspiring.' And that's what made me think, 'Oh I see. This is a man who loves nature more than he loves people.' Then Holroyd said to me, 'The feeling Shaw wanted was of the play bursting out of the house.' The characters are indoors for the first two acts and then they burst out, which is why it's crucial not to take an interval between Acts Two and Three, but to play straight on (although it made for an incredibly long second half – an hour and three-quarters). And it reminded me of *Lear* and *Timon of Athens*, and those plays which are what you might call inside–outside plays; they're set between walls, and then in the second half they turn Beckettian – they go into abstract landscapes out of real places.

The problem to me is that actually he gets this wonderful free interchange between characters; all their masks drop. Ariadne (played by Patricia Hodge) is suddenly free to speak, and she has that wonderful speech about the stables.[14] Some real understanding grows up between the characters who have hitherto been avoiding each other, and the whole thing acquires a warmth that the first two acts haven't had. He melts the characters down together once he takes them out of the house.

Therefore the *deus ex machina* feels contrived to me; it's really a playwright's gesture – 'I don't know what to do with them, so I'll bomb them!' And I think it's sad. Of course, there's a wonderful Brechtian irony at the end, of people who are disappointed not to be destroyed, or disappointed not to be excited by destruction, and who need danger.[15] And of course you can read the First World War into it, and you can say, 'They will, or they did in the First World War find the roles they lacked in life.' There's a critic who finished their lives for them rather wonderfully saying that Ellie goes off to become a nurse, Hector leads a charge, Shotover sits instructing them on how to conduct a battle and inventing new weapons – so that everybody finds a purpose in the

---

[14] 'Why have we never been able to let this house? Because there are no proper stables. Go anywhere in England where there are natural, wholesome, contented, and really nice English people; and what do you always find? That the stables are the real centre of the household; and that if any visitor wants to play the piano the whole room has to be upset before it can be opened, there are so many things piled on it. I never lived until I learned to ride; and I shall never ride really well because I didn't begin as a child. There are only two classes in good society in England: the equestrian classes and the neurotic classes. It isn't mere convention: everybody can see that the people who hunt are the right people and the people who don't are the wrong ones', *Heartbreak House*, p. 141.

[15] *Captain Shotover*: Turn in, all hands. The ship is safe.

Ellie (disappointedly): Safe!

Hector (disgustedly): Yes, safe. And how damnably dull the world has become again suddenly!

Heartbreak House, p. 160

First World War. In other words, war is the thing that will solve these people's problems for them. But I find that a bit facile, and it's structurally not organic.

There's one other thing that intrigued me about your programme note. You mention that this is a play which enshrines despair.[16] Is that something that you find attractive in this play?

He's asking the question which I think anybody's going to ask, which is, What is the purpose of a lot of well-meaning people sitting around? What impact does their well-meaningness have on the world, and is there any possibility left for Romantic action, of all the different kinds, as they conceive it, in a world that appears now to belong to the Mangans, the money-people? So it did seem to me very, very contemporary in that way. He didn't get it so wrong. In fact, when he said, 'The twentieth century is going to belong to the Mangans', he was right, wasn't he?

Amy's View seemed at some level to be a kind of tragedy.

Yes.

But it doesn't end tragically because of that coup de théâtre *that we discussed last time. It seems a very moral thing to me, not to end what is essentially a tragedy with despair, leaving the audience feeling a kind of hopelessness.*

When you say what's the connection between *Heartbreak House* and *Amy's View* – well, I don't think *Amy's View* has *begun* to be understood. Maybe *I* don't understand it. I have this extraordinary feeling of ... Obviously I'm very depressed because I feel that people don't get what it's about. I don't think people understand what it's about. To me, it's a political play about the fact that, at the end, she's saying, 'You can't search for any validation any more in social or political action; in the world outside, you can only find it in yourself and in what you alone do.' So it's about a woman whose world is narrowed and narrowed and narrowed and narrowed until there is nothing – *nothing* but what she believes personally the value of what she is doing to be, which is why the last line of the play is, 'So we're alone.'[17] It seems to be absolutely clear: that is, it portrays a group of people who no longer look to crudely collective action, crudely collective feeling, but who just become atoms. And the only way the atoms can find meaning is by what meaning they choose to put in their own work and *nothing else*. Not a

---

[16] 'Far from the governing tone being either light-hearted or elegiac, it is, on the contrary, full of the feverishness of genuine despair' (p. 255, below).
[17] See *Amy's View*, p. 127.

family relationship, not a social relationship, not a political relationship, *nothing* except that. Which is to me what all that last bit is about – and *crystal clear*. But plainly it is not clear to everyone. So it has been very depressing to me, because I think we're so *in* the situation we're in, that we can't see it. That is how we all now live – that is, when you say, 'Am I in despair?' Well, no, I live a very comfortable life, I'm very happy with my wife; you know, within the blinkers of *just this*, just this.

In a way, the effect of the acceptance of consumer capitalism as the only available model for countries of whatever background has been devastating. Israel or Palestine are trying to be IMF-friendly countries; that is the only model available to them. Does Arafat have any socialist ambitions for his country? None whatsoever! Does he have any view of how his society might be? Acceptable to the IMF is the only way he wants his country to be. In other words we've all just accepted that we become ourselves alone, just the person we are, or maybe the person we love. At least at the beginning Esme has people she loves and relates to, but then it just narrows and narrows and narrows. I don't think people want to hear what the play is saying and I don't think they get it. Some people do who write to me, but not in the way it's written about. I don't think anybody gets it. Do you know what I'm talking about?

Yes, I do. But I remain intrigued by the fact that Amy's View *is finally a morally affirming play, insofar as its final image is one of purification. And there's an enormous emotional kick in that. That is not a negative or despairing image. Yes, the state at which Esme has arrived is in its own way a terrible thing, but it doesn't seem stripped of hope;* Heartbreak House, *on the other hand, seems singularly unredeemed. Ellie's lesson, Ellie's unsentimental education brings her to the point where she says she's been stripped inherently.*

Well, there isn't in Shaw fulfilled love, is there? Nobody fits.

No, the whole idea is mocked.

Whereas in *Skylight* it was clear that the interval – you know, the hour or the two hours they go into the room is wonderful for them both. All the audience gets that. At the beginning of Act Two of *Skylight* the lights go back up and they're very, very happy. Shaw couldn't write that scene because he never showed people fulfilled through love, did he? There is that very powerful bit where Hesione says, 'We were very happy for a short time', but by and large the reason the line is so powerful is because Shaw is suggesting how rare it is. Now that's not true to my view of life. I see people intensely happy and fulfilled through love together, and I like putting that on the stage. So that Esme has known love. And, as people *do* say – and this is the thing they do understand – they say, 'Why do I cry more about Bernard than I do about Amy?' They say, 'It's very odd. Her daughter has died, and you're sitting watching, and you *don't* cry. But the bit that really makes you cry is the speech when she says about Bernard and how they were just happy together for a while, and then it wasn't anything spectacular but we were very, very happy together.'[18] You could feel the whole audience sobbing at this point. It is much more moving than Amy's death, and it is the point to which the play has been headed – because the story is of a woman who doesn't know how to live because her husband died when she was thirty-five and what does she do with the rest of her life? Again it's about fulfilled love not unfulfilled love; they had ten very happy years.

---

[18] 'Life with Bernard wasn't actually spectacular. It wasn't as if we were always in each other's arms. It was just calm. And we laughed at everything. That's all. Nothing crazy. But always with him, I felt whole', *Amy's View*, p. 125.

Richard Eyre

Richard Eyre

Richard Eyre was appointed Assistant Director at the Phoenix Theatre, Leicester, in 1966. He moved to the Royal Lyceum Theatre in Edinburgh, where he was Associate Director, 1967–70, and Director of Productions, 1970–72. During his time as Artistic Director of the Nottingham Playhouse, 1973–78, he nurtured some of the most important talents of the day, including Howard Brenton, David Hare, Ken Campbell, and Trevor Griffiths. From 1988 to 1997 he was Director of the National Theatre in London. Under him, the National prospered both through productions of such musicals as *Guys and Dolls* (revived 1996, first produced by Eyre, 1982), and through new works by Alan Bennett, David Hare, and Tom Stoppard. He was responsible for first performances of all three plays in the Hare trilogy at the National, and directed the memorable first production of Bennett's *Kafka's Dick* at the Royal Court. For television, he has directed Ian McEwan's *The Imitation Game*, Bennett's *The Insurance Man*, and Hare's *The Absence of War*, among others. He was awarded a CBE in 1992, and knighted in 1997.

Our interview was conducted at the Burton-Taylor Theatre, Oxford, on 22 November 1997, at the conclusion of his tenure of the Cameron Mackintosh Visiting Professorship of Contemporary Drama, a post which he held for a year at St Catherine's College, Oxford, 1996–97. Our discussion focussed on the culminating moments of *Amy's View* (see p. 167), although it took in various other aspects of the play. For general observations on the craft of the director, and a compelling account of Eyre's life and career, readers should turn to his volume, *Utopia and Other Places* (London: Vintage, 1994).

Interview

Duncan Wu: *I wonder whether we could begin with* Amy's View. *I'm curious as to what you do when you sit down with a new David Hare play, to find yourself confronted by the moral argument of the piece. How does that affect your work as Director? Do you see it as your job to translate a moral debate to the stage?*

Richard Eyre: Yes. Clearly, I know David's work very well, and I know the moral territory. I guess you can assume that most of the coordinates of that territory are familiar – and that they're shared coordinates. But I don't sit down and consciously think, 'How am I going to illustrate this moral debate?' What I think is, 'How do you animate this text?' And that really means, 'How do you make the characters come alive on the stage?' So that if there is a danger of that turning into a schematic moral debate, you take precautions to ensure that it doesn't appear so. That can really only be achieved by giving a sense of total life to the characters, so that they don't appear as the creatures of the author's moral scheme, but appear to have a sort of autonomous life. And that's just a matter of working with the actors. There is no substitute for very, very hard work.

It begs the question of what you put on stage. In the case of *Amy's View*, here is a play whose tactic, to some extent, is to lull you into a sense of false security; to give you a recognisable, self-contained world (and, coincidentally, it's a world that is *not* that of a country-house play). By the end, you have reached a state of extraordinary bleakness, and that world has been dispelled. So, clearly, the world of the country-house play, and the world of the values of the upper-middle class, in some way have to be evoked. And the designer[1] and I had a very long discussion about how this was to be done. We had a strong aversion towards the traditional set for the traditional country-house play – heavy walls, cornices, doors, French windows, and tennis courts beyond – and we decided straight off that we would find a way of giving a sense of that world, but it would have to be done poetically. That's how part of the debate within the play was poeticised. It was important that the play was both real, and yet had a metaphoric force. I thought if it was realised in a heavy-handed way that it would be bogged down and would actually *deny* life to the characters rather than add to it.

You use that word, 'poetically'. Can you tell me a little more about what you mean when you talk about approaching your work in a 'poetic' manner?

Well, the theatre is a poetic medium, in the sense that it should involve metaphor. I mean, things stand for other things. You can put a room on the stage and it stands for a house or it stands for a way of life. And the degree that it has a poetic force lies in how you actually present it. Let's take an example. If you present (let's say) the world of *Amy's View* – the country house world near the Thames in Pangbourne, a very lush and wealthy part of Britain – in a way that is too over-realised, too detailed, too social realist, then I think you're likely to rob it of poetry, to reduce it to no more than just a piece of

---

[1] Bob Crowley.

stage furniture; it won't resonate. So it's a delicate choice, and the success of the choice can only be experienced by watching the play. There's no way I can explain it to you – well, I can explain it to you and describe it to you, but you would have to see it to understand the success or failure of the poetic nature of the presentation.

Is it something like – I mean, to me a successful theatre experience is when I go to the theatre and I come out having felt moved.

Yes.

As I did when I saw Amy's View. *Is it something to do with that? Are you effectively saying that the disposition of objects on the stage, the disposition of the actors on the stage add up to an emotional experience?*

I'm saying it's *part* of it. It's all contributing in the same way that each word in a poem, each image, is contributing to a cumulative poetic force. If that is understood, then you could say that each gesture has a poetic significance that adds up. I can't say with authority that a production of this play done with solid walls, French windows, doors, in a doggedly social realist way *wouldn't* be moving, because in the end it depends on the power of the actors. But I would say that such an approach would put obstacles in its way. It's not dogma; I mean, in the end it's actually a matter of taste. For me, a realistic approach makes a production less expressive, and if it's less expressive then it's less moving.

I was very struck by that moment which comes at about pages 107–8 of the printed text where Esme and Amy[2] are locked in a kind of emotional battle. It's just at the end of Act Three, where Esme wants her to stay, and she keeps saying she can't. Was that difficult to direct? It seemed to me like a tour de force *in terms of acting alone.*

Yes, it was a very, very difficult scene. It was a difficult scene in that it could only really be done by doing it. It's a very difficult scene to take apart because so much of it is at a very high emotional temperature, and if you take the emotional temperature down then it's no longer about the things that it's about. So it was a scene that had to be rehearsed with your hands inside the furnace – which makes it difficult. And it was a scene that, unlike most of the scenes where I would minutely dissect and analyse and stick together,

---

[2] Played in the Royal National Theatre production by Judi Dench and Samantha Bond. The precise reference is *Amy's View*, pp. 107–10.

generally had to be rehearsed by simply jumping off the cliff and seeing if you arrived intact at the bottom!

One of the things was their movements – it was like a ballet. The movements were incredibly intricate. Afterwards I was thinking about it, wondering how on earth you can prepare actors for this. Do you map out the movements? Or do you let them find their own way through it physically?

A bit of both. I don't really map out movements for actors; I used to when I was much younger. But that's just anxiety because you think you're going to get caught out. The more confident you get, the more you realise that it's much better if you start without intricate planning. That said, you don't exactly begin with a *tabula rasa*. You've made a lot of choices and you think, 'Well, this scene will start there' – and you just work at it. It's like sticking clay on a maquette, you just concentrate on what's happening. So, if an actor does something, you think, 'Oh, that's interesting, why don't you take that, there, and try that out.' You see what they do. You see what their instincts lead them to suggest. With good actors their instincts are gold, and part of being a good director is not clouding their instincts, not obscuring them, trying instead to capitalise on them. You think, 'Ah, I see – if you do that, then it's more interesting if you do that.' It's a dialectic; it's not an instruction. And directing is often a question of *not* directing in the sense of pushing people about, but allowing patterns to emerge. For me the choreography is always very, very important – the rhythm of movement and the shape of movement. But I try to let it evolve and then, if it feels wrong, I'll just nudge it in one direction or another. But essentially it has to emerge, it has to evolve. Having said that, there are some scenes in some plays which need to be very rigidly dictated. Let's say you have a scene where twelve people are sitting round a table; in that case you have to direct, you have to work it out on paper and say, 'In order for that to happen, this character will have to do that, and those characters will have to do something else.' Those situations demand intricate planning and preparation, and you'd begin work on such a scene by choreographing it – in the sense of telling people where to sit or stand on the stage. That's not to say you'd be right in all your instructions, but the more you direct, the more able you are to see whether you're right or wrong. The moment an actor moves, you should be able to tell whether it's right or not. You get to read what you might call the significant mark on the paper; you can tell the difference between the move which means something and one which is just decoration.

The other moment that seemed to me to be weighted with emotion was what David Hare called, in his interview with me, the 'killer' moment – when they pour water over each other at the end of the play.[3] I'm curious to know how you approached that; it must have seemed climactic even when you read the play for the first time.

Yes, clearly we're talking about a poetic moment. That is a poetic moment in that it's clearly in the scheme of the play, and carries much more weight than it would if it merely depicted two actors pouring water over each other just because they are going to do a scene of two people emerging from a shipwreck. It has a basis in reality that, in the context of the play, makes it an intensely moving act of cleansing, spiritual cleansing. Actually, we never rehearsed that. We'd just get to that point, and because we couldn't rehearse the last scene in the rehearsal room I just said, 'Okay, fine! Water, water ...' And that was it, we never actually did it. We discussed it, but left it until we actually got into the theatre. And that was the other thing: nobody knew, except for me, how that end was going to work. I would just say to David, 'Trust me – I'll make it work.' And David, when he originally wrote the play, said to me: 'Your job is to do something brilliant at the end.' Actually the first thing that I did at the end was cut the last line. I don't know if it's in the printed text ...?

No, it's not.

No, but there *was* a last line – which was the first line of the play they were performing, and I said, 'This is wrong; we're in real trouble if we hear a line of the new play – you know, of the play they're performing.' And I said to the actors, 'You've got to trust me, I'll do something that'll work.' Part of the reason I love the end is because it's a pure piece of theatre. There is nothing there on the stage; there's a completely bare stage and two pieces of white silk. All it is is two pieces of white silk, lighting and sound, and you're creating a storm and waves! And it somehow has an enormous emotional force, because it follows all the action of the play and comprises a cumulative encompassing emotional event that ties into the whole use of the theatre in the play as a metaphor for human relationships.

The white silk to me – as a member of the audience, I wasn't thinking in representational terms by that point, and it did seem to me like a fully realised poetic image that embodied in some strange manner the emotional thrust of the play. It was very curious how that worked.

That's obviously the intention, but it's also actually this medium that has been held up as a kind of model for human relationships. Because the thing

---

[3] See p. 167.

about the theatre is that, however absurd and archaic it may be, it is dependent on humanity. I mean, that is the theatre's substance; the theatre's terrain is humanity, and it depends on scale of human body, scale of human voice – there's nothing more, really. So it is a potent image. And being able to conjure it up with that simplicity lends force to the whole poetic metaphor of the theatre, whereas if it was felt to be something complex and technological there would be a false note to it. Do you see what I mean?

Yes I do. David Hare said to me that he had envisaged in that final moment lots of rigging and ship's apparatus, and mentioned the final line that doesn't appear in the printed text. He said that he came to you and said that he didn't think after all that the line should be there, and you said that you'd been waiting two months for him to say that.[4]

It's true. I had actually mentioned it to him before that; I had said, 'Are you sure we need the last line?' I suppose you might say that's a tactic, insofar as I have any tactics. I would prefer not to say to David, 'I think we should cut that line', even if that's what I'd like to say. It's much better if I say, 'Are you sure that we need that line?', and sow the seed of doubt. It is just much better psychology. One is always much more receptive to suggestions rather than harsh pronouncements. If somebody says to me, 'Do you think that scene really works?', it makes me think about it. If somebody says to me, 'That scene just doesn't work!', I just get defensive. I feel obliged to defend my position on this scene because I'm being attacked.

David is a model author to work with. You see, it is interesting that David tends to think in realist terms; you can see it in what he writes – take that opening description, the stage direction of the living room of the house, full of plants, door, hall staircase, on one wall plates are designed and another paintings hung.[5] He writes a room and it's a real room. So he has to make a jump when the play goes into production. I went to him and said that Bob (the designer) and I thought it would be disastrous to see a single painting, because the moment you saw it you would spend your time during the play

[4] See p. 181.

[5] The opening stage direction is as specific as Eyre indicates: 'The living room of a house in rural Berkshire, not far from Pangbourne. The year is 1979. To one side there is a large summerhouse-cum-veranda, full of plants. At the back, a door leading to a hall and staircase. The room has an air of exceptional taste, marked by the modern arts movement of the 1920s and '30s. It is comfortable, with sofas and chairs decked in attractively faded French fabrics. Nothing new has been bought for years. By the biggest chair, discarded embroidery. This was once the home of an artist, Bernard Thomas, and all round the room is evidence of his work, which is rather Cezanne-like and domestic in scale. There are small sculptures dotted around. On one wall are some plates he designed. On another, a box of *objets trouvés*. Yet the art is discreet, part of the general surroundings, and plainly has been there long enough to go unremarked' (*Amy's View*, p. 1).

thinking, 'Was Bernard any good as a painter?' And that, I suppose, is a perfect example of what I mean by literalism and metaphor: if you don't have the paintings, if you simply imagine them hanging on the fourth wall, you don't have that problem, and the painting – Bernard's art (which, of course, is essential to the poetic image running right through the play) – has a force, has a resonance; if the actual things appear, you look at them and think, 'Well, some scene painter is responsible for those, and I see he was vaguely influenced by Bonnard, vaguely influenced by Duncan Grant or Ben Nicholson or whatever' – and it's just irrelevant! It's just literal, as opposed to poetic.

The more I hear you speak about your craft and your work with writers, the more it sounds as if – in a sense – you're very nearly a co-author. You are certainly a collaborator in the project of transferring the text from the page to the stage. I mean, a play isn't really a play when it's written, it doesn't become a play until it's actually – to use your word – an event. And you are, as it were, the conduit by which it becomes the event. To some extent, your job is sometimes to do with rearranging the script.

One thing that is very striking about Amy's View *is the way that the concluding scene is played upstage rather than downstage (which is the way it's written). Was that your decision?*

Yes.

How did that come about?

That was partly because of my uneasiness with the last line, and partly because I just felt that it was a lie – it was too clever by half to do some sort of switch of the audience's point of view, from being backstage to then being in the audience of the play. Do you see what I mean? There *is* a way you could have done it where, as they started their journey downstage, you *could* have switched the perspective and made them walk towards us (i.e. the audience). But I thought it was too complicated; it was too tricky, and robbed it of that important element I was talking about earlier – integral to the play is that metaphor about theatre: it's the human scale that matters. So if they come towards you, you lose that sense of these *extraordinarily* vulnerable people. They are essentially two ordinary people in this enormous space, and if they are going away from you, you get much more sense of the relationship between their human scale and the scale of the theatre surrounding them. And that seemed to me a very, very important statement; you wouldn't get the *vulnerability* of that image if they were walking toward you. It would be too full of content and not sufficiently resonant.

How soon did you realise that? Did you realise that as soon as you read the play or was that something that emerged as you worked on the play later on?

Yes, it emerged slowly, but I always thought about the end, 'I'll find a way of doing it.' I always knew that, somehow, we'd do it. And Bob and I had this rough plan from the outset. But actually, until quite late on we just knew that although the specifics were vague, it would work out. We knew that so long as we had a clear stage, we'd play around, we'd do it and we'd find a way of making it work.

Is there a point at which you go to the author – in this case David Hare – and start negotiating with him about how you see it, or do you deliver it as a fait accompli*? How does that work? Is it something that he realised too as he was working on rehearsals?*

I think he was always a little anxious that, whenever we reached that point in the play during rehearsals, I always said, 'Stop, we can't do the rest of it.' So there is an act of faith involved, and I'm sure it was quite disturbing for him. The first time we rehearsed it in the theatre it was all completely mistimed, and it didn't work at all. So he was sitting there thinking, 'So that's what I've been waiting six weeks for!' Because, of course, unless the lighting cues and the sound cues and the dropping of the silk are perfectly timed, it's just nothing. And that's, of course, one of the things that attracts me about it: it's timing. It's all in the timing.

It's pure theatre.

Yes – which is all in the timing.

Can I ask you one final question, which is a slightly general question. I'm a Romanticist – that's where I come from, that's my area – but for me the joy of the theatre is actually going and seeing the performance and coming out, knowing I've had a sublime experience. And hearing you speak, I'm very aware that you are in the first instance a very practical man of the theatre; that's what you've written so eloquently about elsewhere.[6] But there's also a metaphysical element to your work. It is that element, what we're calling 'pure theatre', it's an image – whatever – that's the thing I find really compelling. It's really much more than the sum total of a series of words. The words are part it – a very crucial part of it, clearly – but it's also a whole series of intangibles. We're talking about the metaphysical. Would you go along with that?

---

[6] See, most notably, Richard Eyre, *Utopia and Other Places* (London: Vintage, 1994).

Yes. I think that's right, and I find theatre without that dimension very dull, it is just plodding. And that's what I mean by that portmanteau term I keep using, 'poetic'. If it doesn't have that poetic element, if it doesn't resonate, if it's merely what it is on stage and nothing more, I'm not interested. That's why, over the years, I have so recoiled from social realism – though not universally, because sometimes there can be a way in which social realism also has a resonance. But if the thing is *merely* what you're seeing in front of your eyes, if it doesn't vibrate at all, then I find it very dull.

Michael Frayn

Michael Frayn, *Copenhagen* (1998)

Copenhagen was first performed at the Cottesloe Theatre, Royal National Theatre, 21 May 1998, in a production directed by Michael Blakemore. It transferred to the Duchess Theatre in the West End of London, 5 February 1999.

It is easy to be foxed by the accumulation of scientific data in *Copenhagen*, by its extended disquisitions on complementarity, wave and matrix mechanics, and of course the Copenhagen Interpretation, but the play takes its momentum less from theoretical physics than from the relationships between its three characters: Niels Bohr, his wife Margrethe, and their visitor, Werner Heisenberg. Shortly after Heisenberg arrives in Copenhagen in 1941 to see his old mentor, Bohr remembers their first meeting in Göttingen in 1922:

> Beautiful summer's day. The scent of roses drifting in from the gardens. Rows of eminent physicists and mathematicians, all nodding approval of my benevolence and wisdom. Suddenly, up jumps a cheeky young pup and tells me that my mathematics are wrong.[1]

Just as that first meeting is more than a mere encounter, the play concerns more than the mechanics of how the atom bomb was put together. The almost paradisal rose garden returns us to the prelapsarian world before man created a means for his self-annihilation, and to a relationship that seems, at least in retrospect, like a kind of love affair that has broken down. As Margrethe observes, the recollection leads Bohr to 'love' Heisenberg again.[2] The reunion cannot fully reawaken their affection for each other – the German occupation of Denmark has put them on opposite sides of a war – but, at least for a short while, they enjoy an echo of the warmth they once felt.

---

[1] *Copenhagen*, p. 22.
[2] *Copenhagen*, p. 23.

BOHR: I open the door ...
HEISENBERG: And there he is. I see his eyes light up at the sight of me.
BOHR: He's smiling his wary schoolboy smile.
HEISENBERG: And I feel a moment of such consolation.
BOHR: A flash of such pure gladness.
HEISENBERG: As if I'd come home after a long journey.
BOHR: As if a long-lost child had appeared on the doorstep.
HEISENBERG: Suddenly I'm free of all the dark tangled currents in the water.
BOHR: Christian is alive, Harald still unborn.
HEISENBERG: The world is at peace again.
MARGRETHE: Look at them. Father and son still.[3]

In this exchange, which consists entirely of internal monologue by the three characters, Frayn maps out the emotional hinterland of the play. The instant at which Bohr opens the door to Heisenberg on his arrival at his house in Copenhagen in 1941 is almost a Wordsworthian spot of time. It reawakens all the emotions felt between the two men two decades before. It returns them, for a moment, to a world at peace, and to a time prior to the boating accident that killed Bohr's young son Christian. 'Father and son still', Margrethe observes, commenting accurately on what held them together. Bohr describes Heisenberg as both a 'child' and a 'schoolboy', in phrases that convey affection without ever belittling his old friend. Most importantly, the revival of those earlier emotions relieves both of them, momentarily, of guilt: Heisenberg, briefly, of the knowledge that he is part of the occupying force, and Bohr from that attached to Christian's death. It is innocent – in Bohr's words, 'pure'. But it can't last.

'We all see you as a kind of spiritual father', Heisenberg tells Bohr, referring to his colleagues in Germany.[4] Margrethe goes on to suggest that he has come to Copenhagen now (in 1941) to seek absolution from Bohr. And at Los Alamos, we learn, Bohr was to become known as 'father-confessor'.[5] The sanctifying of Bohr gives an edge to his status within the relationship; it heightens the intensity of feeling behind it, and conveys something of the potent emotional force between mentor and protégé. And yet, from the very start of the friendship, Heisenberg was correcting Bohr, as if, inevitably, an Oedipal dimension was somehow built into it. Frayn inverts that mythic structure, so that instead of 'killing' the father-figure, Heisenberg defers to him. The visit to Copenhagen, which could have given moral authority to the German quest for the atomic bomb, in fact led directly (within the world of the play) to its derailment. Bohr's angry rejection of Heisenberg when asked whether scientists had the moral right to exploit atomic

---

[3] *Copenhagen*, p. 54.
[4] *Copenhagen*, p. 39.
[5] *Copenhagen*, p. 47.

energy[6] stifles Heisenberg's hunger to develop the bomb that Bohr himself would help create at Los Alamos two years later. Within the mythic structure of the play, the Copenhagen encounter enables the father-figure to exert power over the son, restraining him from possessing the atom bomb, thereby altering the course of the war. The conceit of the play is that the inversion of the Oedipus legend is something in which Heisenberg appears to have colluded. The day after the bomb is detonated, he reveals to his colleagues that he had known how it could be done for a long time: his failure to develop it was a matter of choice.

In this light, Heisenberg took the only course that we, from our present perspective, could regard as acceptable. And that, too, is the subject of the play: if Heisenberg is a 'child', a 'schoolboy', he has to make the journey, during its course, from immaturity to manhood. At the outset, he speaks of the 'impossible responsibility' of his mission to Copenhagen,[7] and is racked with worry as to 'what happens if I fail'.[8] The Copenhagen encounter compels him to grow out of the status of disciple to become capable of making a correct moral decision. It is not an easy one, as he acknowledges: 'Germany is my wife. Germany is our children. I have to know what I'm deciding for them! Is it another defeat? Another nightmare like the nightmare I grew up with?'[9]

How was it that he came to act (or not) as he did? Frayn is careful to give no precise answer. In his Postscript to the published text, he suggests that Heisenberg 'had kept the knowledge of how fast the reaction would go in pure [uranium] 235, and therefore of how little of it would be needed, not to himself but from himself'.[10] In other words, the course Heisenberg took is shown to have been determined almost by an act of psychological repression. It is the essential inscrutability of such processes that preoccupies Frayn. Uncertainty, or indeterminacy, is a concept that pervades the play. It is elemental to the science out of which the atom bomb was forged, and refers us back to the characters' inner worlds, their motivations and actions. In Act One, Bohr and Heisenberg recall their walking tour of Denmark years before:

HEISENBERG: We went to Elsinore. I often think about what you said there. ... the whole appearance of Elsinore, you said, was changed by our knowing that Hamlet had lived there. Every dark corner there reminds us of the darkness inside the human soul ...[11]

---

[6] The question is not posed by Heisenberg until the final recollection of the meeting; *Copenhagen*, p. 90.
[7] *Copenhagen*, p. 12.
[8] *Copenhagen*, p. 10.
[9] *Copenhagen*, p. 42.
[10] *Copenhagen*, p. 112.
[11] *Copenhagen*, pp. 30–1.

The insights of the father-confessor refer his disciple to more than theoretical physics: they embrace the essential unknowability of the human psyche. By implication they also refer back to a variation on the Oedipus myth in Shakespeare, in which a father–son relationship is instrumental to the righting of a terrible wrong. That pattern resonates throughout *Copenhagen*. Like the Danish Prince, Heisenberg's problem is whether to act; nor is he certain of whether he can assume the responsibility of acting. In both cases, the protagonist takes his lead from the father-figure. The irony of *Copenhagen* is that, where the ghost prompts Hamlet to do his duty, Bohr has the opposite effect on Heisenberg (and, in effect, helps him toward the 'correct' decision).

Margrethe is a foil for the impulsive, even Romantic, tendencies of her husband. She notes his mercurial character, and grounds what we see in the dynamics of his relationship with Bohr. 'Not to criticise', he tells her, 'but you have a tendency to make everything personal'. 'Because everything *is* personal!',[12] she replies, defining one of her central functions within the play. Her voice is choric, and it is through her commentary that we understand its characters. But she is hardly a passive spectator. She is the source of jealousy. She recognises immediately that Heisenberg is a replacement for Christian and Harald, 'the two lost boys' of her family.[13] The irony of the play, as she acknowledges, is that Heisenberg's failure to pursue the atom bomb is to make him another 'lost boy':

MARGRETHE: That was the last and greatest demand that Heisenberg made on his friendship with you. To be understood when he couldn't understand himself. And that was the last and greatest act of friendship for Heisenberg that you performed in return. To leave him misunderstood.[14]

Bohr's angry, indignant rejection of Heisenberg may have been unpremeditated, even accidental, but it determined the course of history. Discouraged from his quest, Heisenberg effectively left the field clear for the Americans, and the development of the weapon that was to conclude the war. The price Heisenberg was to pay was that of remaining misunderstood for the rest of his life. Not until the advocacy of Thomas Powers, in his volume, *Heisenberg's War* (1993), and of Frayn himself, through this play, would Heisenberg's story be told. The play is, in that sense, supremely redemptive; the characters tell us as much. As the door opens, Bohr and Heisenberg reveal their emotions:

HEISENBERG: As if I'd come home after a long journey.
BOHR: As if a long-lost child had appeared on the doorstep.

---

[12] *Copenhagen*, p. 75.
[13] *Copenhagen*, p. 29.
[14] *Copenhagen*, p. 91.

The Bohrs have lost two sons but, for a moment, their children are returned to them, and the father–son relationship is restored. And although the play is carried by all three characters, the story it tells, finally, is Heisenberg's. It is his inner world that the play seeks to explore.

Copenhagen seems at first to be an unlikely hit. Its success has been due partly to the skill with which Frayn has worked out the mythic elements of the play, and partly to the fact that it is very much of its time. Concerned with the invention of the weapon to end wars and worlds, it is appropriately millennial. Behind it lurks the spectre of worldwide devastation, and behind that the angst of the post-war psyche.

His success as a comic writer has sometimes prevented critics from appreciating the seriousness of Frayn's intent, let alone the sharpness of his commentary on recent political history. *Benefactors* was one of the most accurate analyses of the peculiar mindset that prevailed in 1970s and '80s Britain, and *Copenhagen*, as it recasts the indecisiveness and questioning of *Hamlet*, seems perfectly to express the anxiety of the West at a moment when an increasing number of third world countries are acquiring the knowledge and means to construct the bomb.[15] More importantly, it dramatises the dilemma of taking responsibility for such acquisitions.

My interview with Michael Frayn was conducted at his studio flat in Camden Town, 23 March 1999. As he has discussed his other writings helpfully elsewhere,[16] and given a lucid account of the scientific background to *Copenhagen* (in the Postscript to the published text), I decided to concentrate on the relationships between the characters. Frayn has published fiction, essays, and a book of philosophy, all of which are invaluable to students of his work; but the best general account of his plays may be found in the Prefaces he has written to the two collections published by Methuen (1985–91).

Interview

Duncan Wu: Copenhagen *has been amazingly successful. How would you account for its appeal?*

Michael Frayn: God knows, I haven't got the faintest notion. I'm absolutely baffled by it. When I wrote it I didn't think anyone would perform it; the idea that anyone would come and see it absolutely never occurred to me. But they do.

---

[15] India and Pakistan tested thermonuclear devices in 1998, and at the time of writing (June 1999) seem to be edging closer to war.
[16] See, for instance, the selection from earlier interviews in Malcolm Page's *File on Frayn* (London: Methuen Drama, 1994).

It is in some ways highly undramatic. Three people on a stage.

Well, it is quite dramatic, it is quite a drama going on. Everyone thinks it's all discussion, but in fact there is quite a lot of plot in there. It's now running in Paris, also directed by Michael Blakemore, with a completely different sort of cast. It got terrific reviews, got off to a very slow start commercially, but it now seems to be picking up and seems to have the same effect as in London: people do come and they listen to it. They get involved in it. I had an absolutely massive postbag about it, far bigger than I've had for anything else – a lot of it from scientists, mostly appreciative, but sometimes pointing out errors that I've had to put right. And a lot of it is from people who knew the Bohrs, or knew Heisenberg, or knew all of them.

It's odd, there's some psychological trick that fiction performs on people. Nearly everyone who knew the Bohrs or Heisenberg says that these are very good portraits of them: they were like this. They often say, 'Even the actors are like Niels Bohr and Werner Heisenberg' – well, that can't be so. It's not possible that I've caught the actual tone of their voices just from reading letters and studying stuff about them, you can't do that! I didn't know them personally, and I was very daunted by that when I wrote the play. I was attempting to make some sort of representation of real people, people who had a real presence and a real character, and there was no way I could get that right. But people have some sort of ability to read into characters in fiction, on the stage, what they want to read; and I think if they feel goodwill towards the whole enterprise, they tend to feel these are accurate representations – these are the people themselves, this is the man, the Werner Heisenberg that I knew, or whatever. I think it is a strange psychological transference of some sort, because it can't be literally true.

Copenhagen *is about uncertainty: why was uncertainty an interesting idea to you?*

I'd read Philosophy at university (Moral Sciences, as it was then called) at Cambridge,[1] and all the ideas associated with quantum mechanics, particularly uncertainty, have obviously got philosophical implications. So if you're interested in philosophy you couldn't but be interested in those ideas.

Why am I interested in uncertainty? Specifically, because it seems to me that there is some kind of parallel between physical uncertainty and epistemological uncertainty. It is extremely difficult (not to put it more strongly) to know why people do what they do, and it's also extremely difficult to know why one does what one does oneself. Not all the time, of course; there

---

[1] Frayn attended Emmanuel College, Cambridge, 1954–57, on a state scholarship. He read Russian and French in his first year, but changed to Moral Sciences for his second and third.

are simple cases – when someone's very hungry, you could be reasonably confident that's why they've elected to eat something. If you're very frightened when you run away, probably that's the reason you ran away – because you're very frightened. When things become more complicated than that, I think it gets much more difficult. What the play is suggesting is that there is some sort of theoretical barrier in the way of our ever knowing. It's not a practical difficulty; there is a theoretical difficulty – as there is in knowing precisely about the behaviour of particles. It's a very precise concept in physical terms, and it's not at all a precise concept when we're talking about human knowledge. But I think there is some sort of parallel.

What do you mean by 'theoretical barrier'?

If we're looking at physical uncertainty, indeterminacy, it's not that it's terribly hard to tell where a particle is and how fast it's going at the same moment; it's just not theoretically possible. There's no way, however you improve your instruments or observations, that you can do it. It's just something which is excluded by the logic of the situation, and I think there is a kind of logic in the situation of people's thinking about themselves which has some parallels (I wouldn't want to push it too far), and means that, however hard you try, and however much effort you put into it, and however astute you become at analysing your own motivation or other people's motivation, there's some point beyond which you can't get. There's a conceptual barrier at some point.

So in terms of pinning down where people stand, we're not so much talking about the physical business of where a particle is at any one point in time, we're talking about where people's intentions can be said to lie.

Yes, and you can make good practical guesses. As the play says, physical indeterminacy applies to everything, even very slow-moving objects in the macro-world. But there the discrepancies are so small that you can effectively disregard them. For all practical purposes, you can tell where you are in the street, even where a fast car is, even where a plane is, even where a planet is going to be in a year's time: you don't have to think about uncertainty because the discrepancies are absolutely sub-microscopic. But they're still theoretically there. It's the same with explanations of why people do what they do: for a lot of practical reasons, you can disregard the problems, you can work on rough approximations, and we do all the time, we have to. All the time we make assessments of people's motives. As Heisenberg says in the play, you'd need a very strange new ethics if you just judged people by external observables[2] – by what they did – and didn't make any estimate as to what their intentions were. It would be very, very curious as applied to the characters in the play. As Heisenberg points out in the play, he is endlessly judged and condemned.[3] But Heisenberg, as far as I know, never caused anyone's death in the world,[4] whereas Niels Bohr, who everyone, including Heisenberg (rightly) regards as a very good man, was actually complicit in the death of an awful lot of people.

I can see the interest in the concept of indeterminacy as a topic for intellectual discourse. At what point did you realise it was dramatically exciting?

I'll tell you how I hit upon the play, which is a fairly direct and simple story. Often when you try to explain how you thought of an idea for a play or a book you can't, the whole thing is so tangled and twisted and indeterminate, and has been going on for so long that you can't quite put it all together. But I can remember quite clearly with this one because about five years ago I read a book called *Heisenberg's War* by Thomas Powers. I came across the story of the trip to Copenhagen for the first time. It had been much written about before; I'd just never come across it. It had been written about by Heisenberg's biographer, David Cassidy; by Bohr's biographer, Abraham Pais,[5] and much disputed by people who'd written articles about it over the years. I'd just never come across it. When I read the story in Powers's book I immediately thought that this crystallises the whole problem of knowing why people do what they do, because there is this very practical question about a really quite striking event. It was a very bizarre thing to do, to go to Copenhagen. Heisenberg knew perfectly well that Bohr was going to be upset about it – of course he knew; he wasn't a very sensitive man, but he was a very intelligent one. There must have been some purpose behind it, but no one has ever been able to give a satisfactory account of what it was. So it just seems to crystallise a lot of this area – if you can crystallise an area, which I suppose you can't!

It was a stroke of good fortune that –

Very good fortune, yes, reading the book.

And also the fact that the area of study concerned lent itself readily to the discussion of indeterminacy.

---

[2] *Copenhagen*, p. 94.
[3] '... explaining and defending myself was how I spent the last thirty years of my life'; *Copenhagen*, p. 47.
[4] *Copenhagen*, p. 93.
[5] *Niels Bohr's Times* (Oxford: Oxford University Press, 1991).

Yes, all luck is usually a combination of external circumstance and some sort of internal situation. And it was because I was interested in this area that the story seemed significant to me. If I hadn't been interested in indeterminacy, and hadn't been interested in human motivation, it probably wouldn't have helped to have read that story.

I remember telling Michael Blakemore about it, explaining this idea to him, when we were working on the previous play, *Now You Know*, at Hampstead.[6] I remember having supper with him one evening, between the rehearsal in the afternoon and the preview in the evening, in a Thai restaurant in Swiss Cottage, and explaining to him about this extremely nebulous and elusive idea for a play. As soon as I had actually written it (and it did take me a long time), I sent it to Michael. He was immediately enthusiastic about it. It's quite a difficult play to read. If you just read the text it is difficult to see that it would work on the stage, and a lot of people read it before it was done and didn't see that it was going to work, but I have to say that Michael did. I haven't put any stage directions on it, so I've theoretically left it entirely up to the director as to how it's done. But since Michael and I have always worked together, we sat down here and talked about it; he put forward ideas, I put forward some ideas – and we agreed that the way to do it was as simply as possible.

Did you revise it partly as a result of things he suggested?

I made some revisions, as always, at his suggestion. He didn't make very many suggestions. What he did persuade me to do was to take out some bits which he thought were just exposition, and although of great interest to me not actually part of the drama; and to simplify and clarify other bits which he thought were opaque. That was what he mostly did. But we did, as we talked about it, hit upon one or two ideas, themes that come out of the story that I hadn't seen before. I hadn't seen, till we talked about it, the parallel between what Heisenberg suspects would have been required of him by people like the Bohrs – that's to say, to sacrifice himself, to throw his life away by getting himself hanged with the Stauffenberg plotters[7] – and what Bohr must have felt about watching his son drown, when (according to a number of eyewitnesses) he attempted to throw himself overboard, and had to be restrained.[8]

---

[6] First performed at the Hampstead Theatre, London, 13 July 1995, directed by Michael Blakemore.

[7] Frayn refers to the Rastenburg Assassination Plot, or July Plot, 20 July 1944, when a number of Hitler's most senior military colleagues conspired to kill the Chancellor, take control of government, and seek favourable peace terms with the Allies. The most stalwart conspirator was Lieut. Col. Claus Philipp Schenk, Graf (Count) von Stauffenberg, who personally carried out the assassination attempt.

[8] The parallel is presented in Act Two; *Copenhagen*, pp. 77–8.

It was only when Michael and I talked about the play that it occurred to me that there was a parallel; that in both cases there was some kind of ethical, aesthetic feeling that both Bohr and Heisenberg should have sacrificed themselves – vainly, because they wouldn't have been able to save anyone by doing it – and that both men, by one means or another, declined that possibility.

Hence that exchange towards the end of the play about jumping or not jumping in to save Christian.

Yes, that's right.

That's interesting, because there's a mythic dimension to the play, isn't there? The father–son relationship between Bohr and Heisenberg is set up at the beginning and runs right the way through. I wonder whether that's one of the things people mean when they tell you that they somehow recognise these people.

Yes, possibly, possibly.

That mythic element: is that a universal, or is that something you think of only in the specific terms of these particular historical characters?

I suppose it does tend to be something that goes through a lot of human relationships, but it is historically specific to these characters. They were very close friends. There was this age discrepancy between them. I think, from the way Bohr talks about Heisenberg, he did have rather fatherly feelings towards him in the 1920s; and I think Heisenberg, by his own account, was rather overawed by Bohr when he first met him, in the way that some might be by a father, and did behave as sons do, rather aggressively, by challenging – the very first thing he did was challenge Bohr's mathematics.[9] They were very competitive – very close and very competitive. Everyone remembers how competitive Heisenberg was. Bohr always thought of himself as very amiable and non-competitive, but everyone else's memories of him were that he was indeed quite competitive, too. And they did have absolutely colossal rows in the Twenties, just as they do in the play. That meeting in 1941 did effectively finish their friendship; they made various attempts after the war to resume it, but never really managed it.

Thomas Powers is one of the very few people who actually comes to Heisenberg's defence; almost everyone who has written about Heisenberg has attacked or dismissed him. Powers is the first person to suggest that Heisenberg has a case. As I said in the Postscript to the published text, I don't

---

[9] *Copenhagen*, p. 22.

quite accept his view that Heisenberg actually did the diffusion equation and kept the answer to himself;[10] I don't think there's any evidence of that at all. It's much more interesting, and likely, that he didn't do the diffusion equation, so the question arises as to *why* he didn't do it, when he had such a forward, aggressive approach to problems in general, and particularly to their mathematical solution.

Powers came over to see the play, and when we talked afterwards he said that he thought that one of the reasons Bohr never wanted to discuss that meeting in 1941 was that he did have a bad conscience about his participation in the Los Alamos programme, and did see, if only unconsciously, that there was a somewhat unfortunate contrast with Heisenberg. Heisenberg had *not* produced a nuclear weapon, for whatever reason, whereas he, Bohr, had helped in producing one, and had acquiesced in its use.

This is yet another question of human motivation – and I think it's even more difficult to arrive at any view of it than the question of why Heisenberg went to Copenhagen in 1941. But it's an interesting possibility. The only other person I've come across who's written generously about Heisenberg is Max Perutz.[11] He went to see the play and sent me a collection of his essays, which I'm reading at the moment. They are wonderful, and in one of them he writes in a very level-headed and sensible way about Heisenberg.

May I take it, then, that the mythic element is not something you're so interested in; you're much more interested in the specifics of motivation?

I think it's the epistemology that is really the take-off point for me. But I think any good play or good book is about more than one thing. It would be difficult to find a good play just about one particular thing, don't you think?

Of course, I wouldn't want to limit it. I just wondered whether the Oedipal myth had shaped your thinking in any way. It could be said that the play inverts Oedipus so that it's the father-figure who comes out on top. Ultimately you could say, given the small number of advocates Heisenberg has had, that he is beginning to win through.

Yes, in this particular instance; but it has to be said that in terms of doing the original sums in the Twenties and Thirties, Heisenberg was a Titan. Everyone recognises that he was an immensely productive and brilliant scientist who made the most fundamental and radical advances which are still part of

---

[10] *Copenhagen*, p. 111.
[11] b. 19 May 1914, Vienna; Austrian-born British biochemist, co-recipient of the 1962 Nobel Prize for Chemistry for his X-ray diffraction analysis of the structure of haemoglobin, the protein that transports oxygen from the lungs to the tissues via blood cells.

physics. There are some who would prefer his discoveries not to be part of physics. I've talked to atomic physicists who say, 'There must be a way round uncertainty, there must be a way round quantum mechanics as formulated in the Copenhagen Interpretation.' But no one can suggest what it is. As you know, Einstein never accepted it, he could not bring himself to believe that the world worked like that – but he couldn't find any way of rejecting it.

Sure, but Heisenberg winds up in a cave with a reactor on the verge of meltdown.[12]

His life went wrong at that point. It has to be said that after the war he attempted to do a lot of fundamental research on something called S-matrix theory, which I can't begin to understand or give you any account of, but it is one of those theories of the sort that Einstein was working on, a general theory of everything, like the unified field theory that eluded Einstein. I'm not in a position to make any comment at all, but S-matrix theory has never been accepted by other physicists. So he did fail in later life in his theoretical physics.

He was very effective in a practical way, though. He was put in charge of German science by the British after the war, and he did actually do what he said he was going to do (which is to say, to restore German physics after Hitler went). He was the head of the Max Planck Institute in Göttingen, and he did get it on its feet again. He was also immensely effective in nuclear policy in Germany. As you know, Germany became very heavily committed to civil nuclear energy, and Heisenberg was certainly an effective voice in that. Germany was also scheduled to become a nuclear power in the military sense – the Americans wanted to arm Germany with nuclear weapons as a bulwark against the Soviet Union – and Heisenberg and Weizsäcker led the campaign against it, and they succeeded. Germany has never had any nuclear weapons.

So that was not ineffectual; he was a very effectual voice. Okay, he failed to build nuclear weapons, but the question of whether that was really a failure or really a success remains very difficult to decide.

Margrethe has a speech: 'That was the last and greatest demand that Heisenberg made on his friendship with you. To be understood when he couldn't understand himself. And that was the last and greatest act of friendship for Heisenberg that you performed in return. To leave him misunderstood.'[13] *What's going on there?*

The suggestion in the play was that maybe – I couldn't push it too far, I couldn't give you any evidence – but it seems to me a plausible possibility that although Heisenberg went to Copenhagen in 1941 for a variety of

---

[12] *Copenhagen*, pp. 50–2.
[13] *Copenhagen*, p. 91.

reasons (I'm sure he had various things in his head not entirely thought out), at the bottom there was some sort of uneasiness, there was something at the back of his mind that he hadn't found yet, some unexamined thing that he wanted to discover. And the way he had always examined things in the past was to talk about them with other scientists and, in particular, talk about them with Niels Bohr. What he hadn't done – and this is, I think, historical fact, though Powers wouldn't agree – he hadn't attempted the diffusion equation in uranium-235. What the play is saying is that if Bohr had remained very calm, and debated the thing rationally with him, he would at some point have said, as he would have done in the 1920s, 'Look, we're absolutely certain it's going to take huge quantities of uranium-235 – but the diffusion equation's only been solved for *natural* uranium. What's the result of doing the diffusion in U-235?' Heisenberg would have said, 'Oh well, I suppose it's the same as natural uranium.' Bohr would have said, 'Come on, do it for U-235.' And Heisenberg would have done it, and probably done it very quickly – by his standards it wasn't a very difficult calculation – and would have discovered that you needed this relatively small amount of uranium-235, so he might just possibly have gone back to Germany and said, 'We might just be able to separate enough U-235 to do it. We don't need to wait for the reactor, we could actually build weapons with U-235.' He might have done that. What Margrethe is saying is that Bohr didn't raise the question: he lost his temper, he never debated the thing with him, so Heisenberg never discovered that he hadn't done the diffusion equation.

Is the implication then that Bohr lost his temper quite deliberately?

No, the implication is that it just happened, but the way it worked out saved us all. This is putting it very strongly, of course. I think it's very unlikely that Germany could have developed nuclear weapons even if Heisenberg *had* done the equation, but it's just possible, it's just possible. And what she's saying is, as it happened, it saved us all from getting nuked by Nazi Germany.

There's this other prong to the argument whereby Heisenberg seems to be stepping back from actually fully realising how things could be done. You say in the Postscript that he held the knowledge from himself.[14]

Yes, it's an impossible area to examine, but this is what the play is attempting to do: to examine a non-event. Why did he not do the diffusion equation? I don't think there's any way of proving it, or even making a very good, strong,

[14] *Copenhagen*, p. 112.

suggestive case, but it is striking that Frisch and Peierls[15] did do the equation. They started from exactly the same position as Heisenberg of being absolutely certain it would take tons of U-235, so it wasn't worth doing – but they did it. Why did *they* do it, and Heisenberg not? You can't help thinking that Frisch and Peierls felt themselves justified in working on nuclear weapons because they were terrified the Nazis were also developing them. They were both refugees from Nazi persecution. Heisenberg never felt that. If you read the Farm Hall transcripts,[16] the Germans never seriously got round to the idea of nuclear weapons. They thought they were exonerated from considering it, they never really pushed it. And they didn't push it, one can't help feeling, because they didn't really want to. They could safely work on the reactor without it involving any serious moral problems about whether they were supplying Hitler with weapons.

In Heisenberg's case, do you see that, even perhaps on a subconscious level, he defers to the father-figure, Bohr?

In the sense that he was waiting to be authorised by Bohr to think the thought, you mean?

Yes.

I think it's quite likely that was part of his thinking; when he was interviewed by David Irving for *The Virus House*[17] he certainly agreed with the idea that he had wanted absolution. Jensen had said that the reason that Heisenberg went to Copenhagen was that he wanted absolution, and David Irving put that to him. Heisenberg said that Jensen had put it perfectly. That runs radically counter to the account Heisenberg gives in his memoirs of why he went, which was trying to get Bohr to persuade Allied scientists to agree to say it was going to be too expensive to attempt, or too impractical to attempt, in return for Heisenberg giving similar advice on the German side. The two explanations can't really be fitted together, but he offered them both, which makes me feel that he had a mixture of things consciously on his mind when he went, and the unconscious reason was not quite any of them.

---

[15] In 1940 Otto Frisch (1904–1979) and Rudolf Peierls (1907–95), both at the University of Birmingham, issued a three-page memorandum that correctly theorised that a highly explosive but compact bomb could be fashioned out of small amounts of uranium-235. This memo ignited the race to develop the bomb in Britain and the United States, advancing it from an issue of academic speculation to an Allied war project of the highest priority.
[16] Transcripts of conversations among Nazi scientists detained by the Allies at Farm Hall, near Cambridge, before and after the detonation of the atom bomb in 1945. First published 1993.
[17] The story of the German bomb programme, published 1967.

I hope I'm making myself clear; it's a very unclear area. That's really what the play is about – it's about an attempt to investigate something that's very unclear, a very uninvestigatable area.

Heisenberg has a memorable speech where he invokes Hamlet: 'We went to Elsinore. I often think about what you said there ... the whole appearance of Elsinore, you said, was changed by our knowing that Hamlet had lived there. Every dark corner there reminds us of the darkness inside the human soul ...'[18]

It's Bohr who said that in the first place, I'm just quoting what Bohr did actually say in life.

It's quite convenient, though, for your purposes?

Yes, of course.

I only say that because Hamlet *is all about another father–son relationship.*

That's true, yes. That's true.

And an Oedipal one at that.

Hmmm. Well. *Hamlet* is certainly about the father, son and stepfather relationship. He's not planning to murder his father, is he? The question is whether he should murder his father's murderer.

It does seem to me that it's very helpful to have that kind of Shakespearean parallel plot in the background, because although Copenhagen *isn't exactly* Hamlet, *you're following that line of narrative, taking reference from similar coordinates.*

Yes, there certainly are parallels. A lot of *Hamlet* is about the difficulty of arriving at a decision, and of knowing whether you're going to do something. In this play, though, it's Margrethe who feels the jealousy – not exactly of her husband's relationship with Heisenberg, but of Heisenberg's coming to seem to displace their son, of being a substitute for their dead son.

Entirely reasonably; she's the only person in the play who seems grounded in any way.

Yes. It is historically true that Bohr did discuss all his work with Margrethe, and she had no scientific training at all. He must have been able to put it in

---

[18] *Copenhagen*, pp. 30–1.

something like plain language. He spoke at length about how everything had to be put into plain language, that this was the point of science, but what he meant by that was the language of classical science: it's not something that I would easily understand, when he tries to translate the language of quantum physics into classical mechanics. So he must have been able to put it more directly still to Margrethe, if he really did talk about it with her.

There's that slightly more human side to him; he's a Romantic.

Yes, he was a *mensch*, I think he really was. But he was also obsessive about his work – they all were – they couldn't have done it otherwise.

One of the slightly daunting things about the after-effects of this play is I've had to speak to various groups of science writers and scientists, including a conference on particle physics in Oxford. There was a Russian physicist there who agreed with the basic thesis; he said that to do anything as difficult as the physics involved in making nuclear weapons, you had to want it not 95 per cent, or even 97 per cent, or even 99 per cent – you had to want it 100 per cent, with your whole heart and soul, otherwise you didn't have a chance of success. He agreed that the evidence was that Heisenberg and his team didn't have that kind of commitment to it, for whatever reason; and our team did. It's very difficult to come to any other conclusion but that the Allied scientists felt they were morally justified because they were trying to produce weapons to forestall someone they regarded as evil. The people on the German side had very similar ideas about the Nazi leadership – that they were evil – and didn't have any great enthusiasm to supply them with weapons.

As you say, that is something Copenhagen *has in common with* Hamlet: *it's about taking moral responsibility for what you do.*

Yes. Possibly you avoid it, which is maybe what Heisenberg was trying to do. I think, whatever view you take of Heisenberg, he was in a terribly difficult situation. He was not in any sense a Nazi, not in any sense a Nazi sympathiser, but he was a rather romantically patriotic German. And that seems to me no less acceptable than to be a romantically patriotic Englishman or American. There are moral drawbacks in all those cases, and for Germans in the Nazi period to find any decent way to behave was very, very difficult.

I am astonished by the ease with which British and American commentators have condemned him. People who were never called upon to make any great moral decisions in their life find it so easy to condemn Heisenberg for not taking a heroic stand. I think you can admire people who are heroes, but you can't *require* people to be heroes – otherwise there's no point in admiring them when they *are* heroic.

If heroism were the default, it wouldn't count as such.

No, indeed. Absolutely. One of the interesting reactions to the play was from Heisenberg's niece, who lives in this country, who had gone to see the play with Heisenberg's grand-daughter. She says that the play made clear to her, for the first time, some of the splits that had occurred in the family as the result of their attitudes to Nazism. Different branches of the family had taken different views about what you had to do about Nazism. Her father was Elizabeth Heisenberg's brother – Heisenberg's brother-in-law – and he had taken the view, in 1936, that the only way to oppose Hitler was to go into exile, and he'd come to this country. Heisenberg had taken the view that he had to stand and do what he could inside Germany, and the two sides of the family have never really been able to come to terms with the other's position. The brother-in-law (that's to say, Elizabeth Heisenberg's brother), as I only very slowly realised, is Fritz Schumacher, the 'small is beautiful' man.[19] She sent me some letters he had written when he went back to Germany after the war in 1945 to see his family again. There he revealed how painful the chasm was between them, how they felt that in some way he had avoided the moral issues that had confronted them, and that he had not gone through the suffering that they had gone through in the German defeat. Although there was some very, very strong family feeling for each other, there was this abyss between them that could never be quite bridged.

This doesn't cast much light on how Michael Blakemore and I work. I'll tell you something about Michael Blakemore: he's too good a director for his own good. If you want to make your reputation as a director, you need to direct the classics, because if you direct a play everyone has seen before, everyone can see what you've done. If there's a production of *Hamlet* and everyone's going round on roller-skates, they know that's the director's idea, because they know Shakespeare's stage directions didn't say anything about going round on roller-skates, and they've seen a lot of other productions where no one went round on roller-skates. So the director gets the credit or the blame for this idea. If you do a new play, no one has the faintest idea what was the director's idea and what was the writer's idea, or what the actors suggested in the rehearsal room. If you're a really good director like Michael Blakemore, and you serve the play instead of thinking how to make it striking and bring a bit of credit to you as director, no one thinks you've done anything; they just think, there's the play, and you just told the actors to stand there and say the lines and that was the end of it. But what a good director does with a new play (and what Michael's always done with me) is to work with the writer first of all, both to get the text right and to make sure

---

[19] Ernst Friedrich Schumacher (1911–1977), British economist who developed the influential concepts of 'intermediate technology' and 'small is beautiful'.

he's understood the play – which is quite difficult with a new text, it's not at all obvious. With *Noises Off*, for instance, Michael persuaded me to rewrite great slabs of the play, because they were not clear. He also put forward a lot of ideas of his own which I incorporated into the play, but he doesn't get the best director prizes because no one can see the work that's gone in. It's like seeing some beautifully made suit: no one can see the sewing because it's so fine that it eludes the eye.

Did you always envisage Copenhagen *in the round?*

I didn't really envisage it clearly at all. Insofar as you can write a play and not envisage it, I tried not to envisage it. I saw it as a set of dramatic situations. When Michael and I talked about it – I can't remember whether he suggested it should be in the round or I suggested it should be in the round – it immediately seemed like a good idea. Partly to create an arena of debate with everyone focussed around it, and partly to make people conscious of the audience, since what the play is finally about is suggesting that we do all need an audience to understand what's going on in ourselves. There's some unconscious reinforcement of that idea given by the fact that the audience actually does surround the action of the play, so the audience are, in a sense, part of the action. It was a bit subliminal – I wouldn't push that too far, but I think it does help. In fact in Paris we can't do that because Paris laws or by-laws (I'm not sure which) absolutely make it impossible for the audience to go on the stage because of the fire risk. So in Paris it's done on a similar set to London except there's no audience round the back.

What about casting? Do you leave that to Michael Blakemore or do you help out?

Everyone asks about casting. Casting's unbelievably difficult. It's astonishingly difficult to look at the text of a new play, and to try and grasp what the characters are like, and to think which out of all the actors and actresses you've seen playing completely different sorts of parts in the past could do these. And everyone pitches in. Anyone who's got any ideas about casting – if a teaboy comes in with ideas about casting you listen to him reverently and with interest! So I certainly thought about that with Michael, and we had endless sessions with the casting director at the National Theatre. We went back and forth, back and forth, going over all the possibilities. I don't think I made any useful contribution to the three we finally picked – except that we did ask Matthew Marsh[20] to read for us, because I hadn't seen him before.

---

[20] Werner Heisenberg in the National Theatre production.

Do you play a part in things like set design, lighting, and so forth?

Not a very big part with Michael Blakemore. Michael and I have worked together so much that I usually let him get on with things in general, and on the whole he does all the initial discussions with the set designer. When there's something to look at – a model or something – I go along and look at it and make possible comments and suggestions. I'm not sure I've ever made any comments which led to anything being changed.

I don't like going to rehearsal if I can possibly avoid it. I also think it's a good thing if someone stays out of rehearsal, because otherwise the thing changes so slowly that no one can see what's happening – it's like watching a snail creeping across the road.

That's why you don't like rehearsals?

Partly, yes. It is a slow process. I can see that it's an interesting process too, to people who are actually involved in it, like the actors and the director. Some writers insist on going to all rehearsals; I wouldn't like to do that. So I go to the first rehearsal, meet the cast and make cheering noises, and then go away again, telling Michael not to bother me unless there's something to look at, like running an Act. Then I can see what's happened, and I can make some comments – this seems to be coming along, that's going in the wrong direction, or whatever.

Is this play very specific to our time?

I don't know, I just don't know. The physics has entered the realm of history. It's historic physics, nowhere near the cutting edge of current thought. But I suppose, because modern physics is very difficult, it hasn't been completely mastered by the lay public. I think a lot of people who see the play, who are not scientists, may have come across the ideas in general terms before, but not in detail. It seems to me that those ideas remain fairly accessible, so the audience can learn something relatively new which is not impossibly difficult.

Do you think there's any sense in which discussions about uncertainty have a particular bearing on the late 1990s?

I should have thought that questions of motivation and the uncertainty of human intentions began very early in pre-history and are likely to continue until the race dies out.

Certainly, the play is about the difficulty of ever getting your hands on certain crucial aspects of human experience. They do elude description and elude examination, and yet they are absolutely central to our lives and to the way we think about ourselves and the way we understand the world. It's very interesting. The uncertainty principle, or indeterminacy, was introduced in 1926, and has been around, effectively unchallenged (people have attempted to challenge it, but no one's ever managed to dispute it), until about six weeks ago, when I saw a headline in *New Scientist* saying 'The Uncertainty Principle is Dead'. You wait seventy years, everything's all right, you get the play on, and then they knock the ground away from under your feet! But actually, when I read the piece it seemed to be slightly less dramatic than that.

There was a team at the University of Koblenz who have actually performed the thought-experiment that Bohr, Heisenberg and Schrödinger were talking about, the one with the two slits.[21] Then, there was not the faintest possibility of ever setting this up in practice. What it was suggesting is that if you could fire a single photon, a single particle of light, at a screen with two slits in it, the photon would pass through both slits, and you could tell this because it would form an interference pattern on the screen behind the slits, which could only be formed by waves coming through different openings. In other words, the particle behaves like a wave. However, if you look at the photon while it's doing this, it ceases to behave like a wave, and behaves like a particle, instead going through only one slit, and there would be no interference pattern on the screen.

These people at Koblenz with modern techniques have actually made it possible to fire a single particle at what's effectively a screen with two slits (it's something technologically more complex than that, although that's effectively what it is), and have demonstrated that it is true that if you don't look at it, it forms an interference pattern – in other words it behaves as a wave. If you do look at it, it behaves as a particle and goes through one slit.

There's a theorist at Cambridge who has been looking at these results, and he says that although this appears to be explained by uncertainty, it's just a mathematical coincidence that uncertainty seems to offer an explanation for it, and in fact there is a much deeper principle involved. But he agrees (as does everyone) that uncertainty is a valid principle; it's just a question of whether it explains the two slits experiment. The deeper principle he calls 'entanglement'. I can't begin to give you any better account of it than this: he says that a quantum particle effectively is two versions of itself. It's a pair of *Doppelgängers* which can be very remote from each other in space. If you hit it with a photon in order to look at it – if you shine some light on it in order to see what it's doing, where it is – the photon doesn't affect the behaviour of the particle it's hitting (as Heisenberg suggested in his original paper), so much as catch the double nature from the particle, and it then itself becomes a pair of *Doppelgängers*. Each of the original particles then has a *Doppelgänger* photon, which affects its behaviour.

---

[21] *Copenhagen*, pp. 25–6.

So in spite of the headline, the uncertainty principle is still alive and well. The suggestion is simply that it doesn't explain the two slits experiment.

Do you see connections between this play and any of the others you've written?

Someone has suggested to me that in formal terms, *Copenhagen* is exactly like *Noises Off*. In each of the plays, the same scene is played three times. *Noises Off* is about this terrible farce: in the first scene you see them rehearse it; then you see them do the same Act backstage; and in the last Act you see the Act from in front again but by this time the action backstage is starting to leak on the stage and make the play unplayable. In this play, they go notionally through the meeting in Copenhagen three times. First they say remembering something is like being there again, and they actually go through the meeting. Then at the end of the Act, Bohr says, 'Let's try it again',[22] and he arrives at the house a second time, and we then switch back to what it was like in the 1920s when they were doing the theoretical research together. At the end of the play he agrees that they still haven't hit upon an explanation as to why he went to Copenhagen, and Bohr says, 'Let's do one final draft.'[23] He arrives at the house again, and this time you just hear odd lines of that scene, while we hear the thoughts of the characters as they look at each other, and try to work out what the other is doing.

Are you conscious of any Romantic tendencies in your writing? I ask because I see the aim of the play as being to redeem the various personages from their historical reality and to lend their plight in 1941 a kind of permanence, within the context of the literary work.

The whole nature of the play means that we're not going through those events for the first time round, but that we're trying to fix them in some way out of the flux of the past. Whether the play will go on having any resonance I don't think you can tell. You just have to see. Some plays and books seem to go on being meaningful even when they seem to be very attached to the times they were written in; some that appear to have a classical timelessness get swept away by time.

We had quite a lot of difficulty in the rehearsal room with the time zones in the play, incidentally. The cast quite often were confused as to where they were; whether they were now in 1941 or 1925 or 1922, or in some timeless point in the future. I suppose one's got to get it clear for practical purposes, but it does seem to me to be not a particularly artificial convention that we do, all of us, live in different time zones. In the most ordinary way we are

---

[22] *Copenhagen*, p. 53.
[23] *Copenhagen*, p. 88.

remembering things that happened yesterday and things that happened twenty years ago. We are worrying about things that might or might not happen tomorrow, or next year, and we switch back and forth from one to the other quite informally and effortlessly.

One of the reasons they sent for Michael Blakemore to do the play in Paris was that they got half way through rehearsals with another director who was doing an extremely elaborate production which involved a lot of white tulle. The white tulle was used (insofar as I can understand it) to indicate when characters were remembering things; there were lots of translucent white curtains that came in when characters were remembering things and then went out again when they were in the present. What it must have been like I cannot imagine! I can see that might be workable if you just have the occasional flashback, but not where people are moving backwards and forwards all the time. What they did with the curtains I can't think; they must have been flapping back and forth, and in and out, and up and down.

It sounds more like Noises Off.

Anyway, they fired the original director rather brutally and asked Michael Blakemore to go over. He did away with the curtains, that was the first thing he did!

Michael Blakemore

Michael Blakemore

Michael Blakemore began his career as an actor with the Birmingham Repertory Theatre, and then with the RSC, 1952–66. He became a co-director at the Citizens, Glasgow, 1966–68, and went on to become Associate Director of the National Theatre, 1971–76. He has directed, among many others, Peter Nichols' *A Day in the Death of Joe Egg* (1967), *Arturo Ui* (featuring Leonard Rossiter in one of his great comic stage roles, 1969), David Hare's *Knuckle* (1974), Nichols' *Privates on Parade* (1977), and Miller's *All My Sons* (1981); for the National he directed Nichols' *The National Health* (1969), O'Neill's *Long Day's Journey into Night* (1971), and *Macbeth* (1972). He has directed three films: *A Personal History of the Australian Surf* (1981), *Privates on Parade* (1983), and *Country Life* (1995), and is the author of a novel, *Next Season* (1969).

His collaboration with Frayn dates back to *Make and Break*, produced at the Lyric Theatre, Hammersmith, where he was Resident Director, 1980. He has gone on to direct six more works by Frayn: *Noises Off* (1982), *Benefactors* (1984), *Uncle Vanya* (1988), *Here* (1993), *Copenhagen* (1998), and *Alarms and Excursions* (1998). He also directed a revival of Frayn's translation of *The Seagull* (1990).

Copenhagen presents certain obvious challenges to any director. With three actors holding the stage in dialogue for the entire play, any successful production must be regarded as a *tour de force*. I visited Michael Blakemore at his home in Belsize Park, London, on 26 March 1999. He had recently returned from Paris after completing work on the first French production of the play. I asked him, among other things, about the challenges in mounting a production of this unusual work.

Interview

Duncan Wu: *How would you describe your job as director?*

Michael Blakemore: The director's job is to realise the text through the language of acting and through the language of theatrical presentation. If the play is a good one – and I usually attempt to do good plays – the first obligation on me is to bring out what is in the text, but which may be concealed. It is not enough for the text just to be read aloud: that is a frequent academic misconception, particularly with the classics – the belief that, if the text is simply delivered, it will somehow live the way it lives on the page in the mind of the reader. In a public performance something else has to happen; it has to go through another process, and that process is the text filtered through the minds of actors, and actors with their director thinking about resonances and depths within the text that maybe haven't yet occurred to them.

Once one's gone as far as one can, trying to realise the intentions of the author, then I think it's sometimes possible for the director to go a little bit further – to extend the writing. It's always, I think, derived from what's there initially. Often moments of invention that I'm particularly proud of have been credited to the author. This is irritating to one's vanity, but at least means I've done my job properly.

You mention the author's intentions. In the case of authors who are absent for whatever reason, are those intentions that you surmise?

Yes. I don't believe that a play means something absolutely concrete for all time; it's something which alters its character according to the times in which it's presented. There is a certain sort of flexibility to interpretation, and indeed the author himself may not be *entirely* aware of possibilities within his play, and in twenty years' time a director will get the text and do something with it that the author didn't envisage.

But I think if you're doing a new play you have to assume that the man who wrote it knew what he was trying to do, so the first thing with Michael Frayn, or any playwright that I work with, is I spend a lot of time with them, going line by line through the text, and I simply ask dumb questions – 'What exactly do you hope to achieve here? What exactly does that mean? What sort of person do you think this is?' I ask those questions going meticulously through the text. When I think that I have got as much from him as I can, then I work on it myself, and hopefully an additional layer is added. Then the actors come on board, and I pass on to them the thoughts that I have which are derived from the talk I've had with the dramatist, and then you get their input. And of course all these different inputs represent different stories, because they are built on a variety of different personalities and different temperaments. Hopefully it comes out at the end as a successful amalgam of all these elements.

In terms of the writer–director relationship, are you a bit like an editor?

Initially one is like an editor, and in certain plays I've had quite a big editorial contribution. This was true of *Noises Off*,[1] which was easier because it's a farce, and there's something mechanical about farce, and therefore it's possible to approach it almost mathematically. This isn't true of other sorts of plays. On the other hand, with *Benefactors*[2] or indeed *Copenhagen*, I made a few suggestions about cuts or clarifications, but virtually directed the play I first read. But it was nevertheless discussed at great length, and there were small changes made – which I suppose was due to my editorial input in that we arrived at certain alterations together.

You and Michael Frayn have been working together since 1980. It must be quite liberating for him to know that he can depend on your expertise for such things as the technical challenge of keeping three people on stage for two hours. I notice that there are comparatively few stage directions in the printed text of Benefactors.

And none in *Copenhagen*.

Do you think that he's got into the habit of regarding you as a partner in the process of production?

I think that is true. I hope he trusts me. He'll listen to anything you have to say, and will get very excited if you have an idea that he thinks will energise the piece. But he also knows that if he says, 'No, I don't like that', there's a point beyond which I won't argue: he wrote the play and I *must* accept his authority. But otherwise he just leaves me to get on with it. Our arrangement is that he knows he's welcome at rehearsals any time he likes. He usually comes to the first reading – with *Copenhagen* we sat around a table reading it for the first week and he was there to elucidate, or help, or explain things – then he goes away, and says, 'Ask me back when you want me back.'

This is good for me because, if an author is constantly in attendance (which I don't mind and, in the case of the other plays, that's how it's been), he becomes sucked into the process, the politics of the rehearsal room, and this can affect his objectivity. But if the author stays away and you say, 'I think we've got something to show you, come back and tell us what you think', he will see his play as if for the first time – and will know at once what he likes, what he doesn't like. And that's very useful.

---

[1] Three-act play first performed at the Lyric Theatre, Hammersmith, 23 February 1982, directed by Blakemore. It transferred to the Savoy Theatre, 31 March 1982, opened in New York the following year, and was filmed by Peter Bogdanovich in 1992.
[2] Frayn's two-act play was first performed at the Vaudeville Theatre, London, 4 April 1984, directed by Blakemore; another production opened the following year in New York, and it was televised in 1989.

Do you ever find yourself going down dead-ends when you're in rehearsal, which you're happier the writer isn't there to witness?

No, I don't mind that particularly. The only thing about the writer, if the writer attends, is: he's either got to be there the entire time, so that we get used to him, or come when we've got something to show him. In a rehearsal room you're asking people to shed their inhibitions and this requires candour and trust. Everyone there becomes bonded by the terrors ahead and a person who comes in from outside (particularly if he has the authority of the author – who is, after all, the court of final appeal) can introduce tension into the rehearsal room, which isn't productive. If the author's there every day, fine; if he's not going to be there every day, it's nice if he comes when we're ready to show him something.

Do you experiment when you're rehearsing a play? Do you ever do improvisations, or do you just stick to the text most of the time?

I do stick to the text. There is a school of directors (I think Max Stafford-Clark is one of them) for whom certain experimental techniques are central. I come out of a slightly earlier tradition and that's not the way I've worked. But sticking to the text there's still a variety of ways it can be explored.

   Copenhagen is a very particular play, because it deals with scientists, people who practically define themselves by the lucidity and passion they bring to the espousal of their ideas and theories. This clarity of thought is a requirement of any production of the play with whatever cast. So a lot of our early work was simply sitting around a table, making sure that the actors understood every scientific postulate in the play (although they didn't need to be experts in theoretical physics!). We had to make sure that they were so at ease with these concepts that they could embrace the dialogue with real authority. Some of this science was quite tricky to grasp.

You can say that again! I found it very tricky, it's quite a brain-twister.

And a lot of this theoretical physics appears to fly against common sense. The idea that the universe *only* exists inside the human head, and has no objective reality, is a very curious idea to most people. Indeed I remember David Burke,[3] when we were rehearsing the speech in which he expresses this, said, 'But I don't believe that, I don't believe that when I die, the universe as I see it won't go on existing.' And of course, that is a commonsensical conclusion. But as

[3] David Burke played Bohr in the Royal National Theatre production of the play. The speech to which Blakemore refers is on page 73 of the published text.

he got more familiar with the ideas in the play, as he became steeped in them, he was able to play that speech with real conviction.

In what way is it advantageous to work with the same writer repeatedly over a long period?

It's lovely to do a body of work together, and to have a very good professional relationship. There is a certain antagonism, I think, between writers and directors, built into the job, because the director *has* to accept that the play is, as it were, the first cause. There would be no production without it, and his artistic vision is at the service of someone else's. There's a certain collision which can be fruitful, but can also be painful, and often director–writer collaborations last about three shows, before they begin to get a little bit ragged. Elia Kazan, who directed Arthur Miller and Tennessee Williams, always resented the fact that the playwright had to come first. He served his playwrights, but he didn't like it: that's why he went into movies and wrote novels. He said, 'I never want to work on another line that some other man has written.' He wasn't a bad novelist, but he wasn't as good a writer as the people whose work he had directed. In the movies, of course, there's the cult of the director, and the contribution of the poor old writer is taken entirely for granted. Critics talk about the themes and so forth as if they had no existence in the screenplay. So there is that rivalry, I suppose.

I had a successful collaboration with Peter Nichols earlier in my career, but it really did break down after about three shows.[4] I don't know what the reasons were, but certainly Peter was a little bit resentful of the contribution that I made, and I suppose I was resentful because he wasn't quite acknowledging that contribution. For whatever reason, we didn't continue; he wanted to get somebody else to direct his fourth play, because he felt that somehow his work was overshadowed by my participation in it – which wasn't the case at all, they were plays that stood on their own. We eventually got together again with *Privates on Parade*.

But this hasn't happened with Michael Frayn.

No it hasn't. Because he's an extremely reasonable man. I've often described Michael as a man of passionate moderation. He's acutely aware of someone else's point of view and will give it every consideration. But he's also a person of strong opinions; if he thinks something is wrong you can't budge him.

---

[4] Blakemore directed *A Day in the Death of Joe Egg* (1967), *The National Health* (1969), *Forget-Me-Not Lane* (1971) and *Privates on Parade* (1977).

You must have a unique overview of his oeuvre, *having been so close to it for so long.*

He's so totally unpretentious, and is happy with the idea of a play being an entertainment; he loves making people laugh. He's modest (though he doesn't underestimate his achievements), and this modesty perhaps has prevented him from being ranked where he should be, and where *Copenhagen* has undoubtedly put him: among the top playwrights. Of the plays I've done (and I've done a number of very good plays), there are only two which I think have an excellent chance of being done in sixty years' time.

And they are?

One is *Noises Off*, which seems to me about the most brilliant farce, the cleverest farce, that anybody has ever written, and the other is the totally different *Copenhagen.*

Noises Off *is such a good farce I'd say it transcends the form.*

It transcends the form, yes. As well as having all sorts of concealed ideas in it – because Michael's discipline was Philosophy. But he is not ashamed of being able to make people laugh, and believes (as I do) that laughter is a very important and civilising function.

What do you think Copenhagen *is about?*

Oh dear, that's the sort of question I dread. I think you could say it's about uncertainty.

That's what Michael says.

I think that's correct, then, it's about uncertainty. The play applies to our personal lives some of the discoveries made in theoretical physics, and tries to draw a parallel between what we know or don't know about physics, and what we know or don't know about our own behaviour. It's also about the consequences of our actions, and the way our actions lead us into areas which we cannot foretell, often with ominous consequences. Uncertainty! I'm glad I got away with that one!

That's a perfectly persuasive answer.

Why I admire it so much as a play is because, increasingly, the theatre is in competition with movies (most people's preferred entertainment) and television. And in order for the theatre to maintain its vitality and its interest, it has got to do something that the other, better-equipped mediums, can't do. *Copenhagen* is entirely a play: you couldn't have that experience in a movie theatre, you couldn't have that experience in a novel or in a television programme. It's entirely a play. So when you go to see it and you're sitting in the theatre, you think, I'm glad I'm here because I'm having the sort of experience I couldn't have anywhere else.

That is also true of *Noises Off*. They tried to make a film of *Noises Off*, and it didn't begin to work, because *Noises Off* needs live actors. In that second Act you're watching actors acting people at great physical risk, when they themselves are also putting themselves at risk. Falling downstairs and so on. It's a double thing, it's actors acting danger, and at the same time you think *they're* in danger. It has the *frisson* of acrobatics or the high wire.

At first sight, to the untutored eye, the printed text of Copenhagen *doesn't look very interesting dramatically, and I think it would take somebody with some experience to see in what ways it is. Why did you think it was?*

You're right to say that, because we had a lot of trouble casting this play. Many people who read it didn't like it, because to a careless reader or even just a reader reading it for the first time, it can seem a bit like a staged lecture: for most of the time you're grappling with the scientific concepts, which are not easy to grasp at a single reading.

It seemed to me when I read it that there were really two plays going on: there was the play of scientific ideas, which would need to be presented with the utmost clarity. But underneath there was another play about the emotions generated by the discovery and promotion of these ideas. The way, for instance, our sense of ourselves is defined by the work we do and our pride in it; the passion generated by the ideas we believe in and which to an extent we feel we own. Any woman in the audience could understand the wife's suspicion of this bright young man arriving in her house like the proverbial cuckoo in the nest. There was all this going on underneath the science: the egotism of these people, the fury with which they justified themselves, the rages between friends. Other things, too. The way we all tend to sentimentalise the past, and make it seem much more pleasant than it actually was – because the past, it's got a ribbon round it, and it's neat and tidy, unlike the uncertainty of the present, endlessly created within the moment, messy and full of danger. There were these two plays, and the task of rehearsing it was, first of all, to make sure that the science was properly dealt with, and then to unearth all this conflict, this to-ing and fro-ing of right and wrong that these highly intelligent people share with the rest of us.

There's a mythic element to it. It's a play of relationships. It's almost like a sort of love affair, the father–son relationship that is constantly being returned to.

Yes, that's right. And the suspicion of the woman, and her dislike of this son-figure that the man has adopted.

There are other things, too, that, when Michael wrote it, and when I first read it, we weren't aware would work in the play's favour. The first of these is that it deals with an *extremely* important subject, namely atomic annihilation. The moment somebody says 'plutonium' in the play, everybody in the audience sits up and starts paying close attention. This also applies when the universe as merely an aspect of human perception is being discussed. Again people think: Now this is important. I ought to listen to this.

The other thing is that (and I don't think either of us realised this until the play was in front of an audience) many of the scientific theories in the play find a parallel in the very act of public performance. In the play it's explained that it's impossible to know everything about the behaviour of an electron, because in order to observe it you have to shine a light on it – it has to be hit by a photon – which will alter the behaviour you're trying to observe.[5] This is exactly what a theatrical performance is like: the actors rehearse the play by themselves in a room, and they think they know what they're doing, who they are. You then put it on a public stage, and an audience, like a lot of photons, shine their attention on it. Now the play is suddenly something different. It is altered by the presence of the audience, and the actor at last has a clear idea of the power of his part.

Towards the end of the play I was concerned whether we would be able to hold the audience's attention during that third, difficult examination of Heisenberg's visit to the Bohrs' house in 1941. Heisenberg struggles to analyse the way he perceives the two other people in the room with him – 'Bohr has gone even as I turn to see Margrethe.'[6] But this, of course, is exactly the way the audience are watching the actors on stage, and they listen to a description of their own behaviour spellbound. Theatrical performance actually animates all the things that the play is discussing. I don't think that audiences consciously realise that, but it's something they sense.

The heart of the play is an intangible, isn't it?

Yes.

We're talking about something sublime, almost metaphysical.

---

[5] *Copenhagen*, pp. 68–70.
[6] *Copenhagen*, p. 88.

Yes, we are I think. It's exciting on a level that you don't quite understand; that's the interesting thing about it. Most audiences can pretty much grasp the ideas; they can get the general feeling of them. They certainly understand the significance of the almost accidental invention of this terrible weapon, that came out of these self-absorbed scientists using their minds to have fun, to play games. To play games and to win: that's what they're about. They were privileged people, they had tenure, all they had to do was sit around and think. And out of this apparently harmless, enlightened activity came these terrible consequences.

The play makes reference, whether implicitly or explicitly, to other works – Hamlet *and* Oedipus *spring to mind.*

Hamlet is referred to in the text. The characters talk about Elsinore as representing the darkness inside the human soul.[7] I would think that is less a deliberate reference on the part of the author, than the sort of reference that would come naturally to the widely educated characters in the play. *Hamlet* and *Oedipus Rex* are part of their mental furniture to refer to when and where they apply.

I mentioned to Michael the fact that Hamlet is about another father–son relationship, and he said that he hadn't thought of that.[8]

I think the *Hamlet* reference is introduced into the play simply to make the point that, at the bottom, there's a nasty little vacuum inside us all.

How would you regard Bohr's recollection of his first meeting with Heisenberg, when he describes the rose garden and those wonderful surroundings?[9] Is it sentimentalised?

No, I don't think it is, particularly. What are sentimentalised are those memories of the Twenties at the beginning of the second Act, when they are recalling their hike through Europe, and their joint discoveries, and all that sort of stuff.[10] Margrethe is listening, and says, 'No, no; it wasn't like that at all.' But I think Bohr does remember that first meeting very accurately, and with great affection. I think that's fairly truthfully remembered, to the extent that anything can be.

---

[7] *Copenhagen*, pp. 30–1.
[8] See p. 223, above.
[9] *Copenhagen*, p. 22.
[10] *Copenhagen*, pp. 57–63.

That's an element of the text that needs to be preserved in terms of all the values that Bohr attaches to it.

Yes, I think so.

It must have been a particular challenge approaching a play with the same three characters on the stage the whole time.

It was hard. I loved the play and I would have wanted to do it whoever had written it. But I also wanted to do it because I have an ongoing relationship with Michael. We've done some plays that have been successful, and we've done some that have been shot down – I think of one in particular, which was most unfairly criticised, a play called *Here*, which I think is an extraordinary play.[11] I always found *Copenhagen* a thrilling read, and I just hoped other people would, but I had no idea (and I don't think he did either) that it would be the success it has been. We thought it would appeal to a smallish audience, who were possibly interested in the things it dealt with, but we didn't have any idea it would have the wide catchment it has had.

Do you know why that is?

I think for those reasons we've discussed. It does insinuate itself into the minds of an audience. But initially it was a forbidding play to attempt. Michael had no precise idea how it should be staged. At one point he suggested we maybe had a couple of armchairs on the stage, but I thought that would be far too stolid and constant a presence: I wanted to do it with as much flexibility as I possibly could, because it's constantly going back and forth in time, and what was required was an absolutely neutral background against which you could flip into the past then back into the present almost in the course of a single sentence. I had this original vision of just having a circle, like a drawing of an atom, and doing it in the round so that, wherever possible, some of the scientific concepts could be somehow acted out.

So that was your idea, of doing it in the round?

Yes – but it came out of talking with Michael. Originally I didn't want to have any chairs, I just wanted it to be round and maybe have it rather like a fishpond, a sort of lower area, so there would be two circles, and the actors would be able to sit on the rim of the inner one. We tried that with the designer,

---

[11] First performed at the Donmar Warehouse, London, 29 July 1993, directed by Michael Blakemore.

Peter Davison, but it looked odd, like an upside-down straw boater or an empty Jacuzzi. So we scrapped it.

Finally we just had the circle and three lightweight chairs of a Thirties design. Peter completed the surround of seating by building something that evoked the lecture theatre. The only other overt production technique I used was some very specific sound effects. Each time Heisenberg re-enacts his visit I wanted the doorbell to have an unsettling resonance as if it was echoing down time – in memory. I wanted a sound that the audience, too, would remember whenever that moment was revisited. And I think that works very well.

The other sound effect, which didn't occur to me until halfway through rehearsals, was the bomb going off,[12] and it's dramatically very useful. As in a Shakespeare play where you have the battle or the duel, it provides a focus, a climax to the events before the play, before the story is wound up. The bomb is the thing, the possibility, the play has been about; and of course the sound effect is not a bomb that went off, but a bomb that *might* have gone off, had Heisenberg done his calculations – and indeed might go off in the future.

The bomb's not marked in the script.

No, it's not marked in the script. There are no stage directions of any sort. It's one of those things that you stumble on, but it worked very well. Discovering such things is really a matter of luck. Sometimes they work, sometimes they don't. You're never quite sure until an audience tells you.

But I think we were lucky with *Copenhagen*. It involved long sessions with Michael and with the designer. Once I'd done everything I could with Michael, I worked very hard on the text by myself, because I knew that somehow we had to get as much variety, and as much movement, and as much clarity into it as possible.

Fortunately it begins with a strong, naturalistic scene; this is Heisenberg's first arrival at the house, which plays through like a straightforward scene. This leads into the dinner party, which again is a straight scene, so the audience are lured into the story in a way that's familiar to them. Now the play can go all over the place, which it does.

There are some odd elements in that first scene, of course. The first thing is that they're all dead.

---

[12] In Blakemore's production the sound of an exploding atom bomb was interpolated between Heisenberg's 'Hold on ...', and Bohr's 'And suddenly a very different and very terrible new world begins to take shape'; see *Copenhagen*, p. 91.

Yes, that's the initial premise. They're in some kind of unspecified waiting-room, where there's nothing to do but examine and re-examine their lives.

The second thing is that Margrethe hovers above things somewhat, as a choric figure.

Yes, that's right. She represents us, I think. She is not a scientist but she's a highly intelligent woman who can understand science and scientists. She hasn't got what they've got: the power of original thinking. Nor has she got any of the egotistical pride and jealous passions that go with their abilities. She can see the trap of the creative mind, the vanity that attaches to it.

You've already mentioned the final retelling of the story towards the end of the play.[13] You must always have seen that as a particularly important section.

It was the one section of the play I thought we'd never get away with. So much has already been asked of the audience, and now suddenly this! I thought they'd give up and not listen. But they don't: you can hear a pin drop.

Why do you think that is?

Because the play deals with a total shake-up of our commonsensical view of what happens when we open our eyes and regard the world. In a sense, this scene is particularising that; it's saying, 'Let's really analyse what happens when three people meet.' A lot of ideas have been bandied about in the play by this time – the idea, for instance, that when you're doing something you can't be thinking about it, and when you're thinking about it you can't be doing it; ski left, ski right, or think about it and die. In this scene, the third enactment, ideas are being explored and tested in terms of our moment-to-moment life. It's absorbing.

Then there's the episode in which the two particles collide for the third and last time. For me, it's close to being a transcendental moment of theatre; Margrethe calls it a 'great collision'.

HEISENBERG: He gazes at me, horrified.
MARGRETHE: Now at last he knows where he is and what he's doing.[14]

It's a moment that we've been prepared for; we've already seen it twice, and yet it's oddly compelling right then.

---

[13] *Copenhagen*, pp. 88–91.
[14] *Copenhagen*, p. 90.

But we've never seen that, you see. We've heard about it, but we've never seen it. It's been described on the other visits, and this is the first time it's been staged. Of course, the minute you see it, it's anti-climactic, because we know no more than we knew before. Not until Bohr suddenly has his idea for a thought-experiment, when he jumps to his feet and says words to the effect, 'Hold on, wait a moment, what if I hadn't reacted with horror? What if I hadn't gone charging off into the night? What if I'd played the part that he was expecting me to play, of the father and the adviser, and said to him, "Have you done the calculation?"' That's where it gets uncannily dramatic, and you suddenly see how the past, which reached a junction and went off in one direction, might just as easily have switched and gone off on another. Arbitrary causes leading to absolute conclusions.

I was totally persuaded I'd seen it before, but you're quite right – I hadn't. The thing is, it's been referred to, and one has envisaged it, and thought one had seen it – but of course that's wrong.

No, till that moment it's never been staged. It's begun to be staged, we do see them beginning the walk, and the great advantage incidentally of that circle is that you can stage walks as long as you like. The play's all about walking – when you walk, you talk, says Bohr.[15] When Heisenberg's going to the house, and he's walking through the night, as long as he's moving on the perimeter of that circle the audience will believe in his journey.

Michael very cleverly has a sort of time-jump when Bohr and Heisenberg walk out earlier on, so that you don't see what actually happens; all you see is the two men coming back to the house.

Yes, you see them leaving. The first time you see them leaving the house Margrethe's left on stage with her thoughts, and when they come back they're not speaking.[16] The second enactment doesn't deal with the walk at all,[17] and only on the third occasion do you see what actually happened on that walk.[18] In the second half of Act One, the walk is endlessly discussed but it's discussed in the past tense, it's not staged.[19]

The thought-experiment of that third meeting is a kind of fantasy, as to what might have happened.

---

[15] *Copenhagen*, p. 57.
[16] *Copenhagen*, p. 31.
[17] *Copenhagen*, p. 55.
[18] *Copenhagen*, p. 90.
[19] *Copenhagen*, p. 36.

That's exactly what it is. It's very like when some ghastly accident happens, or rather *doesn't* happen, and someone says, '*Thank God* I forgot to turn the gas on.'

Yes, in this case it's the opposite, because the terrible new world could have taken shape. It's a dystopic fantasy.

Exactly. The other scenario you could apply to the actual building of the Los Alamos bomb: 'If only we hadn't done that, if only we hadn't made that discovery, it would never have been invented.'

Margrethe has a speech: 'That was the last and greatest demand that Heisenberg made on his friendship with you. To be understood when he couldn't understand himself. And that was the last and greatest act of friendship for Heisenberg that you performed in return. To leave him misunderstood.'[20]

It's a very dense and complicated speech.

Can you tell me about it?

I think what she's saying is that Bohr did not behave characteristically, didn't behave as Heisenberg hoped he would. 'That was the last and greatest demand that Heisenberg made on his friendship with you': he wanted Bohr to help him with this moral and scientific problem, and be his mentor. 'To be understood when he couldn't understand himself': in other words, to be given the prod that Bohr gives him only in retrospect, by asking the question, 'Have you done the calculation?' 'And that was the last and greatest act of friendship for Heisenberg that you performed in return': which was not to behave as he expected you to behave, to be a mentor, but to react with anger and resentment.

Is the implication, then, that there was a deliberation about Bohr's being impatient, because he was deliberately enabling Heisenberg to avoid the moral responsibility?

No, I think the implication is it was sheer accident, and thank God it happened that way. 'Thank God you got angry.' It is absolutely arbitrary. We don't know how we're going to behave, and instead of behaving as Heisenberg wanted him to behave, and as he'd always behaved in the past – instead of doing that, Bohr got angry. Just accident.

So there's another act of generosity on Bohr's part?

---

[20] *Copenhagen*, p. 91.

'And that was the last and greatest act of friendship for Heisenberg that you performed in return' – to be angry. You saved Heisenberg from himself.

From having that knowledge and potentially going on to develop that weapon.

That's right. The implication being not that he wanted to develop a weapon for Hitler, but that his scientific vanity was such that, once he'd smelled the solution, he could not help but go on and be the one who'd solve the problem. It's clear that he wasn't at all sympathetic to the Nazis; he loved his country but he wasn't sympathetic to the Nazis – he just felt, if his country was at war, he should be there.

The thing that you've been coming back to is that element of vanity. Those two men are extraordinarily vain.

Yes, indeed, but not in the ordinary way of vanity. Not like a businessman saying, 'I'm earning £500,000 a year', not in any banal way, because in many ways they're modest, unpretentious men, very helpful and sweet to other people – but about their ideas.

In the way that people who live in their heads are vain.

Exactly. Scientists and artists, they both take voluptuous pride in their work. For instance, the idea of a book they wrote going out under somebody else's name! The human mind is extraordinarily proprietorial and protective of the things it invents, the things that it adds to the universe.

By contrast, Margrethe has that wonderful line, 'everything is personal',[21] and I felt that her function was to ground the intellectual ideas, and the dynamics of the play, in the realm of the personal.

That's right. That is her function, just to say, 'Hold on a second, you are like everybody else, you're not exceptions, you're as jealous and as emotionally turbulent as everybody else.' She also sees their behaviour in the ways it will affect her family. Bohr and Heisenberg see themselves as having their scientific lives apart from their family lives. She says, 'No, they're one and the same thing: one will affect the other.' That's why she reminds Bohr about how, whenever she gave birth, he'd get an assistant and go for a long hike through the Danish countryside, just to get away from the nappies.[22]

---

[21] *Copenhagen*, p. 75.
[22] *Copenhagen*, pp. 58–9, for instance.

Why is the drowning of Christian, Bohr's son, constantly invoked? It's recalled very powerfully towards the end of the play when Bohr is told by Heisenberg it wouldn't have helped if he had jumped in after Christian.[23] What's going on there?

First of all it's factually true. It's that irreducible core of grief that is at the heart of any human life. It's as inexplicable as all the other things that happen. It's just there, you can't say anything about it; terrible things happen, and sad things happen, and we're extremely lucky if we manage to escape them – but nobody ever does, really. It's like when they talk about Elsinore and the darkness inside the human soul. There's a darkness in the lives we all have to lead, which is at odds with this game-playing and scientific exhilaration. Something will always creep in under the door; you can never escape it, no matter how brilliant you are.

Do you mean uncertainty as to what our own motives are?

No, just the external things that happen to us as living organisms. Accidents will happen to us and people we love will die, and there will be disasters.

Is there any darkness in his own motives? It seems that Bohr is constantly tortured by the thought that he didn't jump in after Christian, even though it wouldn't have helped.

It is clear that it wouldn't have done any good if he'd done that; he simply would have drowned himself. But it's the only thing that Bohr can think might have made a difference. I don't think we're being asked to believe, maybe he should have jumped in, maybe he failed – it's just that that event cannot be ameliorated philosophically, there's nothing you can say about it except that it happened and that Bohr was marked by it for the rest of his life.

Tragic even.

Tragic, yes tragic.

Do you think such labels as 'tragic' and 'comic' are helpful when one's thinking about a play like Copenhagen?

One of the great things about the British tradition of writing plays is that the categories 'tragic' and 'comic' are deliberately blurred, beginning with

---

[23] 'What would it have achieved if you'd dived in after Christian, and drowned as well?', *Copenhagen*, p. 78.

Shakespeare. You get the gravedigger's scene, or Polonius and Reynaldo in *Hamlet*, funny scenes – and a lot of Hamlet himself is dryly funny – as opposed to the French tradition, where it's tragedy or comedy, one or the other. I like that mix, and I think that Michael does. There's a lot of laughter in *Copenhagen*.

It is a funny play in many ways.

Yes. There's a lot of quite strong laughs in it, although it's obviously much less funny than, say, *Noises Off*, which is designed to generate laughter, and nothing else.

Is Copenhagen *Michael Frayn's masterpiece?*

I think so, but it's an odd word, isn't it? It's got a neatness that I don't altogether like. What I particularly admire is that it's so completely a work for the theatre – not a film, not a radio play. You can't imagine experiencing it anywhere but in a playhouse. It's an important subject which is brilliantly handled. It's not as if Michael had said rather arbitrarily one day, 'Now I'm going to write a play about science.' It comes out of lifelong preoccupations.

I don't know if he told you, but when he was doing his National Service he was one of those people who was allowed to study Russian instead of the usual training, and he shared a billet with somebody who was passionate about theoretical physics, and got him interested, too. So that was one of his early enthusiasms. Possibly because a lot of the propositions like uncertainty bleed naturally into philosophy, which was Michael's subject. So this scientific material had been swilling around in his head for years, when he read this book by Thomas Powers about Heisenberg.[24] It greatly excited him, and suddenly he saw the possibilities of the play. I think good writing mostly comes out of the preoccupations of a lifetime. It's not someone arbitrarily choosing a subject; you have a moment of insight, and suddenly all the things you've been interested in are brought into focus in this project that's just occurred to you.

Do you think that there's something contemporaneous about it – that it could only have been written and produced now, at this point in our history? Or do you think it's one of those plays that could have been written at any time in the last thirty years?

It's very hard to make a judgement on that at this time. It'll be much more apparent in about ten years. The play certainly benefits from the theatrical

---

[24] *Heisenberg's War* (London: Jonathan Cape, 1993).

experiments that have been going on for the past thirty years, and it comes out of an awareness of the competition that the theatre is up against – of what films can do. The meticulous naturalism of a terrific playwright like Granville-Barker – I don't think anybody would embark on that now, because it can be done so much better in movies and television. So in a sense the form of *Copenhagen* has been imposed on Michael by the competition, and by what the theatre can still do. In many respects it's quite similar to *Benefactors*, but it dispenses with even the rudimentary sets of that play. That had a cast of four and depended more on realistic props – an Aga stove, a dining-room table, but there was a similar fluidity.

I thought it was very similar to Benefactors. *Do you think there's something thematically similar between the two?*

There may well be something thematically similar, I haven't even begun to think about that. Formally, I think they're not dissimilar. But this is far more audacious. By and large, *Benefactors* proceeded with scenes, quite clear scenes; it also tried to get rid of any extraneous naturalism, though not to the same extent as *Copenhagen*.

Whereas Copenhagen *throws out the whole concept of scenes.*

Yes, absolutely. No props. Absolutely no props, the only prop in the play is Bohr's pipe.

Besides the furniture.

Three chairs. Three chairs and a pipe. And you could do without the pipe if you wanted.

The programme for the Royal National Theatre production of the play is an invaluable guide to the background materials. There's a foldout chronology as to when each of the discoveries was made, from 1895, leading to the invention of the atom bomb in 1945. Interestingly, the chronology is circular in design, and it seems to me that it's a map for watching the play, for working out why it's performed in the round, and what the significance of that might be. There's so much information here and in Michael's Postscript to the printed text; do you see there being problems in the future for anyone who does this play without Michael or you? Or do you think that's not really a problem?

Yes, this additional information was Michael's work. I think I suggested a family tree of the bomb, but I didn't know how to go about it; he devised it.

My vanity was enormously tickled when they did the play at the Theatre Montparnasse in Paris, and the French producer rang me up and said, 'We need you, we need you.' So I went over, threw out their set, and started again. However, I would love to see another production that approached the play in an entirely different way, something that I hadn't remotely envisaged.

So other approaches could work?

They might, I don't know. The first rule of the theatre is that no one is indispensable. However, the first production of a new play is very important because it can either destroy it, or it can establish a way of doing it which then becomes *the* way to do it – and is copied all over the world. In any event, a good first production represents a backstop position. I think that one of the reasons why Michael wrote it without any stage directions was to give whoever attempts it a free hand. Certainly there have been different sorts of productions of *Noises Off* all over the place, one of which dispensed entirely with the third Act.

That's not possible, is it? How can you do that?

This guy thought it was. He just did. He stopped it after Act Two and said, 'That's the end of the play.'

But it doesn't make any sense without Act Three.

It doesn't, no. But he felt that he couldn't top the second Act, so he said, 'We'll end it here.' I think this was a production in the Balkans, not surprisingly.

APPENDIX I
Howard Brenton's Programme Note for '3 Plays for Utopia: A Howard Brenton Season' (1988)

The Royal Court produced three plays by Howard Brenton in spring–summer 1988 under the rubric, '3 Plays for Utopia': *Sore Throats*, *Bloody Poetry*, and *Greenland*. The scandal surrounding *The Romans in Britain* was still recent history, and the season served the useful purpose of clarifying Brenton's essential seriousness of purpose, and outlining his distinctive concerns as a playwright.

His programme note, below, appeared as the preface to *Greenland*, which was published to coincide with its first production on 26 May 1988. As it may be difficult for some readers to obtain, and is important for all students of Brenton's work, I reproduce it herewith by kind permission of the author.

3 Plays for Utopia: A Howard Brenton Season

On Writing the Utopian Plays

I first had the idea of writing a 'Utopian' play eleven years ago. I was on Epsom racecourse at the Derby of 1977 (Piggott on The Minstrel). It was one of those far-fetched ideas that can come to a playwright on a glorious summer's day – and then take ten years to finally achieve.

My first attempt at a play with Utopian themes was *Sore Throats* (1978 RSC at the Warehouse Theatre). It begins far from human dignity and peace. The first act is the most violent writing I have ever done. My instinct was that if you are going to show people moving towards a transformation into citizens of a Utopia or, in *Sore Throats*, a Utopian state of mind, you have to show them first at their vilest and their most unhappy. A playwright who shirks from writing about people at their worst, will not be believed when trying to write about them at their best. The three characters in *Sore Throats* set out on a crazy voyage in the play's second act. I finally imagined where to in the new play of this season, *Greenland*.

After *Sore Throats* I attempted an adaptation of William Morris's novel *News From Nowhere*. This has the reputation of being one of the great loony books of the left. I found it less silly that it is meant to be. But I couldn't make it work. Morris wrote in an historical innocence that we do not have. Then I tried a straightforward text, set a thousand years from now. It was incomprehensible. It was also unlivable – in trying to describe a heaven on earth, I had described a hell. I despaired of the idea and burnt everything I'd written for it (my small garden is rich with the typing paper ash of abandoned Utopias – at least they help the runner beans grow).

Then Roland Rees of Foco Novo Theatre asked me to write a play about the poet Shelley. What interested me about Shelley, Byron and their circle was that they were would-be Utopians, not only in their work and their views, but in the way they tried to live. So the play about them, *Bloody Poetry* (1984, Foco Novo Theatre, Leicester Haymarket and Hampstead Theatre), was a window opening for me. Byron, Shelley, Mary and Claire are moderns. They belong to us. They suffered exile from a reactionary, mean England, of which ours in the 1980s is an echo. They were defeated, they also behaved, at times, abominably to each other. But I wrote *Bloody Poetry* to celebrate and to salute them. Whether they really failed in their 'Utopian dreams' is not yet resolved.

In *Greenland* I come clean. Over half the play is set seven hundred years in the future. I have tried to dramatise how I hope my children, or my children's children's children, will live and think. The 'Greenlanders' in the play are strange, and their sense of humour is disturbing, but I would love to meet them.

Shelley said to me, when
I asked for a tip, 'Write first
For a new world within –
Always of
Men, women, nature and society –
Never forget
The world is old
But its great age has yet
To be made
Let alone told –
And declare you are a public enemy
Of kingly death, false beauty and decay'.
Ta, Percy. I'm on my way.
(Sonnet 30 from *Sonnets of Love and Opposition* by Howard Brenton)

APPENDIX II
David Hare's Programme Note to Shaw's *Heartbreak House* (1997)

David Hare's production of George Bernard Shaw's *Heartbreak House* opened at the Almeida Theatre, Islington, London, 14 August 1997. It is the subject of the second of my interviews with him, pp. 186–97, above. The programme carried an important essay by Hare about the play, explaining why he wished to direct it, and what it signifies. I thank him for permission to reproduce it here.

In the confident days of post-war expansion, most regional and national companies were able to rotate the same classic authors to make up a dependable repertoire of plays which Ken Campbell once wittily christened 'brochure theatre'. At your local theatre you could reasonably expect to see Shakespeare playing in a regular team of writers who usually included Wilde, Ibsen and Arthur Miller. But more recently, as theatres have suffered disastrously from public underfunding and as the comfortable literary consensus which underpinned their choices has disappeared, so artistic directors have needed to adopt a bolder and more improvised approach to creating a modern repertory. Some famous writers have continued to thrive. Chekhov's four best-known plays are still relentlessly revived. But the most eminent victim of this enforced shake-down has been the problematic figure of George Bernard Shaw. Sometimes it is as if we no longer quite know what to do with him.

On the publication of the final volume of Michael Holroyd's brilliant three-part biography in 1992, several reviewers noted how unfortunate it was that the fifteen years it had taken Holroyd to write the book had coincided with an irreversible decline in his subject's reputation. It would be hard, they insisted, to imagine a playwright more thoroughly out of fashion. Shaw, for all his extraordinary longevity and range, was associated with an era of rational Fabianism which no longer spoke to the modern world. Moreover, his plays, with their notorious long sentences and stagy attitudinising, implicitly embodied a fearful attitude to sex which our own more full-blooded age found spinsterish and immature. The characters were authorial mouthpieces – puppets, not people. The playwright once described as 'the creator of modern consciousness' seemed, in the way of many things new, to have become a victim of the fact that he had so completely dominated his own time. He had, in short, been superseded.

If these reviewers had looked a little harder they would have found that their supposed reassessments of Shaw more truly reflected the doubts which some audiences and critics had enjoyed about his work from the beginning. The character of Shaw himself often commanded an interest and authority far wider than any of the individual plays he actually wrote. If *Heartbreak House* is, as its author suggested, his *Lear*, then it has to be said that from its first presentation it has suffered a far more mixed press than Shakespeare's accepted masterpiece. Billed, perhaps misleadingly, as a fantasia in the Russian manner on English themes, it played at the Royal Court in Shaw's own 1921 production at over four hours. It thereby attracted a level of dismissive vituperation which Shaw's recent detractors could hardly hope to emulate. From the outset, Shaw's attempts to mix high farce with divine tragedy, and to marble an apparent comedy of manners with grave presentiments of impending catastrophe have brought out an anger and exasperation in some spectators which has never truly abated.

The purpose of reviving *Heartbreak House* here at the Almeida just before the millennium (without altering or updating the text) is to take a timely look at the century's original state-of-England play, aware that it does indeed exhibit some of the strengths and weaknesses of that singular genre which has given twentieth-century British drama so much spirit. In gathering together a collection of Bloomsbury-like Bohemians in a Sussex house, the play now appears to set off in a now-familiar Chekhovian direction, analysing the state of a nation, and its dangerous indifference to its own fate by portraying the life and loves of a representative group of middle-class people. Shaw looks ahead to the coming century and sees it as no friendly place for romantics or adventurers, but belonging instead to the narrow new class of depressing capitalists who are determined to reduce life to its lowest common denominator. Who can say he was wrong? Yet even in this overall scheme, so uncannily prophetic about the world we now live in – Captain Shotover, let it be noted, is working on Ronald Reagan's Star Wars strategy, the weapon which will destroy all other weapons – there is a wildness of texture, a sheer strangeness of vision which is often so personal and peculiar that we may almost rub our ears, in danger of disbelieving what we have heard.

Many commentators have rightly drawn attention to the zaniness of Shaw's humour. His playfulness with the form of theatre itself is taken to prefigure the arrival of absurdists like Beckett and Ionesco. But less noticed, it seems, is Shaw's underlying steel. Under the surface of the whole enterprise lies the extraordinary contention that it is not anyone's business to try and be happy; that happiness, indeed, may only be a failure and a lure. Using a method of reversal which is notably Brechtian – strong characters turn out to be weak, rich characters turn out to be poor – Shaw explains with remorseless clarity how easily the wish to enjoy life turns into a hopeless infatuation with dreams. He shows how each of us drifts off from the world into which we are born to dream far too lazily of a world in which things might be different.

No wonder this uncomfortable portrait of a society in which people are habitually distracted from their better purposes is one which theatregoers have occasionally found hard to contemplate. But they have also often not been helped by a common view of the play which emphasises its frivolity and rhetoric at the expense of its deeper feelings. Far from the governing tone being either light-hearted or elegiac, it is, on the contrary, full of the fever-ishness of genuine despair. Underneath the banter, underneath the central story of a young girl growing up in the course of a single evening, lies a sense of wasted passion which belies Shaw's reputation as a cold or cerebral writer. 'It has more of the miracle, more of the mystic belief in it than any of my others', wrote the author of his own favourite play. It also, he might have added, has more of the heart.

Bibliography

Dramatic Works (including translations, collaborations, and filmscripts)

Alan Bennett

Office Suite (London: Faber and Faber, 1981)
Objects of Affection and other plays for television (London: BBC, 1982)
A Private Function (London: Faber and Faber, 1984)
The Writer In Disguise (London: Faber and Faber, 1985)
Two Kafka Plays (London: Faber and Faber, 1987)
Prick Up Your Ears: The Screenplay (London: Faber and Faber, 1987)
Single Spies (London: Faber and Faber, 1989)
The Madness of George III (London: Faber and Faber, 1992)
The Madness of King George (London: Faber and Faber, 1995)
The Wind in the Willows (London: Faber and Faber, 1996)
Alan Bennett: Plays 1 (London: Faber and Faber, 1996) (formerly published as
    Forty Years On and Other Plays (London: Faber and Faber, 1991))
Alan Bennett: Plays 2 (London: Faber and Faber, 1998)
The Complete Talking Heads (London: BBC, 1998)
Alan Bennett, Peter Cook, Jonathan Miller, Dudley Moore, *Beyond the Fringe:
    A Revue* (London: Samuel French, Inc.: 1963)

Howard Brenton

Brecht, Bertolt, *The Life of Galileo* tr. Howard Brenton (2nd edn, London:
    Methuen, 1981)
Brenton Plays: One (London: Methuen Drama, 1986)
Brenton Plays: Two (London: Methuen Drama, 1989)
H. I. D. (Hess is Dead) (London: Nick Hern Books, 1989)
Berlin Bertie (London: Nick Hern Books, 1992)
Johann Wolfgang von Goethe, *Faust Parts I and II* tr. Howard Brenton
    (London: Nick Hern Books, 1995)
Howard Brenton and Tariq Ali, *Iranian Nights* (London: Nick Hern Books,
    1989)
——, *Moscow Gold* (London: Nick Hern Books, 1990)

——, *Ugly Rumours* (London: Nick Hern Books, 1998)
Howard Brenton and David Hare, *Pravda* (2nd edn, London: Methuen, 1986)

David Edgar

Edgar Plays: One (London: Methuen Drama, 1987)
Edgar Plays: Two (London: Methuen Drama, 1990)
Edgar Plays: Three (London: Methuen Drama, 1991)
The Strange Case of Dr Jekyll and Mr Hyde (London: Nick Hern Books, 1992)
Pentecost (London: Nick Hern Books, 1995)

Michael Frayn

Plays: One (London: Methuen Drama, 1985)
First and Last (London: Methuen Drama, 1989)
Plays: Two (London: Methuen Drama, 1991)
Now You Know (London: Methuen Drama, 1995)
Alarms and Excursions (London: Methuen Drama, 1998)
Copenhagen (London: Methuen Drama, 1998)

David Hare

The Asian Plays (London: Faber and Faber, 1984)
The History Plays (London: Faber and Faber, 1984)
Paris by Night (London: Faber and Faber, 1988)
The Secret Rapture (London: Faber and Faber, 1988)
Strapless (London: Faber and Faber, 1989)
Racing Demon (London: Faber and Faber, 1990)
Heading Home, Wetherby and Dreams of Leaving (London: Faber and Faber, 1991)
Murmuring Judges (London: Faber and Faber, 1991)
The Absence of War (London: Faber and Faber, 1993)
Amy's View (London: Faber and Faber, 1997)
Ivanov adapted from Chekhov (London: Methuen Drama, 1997)
Via Dolorosa and When Shall We Live? (London: Faber and Faber, 1998)

Other Writers

Caryl Churchill, *Serious Money* (London: Methuen/Royal Court Writers series, 1987)
——, *Blue Heart* (London: Nick Hern, 1997)
Sarah Kane, *Blasted and Phaedra's Love* (London: Methuen Drama, 1996)
Mark Ravenhill, *Shopping and Fucking* (London: Methuen Drama, 1996)
Bernard Shaw, *Heartbreak House* ed. Dan H. Laurence (London: Penguin Books, 1964)
David Storey, *Plays: One* (London: Methuen Drama, 1992)

Non-Dramatic Works

Peter Ansorge, *From Liverpool to Los Angeles: On Writing for Theatre, Film and Television* (London: Faber and Faber, 1997)

Alan Bennett, *The Lady in the Van* (London: London Review of Books, 1990) (first published, *London Review of Books*, 20 October 1989)

——, *Writing Home* (London: Faber and Faber, 1994; 2nd edn, 1997)

——, *The Clothes They Stood up In* (London: Profile Books, 1998)

Richard Boon, *Brenton the Playwright* (London: Methuen Drama, 1991)

Howard Brenton, 'Disrupting the Spectacle: Howard Brenton talks to Peter Ansorge', *Plays and Players*, July 1973, pp. 22–3

——, *Diving for Pearls* (London: Nick Hern Books, 1989)

——, *Hot Irons: Diaries, Essays, Journalism* (London: Nick Hern Books, 1995)

Angela Carter, *Nothing Sacred: Selected Writings* (2nd edn, London: Virago, 1992)

Maria Delgado and Paul Heritage, *In Contact with the Gods? Directors Talk Theatre.* (Manchester: Manchester University Press, 1996)

John Dexter, *The Honourable Beast: A Posthumous Autobiography* (London: Nick Hern Books, 1993)

David Edgar, *The Second Time as Farce: Reflections on the Drama of Mean Times* (London: Lawrence and Wishart, 1988)

——, 'English in Revolt', *Daily Telegraph*, 15 July 1995

Richard Eyre, *Utopia and Other Places* (London: Vintage, 1994)

Michael Frayn, *Speak after the Beep* (London: Methuen, 1997)

—— 'Drama of the uncertainty principle', interview with Alastair Macaulay, *Financial Times*, 6/7 February 1999

David Hare, *Writing Left-Handed* (London: Faber and Faber, 1991)

——, *Asking Around: Background to the David Hare Trilogy* ed. Lyn Haill (London: Faber and Faber, 1993)

——, *Platform Papers 9. David Hare* (London: Royal National Theatre in association with the Almeida Theatre, 1997)

Tony Mitchell, *File on Brenton* (London: Methuen, 1987)

Richard Nelson and David Jones, *Making Plays: The Writer–Director Relationship in the Theatre Today* ed. Colin Chambers (London: Faber and Faber, 1995)

Malcolm Page, *File on Hare* (London: Methuen Drama, 1990)

——, *File on Frayn* (London: Methuen Drama, 1994)

Malcolm Page and Simon Trussler, *File on Edgar* (London: Methuen Drama, 1991)

Susan Painter, *Edgar the Playwright* (London: Methuen Drama, 1996)

Dennis Potter, *Seeing the Blossom: Two Interviews and a Lecture* introduced by Melvyn Bragg (London: Faber and Faber, 1994)

Roland Rees, *Fringe First: Pioneers of Fringe Theatre on Record* (London: Oberon Books, 1992)

The Joint Stock Book: The Making of a Theatre Collective ed. Rob Ritchie (London: Methuen Theatrefile, 1987)

Mary Shelley, *Frankenstein* ed. M. K. Joseph (Oxford: Oxford University Press, 1980)

Max Stafford-Clark, *Letters to George* (London: Nick Hern Books, 1989)

Heidi Stephenson and Natasha Langridge, *Rage and Reason: Women Playwrights on Playwriting* (London: Routledge, 1997)

Daphne Turner, *Alan Bennett: In a Manner of Speaking* (London: Faber and Faber, 1997)

Duncan Wu, 'Realistic Revolutions' (review of Brenton, *Bloody Poetry*, Royal Court Theatre), *TLS*, 22–8 April 1988

——, 'In search of Utopia' (review of Brenton, *Sore Throats* and *Greenland*, Royal Court Theatre), *TLS*, 17–23 June 1988

——, 'Out of the gutter' (review of Brenton, *Diving for Pearls*), *New Statesman and Society*, 16 June 1989, p. 37

——, 'In the air' (review of Hare, *Writing Left-Handed*), *New Statesman and Society*, 21 June 1991

——, *Six Contemporary Dramatists: Bennett, Potter, Gray, Brenton, Hare, Ayckbourn* (2nd edn, Basingstoke: Macmillan, 1996)

Index